New Perspectives on Resilience in Socio-Economic Sph

Andrea Maurer (Ed.)

New Perspectives on Resilience in Socio-Economic Spheres

Springer VS

Editor
Prof. Dr. Andrea Maurer
Universität Trier, Deutschland

ISBN 978-3-658-13327-6   ISBN 978-3-658-13328-3 (eBook)
DOI 10.1007/978-3-658-13328-3

Library of Congress Control Number: 2016939378

Springer VS
© Springer Fachmedien Wiesbaden 2016
This work is subject to copyright. All rights are reserved by the Publisher, whether the whole or part of the material is concerned, specifically the rights of translation, reprinting, reuse of illustrations, recitation, broadcasting, reproduction on microfilms or in any other physical way, and transmission or information storage and retrieval, electronic adaptation, computer software, or by similar or dissimilar methodology now known or hereafter developed.
The use of general descriptive names, registered names, trademarks, service marks, etc. in this publication does not imply, even in the absence of a specific statement, that such names are exempt from the relevant protective laws and regulations and therefore free for general use.
The publisher, the authors and the editors are safe to assume that the advice and information in this book are believed to be true and accurate at the date of publication. Neither the publisher nor the authors or the editors give a warranty, express or implied, with respect to the material contained herein or for any errors or omissions that may have been made.

Lektorat: Cori Antonia Mackrodt, Katharina Gonsior

Printed on acid-free paper

This Springer VS imprint is published by Springer Nature
The registered company is Springer Fachmedien Wiesbaden GmbH

Table of contents

Introduction:
New Perspectives on Resilience in Socio-Economic Spheres 1
Andrea Maurer

Part I THE SOCIAL SCIENCE PERSPECTIVE

The Notion of Resilience:
Trajectories and Social Science Perspective 9
Wolfgang Bonß

Resilience in Catastrophes, Disasters and Emergencies 25
Socio-scientific Perspectives
Daniel F. Lorenz and Cordula Dittmer

Part II RESILIENCE IN THE ECONOMIC SPHERE: THEORETICAL AND EMPIRICAL EVIDENCE

Resilient Financial Systems:
Methodological and Theoretical Challenges of Post-Crisis Reform 63
Renate Mayntz

In Search of the Golden Factor:
Conceptualizing Resilience in the Framework of
New Economic Sociology by Focusing 'Loyalty' 83
Andrea Maurer

Consumer Organisations
and the Social Resilience of Markets 111
Sebastian Nessel

Part III RESILIENCE IN THE SOCIAL SPHERE:
         THEORETICAL AND EMPIRICAL EVIDENCE

Responses to Discrimination
and Social Resilience Under Neoliberalism 143
The United States Compared
Michèle Lamont, Jessica S. Welburn, and Crystal M. Fleming

The Resilience of Punctuated Cooperation 177
Hendrik Vollmer

Contributors 197

Index 201

Introduction:
New Perspectives on Resilience in Socio-Economic Spheres

Andrea Maurer

Why do so many people think about resilience today? This compilation of papers comes from social scientists who discuss the relevance of resilience in socio-economic spheres from different point of views. The aim is to offer new theoretical perspectives on resilience and new ways of giving empirical evidence.

The selection shows that the notion of resilience is used to analyze disruptive processes as well as how to handle these processes more or less successfully, in a wide range of socio-economic spheres. The selected papers do not only show that research on resilience is to be connected with classic concepts but also help to identify and overcome theoretical challenges. For example, there is a discussion, which moves against theories of modernization, saying that modern societies are faced with general risks which cannot be foreseen or planned but which can be overcome by different social mechanisms or factors in complex ways which are to be analyzed with the help of middle range theories, case studies or diverse institution theories. A second line of discussion provided by the collection helps to translate the general idea of disruption by using different theories and by focusing on concrete spheres. Disruptive or existence-threating events are defined in the framework of a particular theory of typical social action systems like social relationships, groups, organizations, societies, social systems, world society and the like. Thus, research on resilience can be based on various methodologies, theoretical programs and empirical research studies. The overall guideline is to formulate theses about social factors from a particular theoretical or empirical point of view, which help overcome the threats and gain stability. Most of the papers illustrate that such theses can be empirically proven and used for giving practical advice. This attracts practitioners from different fields, such as politicians, environmentalists, business owners or consumers to name a few. In other words, the notion of resilience supports the aim of solving various socio-economic problems by identifying social factors which support particular actors, groups and organizations when dealing with disruptive events, such as social or economic crises in modern societies.

Sociologists, as well as other social scientists, only recently started conceptualizing the notion of resilience and doing theoretically guided empirical research on the topic. Although the notion of resilience can be transported easily from individual problems to natural desasters to social action systems confronted with disruption it is not transdisciplinary. Furthermore, it is not a coherent concept or research program. What makes the notion of resilience interesting for social scientists in general and sociologists in particular is opening up the black box of disruptive and unforeseen processes or events. It also offers a heuristic basis to figure out which *social factors* support one's overcoming of such existence-threating events. Some concepts offer a closer look at what happens after or during disruptive processes and therefore help to identify why some social factors trigger and others stop the threats. Within sociology, disruptive processes can be seen as loss of mutual expectations, essential functions or moral values, to name a few, in social groups, institutions, organizations or social systems. Only based on a theoretical description of what defines the particular figure of a social group, institution, organization, society or social system can one identify social factors which help to stop disruptive processes and regain normality. Because of its broad spectrum, the notion of resilience can be combined with different sociological approaches. This is a big advantage as well as a big challenge. For example, resilience can be discussed by starting with the assumption of a social system being functionally differentiated and based on codes but also with the assumption of a socially integrated group or a market. Research on resilience then looks at social factors helping to reestablish either codes, values or utility expectations during and after disruption. The overall idea is to figure out how disruptive processes and threats of the basic foundations can be stopped and how codes, moral values or utility expectations be restored.

This book covers recent attempts in sociology to conceptualize "resilience" theoretically and to offer particular insights in the factors which enable social groups, institutions, organizations, societies or social systems to deal with various disruptive processes and to regain stability. The readings are organized into three parts: firstly, new theoretical perspectives are offered. Secondly, social resilience in economic sphere is discussed. Last but not least, social-cultural resilience of groups and individuals is analyzed.

In the first part of the collection new theoretical perspectives on resilience are outlined. The first chapter by *Wolfgang Bonß* brings in the new idea that modern societies are unavoidably confronted with risks which can not be dealt with through classical political ways of planning. So, resilience is defined as the ability to absorb and prevent risks by constantly rearranging and adapting. *Daniel F. Lorenz* and *Cordula Dittmer* react to the broadness and use of the term in very different spheres, concerning its transformative capital, the capacity of agency, and integrative empowerment by focusing on the field of power relations and asymmetric developments. They highlight the abilities of humans and the emancipatory force of resilience. They are doing this by analysing the role of social and cultural interpretative patterns for the construction of meaning by individuals confronted with catastrophes.

In the second part, the notion of resilience is used to discuss economic crises and to look at them by asking what makes some economic actors or action systems more resilient because of special social factors which help to reduce and overcome disruptions. In her article, *Andrea Maurer* conceptualizes resilience in the framework of new economic sociology. Her main idea is to describe disruption as a breakdown of mutual expectations in the economic sphere and then look for such golden social factors which help actors in economic sphere to overcome shocks or crises. Along with the widely known network and institutional analyses the notion of "loyalty" by Albert Hirschman is highlighted as a social factor which helps to overcome existence-threating in the economy. This is because loyalty motivates members to stay when benefits are quite unsure and it works as a social signal which increases the expectation of benefits. Both mechanisms go along which each other so social commitment can bring benefits back.

Renate Mayntz deals with the international financial crisis. Her starting point is to view the financial crisis as having been unleashed by a disturbance in the US housing market. Proof is given that the financial markets are not self-regulating. Ironically, adaptive responses to prior changes in the environment of the financial system had made it vulnerable, rather than resilient to external disturbances. Political intervention to re-establish financial stability requires both data and causal knowledge about the dynamic of the financial system. In 2008 both were deficient. The stress test of European banks, the international Data Gaps initiative, and efforts to develop indicators of financial soundness responded to these deficiencies. In analysing the data collection and measuring enterprises, their underlying causal models of financial stability and of resilience are discussed. Resilience is defined as a property of social systems which emerges either by intention or by chance.

Sebastian Nessel also deals with a disturbance of markets but takes this within the framework of new economic sociology as proof that markets are not to be seen as normally self-regulating units but as social action systems which are characterized by particular actors who interact in social fields like markets. By using the theoretical concepts proposed by Pierre Bourdieu and Neil Fligstein, Nessel offers empirical evidence that consumer organizations are an important social factor within markets. They help especially when actors are confronted with unexpected processes or with a disruption of mutual expectations.

The third part presents papers dealing with factors which help the social sphere deal with existence-threatening events. The paper by *Michèle Lamont, Jessica Welburn,* and *Crystal M. Fleming*[1] discusses how stigmatized groups, especially in the US but also in Israel and Brazil, overcome stigmatization and increase individual well-being. For this the notion of "Anerkennung" (appreciation) is central. Based on work by Laurent Thevenot and Michèle Lamont different stigmatized groups of Afro-American in New York, Afro-Brazilians in Rio de Janeiro and Jews from Arabia are compared. Evidence is given that especially in precarious social circumstances group membership provides resources to overcome stigmatization. Special repertoires are reconstructed which support the reestablishment of social appreciation. The social-cultural context is named as particular social factors, which enable groups or group members to activate particular repertoires. Common experience and shared identity help to overcome weaker discrimination from the outside.

Hendrik Vollmer, with reference to Harold Garfinkel and Pierre Bourdieu, offers a completely different view on resilience. He suggests not focusing on resilience as a resource which helps to overcome problems but focusing on it as an attribute of individuals or groups who cope and do not succumb to disruptions. Thus, he offers a set of phenomena which address the topic of resilience by demonstrating particular forms of resilience. It is seen as a "practical sense" found in a social group or society. The expression of resilience in this sense, is 'punctuated cooperation'. It is shown, through examples, that sociology can do research on resilience by looking on what individuals are doing practically.

Although there are a lot of new insights into and research on social resilience in sociology today, some important open questions and challenges for the future still remain. First of all, there is no overall theory on resilience, only a number of concepts translating resilience into different theoretical views and heuristics. One important line of discussion is to look for certain social factors which characterize social units which adapt to or deal better with disruptive events and processes then others. Sociology can help identify why and how social factors help social groups,

---

[1] Originally published in *Hall, Peter A. and Michèle Lamont* (ed.), 2013: Social Resilience in the Neoliberal Era. Cambridge: Cambridge Univ. Press, pp. 129-82.

institutions, organizations, societies or social systems overcome crises and carry on. On the other hand, there are some critical voices saying that resilience cannot be designed or planned, rather it is to be seen as an emergent social effect. At this point, it is an open question whether sociologists can and should do systematic research on resilience. It is my hope that this compilation enforces both a discussion about the theoretical foundations as well as the normative restrictions of research on resilience.

Dr. Cori Mackrodt, VS Springer's editor in chief, has accompanied this volume with her great experience and offered ideas whenever needed. Janosch Stolle, from the University of Trier, was of great help by translating part of the articles. Last but not least, I'm deeply grateful to Laura Lehto and all contributors from different disciplines and countries for their patience and inspiration.

Acknowledgements

The editor wants to thank the following for kindly given permission to translate and/or reprint articles.

Springer VS: Bonß, W. (2015). Karriere und sozialwissenschaftliche Potenziale des Resilienzbegriffs. In M. Endreß & A. Maurer (eds), Resilienz im Sozialen. Theoretische und empirische Analysen (pp. 15-31): Wiesbaden: VS Springer [revised and translated version]

Springer VS: Nessel, S. (2015). Verbraucherorganisationen als Resilienz- und Vulnerabilitätsfaktor von Markterwartungen. In M. Endreß & A. Maurer (eds), Resilienz im Sozialen. Theoretische und empirische Analysen (pp. 153-180): Wiesbaden: VS Springer [revised and translated version].

Michèle Lamont, Jessica S. Welburn, and Crystal M. Fleming (2013). Responses to Discrimination and Social Resilience Under Neoliberalism: The United States compared [open access] and published in: Hall, P., & Lamont, M. (eds), Social Resilience in the Neoliberal Era (129-157). Cambridge: Cambridge University Press

Part I
THE SOCIAL SCIENCE PERSPECTIVE

The Notion of Resilience: Trajectories and Social Science Perspective

Wolfgang Bonß[1]

The keyword of resilience has gained a tremendous trajectory within the last years. If you search for resilience in Google Ngram Viewer, a program which allows you to monitor the use of specific terms within books, it shows, that this term was not used in German-speaking countries (except for a short period between 1942 and 1950) until the 1970s.[2] This changed, slowly after 1990 and significantly after 2000. Since then, the use of this term within the German-speaking literature has doubled.[3] Media coverage of political discussions and research proposals on the topic of resilience are increasing too. Almost everywhere, a growing use of the term resilience is apparent. The term has also been transferred to several new problem areas without making it clear, what resilience stands for in general or in the specific field of the problem.

---

1 Revised version of an originally in German published article (Bonß, W. 2015. Karriere und sozialwissenschaftliche Potentiale des Resilienzbegriffs, pp. 15-31 in: Endreß, M. and A. Maurer (ed.), 2015: Resilienz im Sozialen. Wiesbaden: Springer VS.). The article is translated into English by Janosch Stolle, Andrea Maurer, and Laura Lehto.
2 See: https://books.google.com/ngrams/graph?content=Resilienz&year_start=1900&year_end=2010&corpus=20&smoothing=3&share=&direct_url=t1%3B%2CResilienz%3B%2Cc0 (Access: April 18th, 2014).
3 Within the English-speaking literature the term is already in common for a longer period of time, but even here the use more than doubled since 1990 (cf. https://books.google.com/ngrams/graph?content=resilience&year_start=1950&year_end=2014&corpus=15&smoothing=3&share=&direct_url=t1%3B%2Cresilience%3B%2Cc0 (Access: 18. April 2014).

A Google search shows that from a quantitative perspective, the growth is interrupted. The search for the term on December 1, 2013 provides about 9.280.000 results, on April15, 2014 it had increased already to 10.100.000. Although, the number of Google results does not tell anything about the quality or relevance, it does tell us that social attention to it is increasing.

In this paper I will discuss how the notion of resilience gains new perspectives in the context of new developments in society and the theories. Furthermore, I am going to introduce resilience as a new way of dealing with the question of uncertainty. For this, the notion of resilience can help sociologists to overcome classical views on uncertainty and provide a better understanding that does not highlight avoidance of but the identification of risk potential. So, through the reconstruction of the resilience discourse, some new insights will be offered.

1 Traditional lines of resilience

The Oxford English Dictionary[4] defines resilience in two ways. On the one hand it stands for "the ability of a substance or object to spring back into shape; elasticity". This is a more scientific oriented definition that refers to the elasticity of raw materials. On the other hand, resilience is defined as "the capacity to recover quickly from difficulties; toughness". Hereafter resilience will be understood in the ability of technical and/or social systems to be tough when facing disturbances, regardless of their kind. This highly general definition, with the commonly known keyword of "toughness", encompasses nearly all possible varieties of the term of resilience, which indeed could be formulated highly diverse in detail. If you temporarily omit the scientific- or raw material oriented definitions, three traditional lines of the social-scientific definition can be separated from each other.

1. The oldest variant represents the psychological research for resilience, which was founded by Emmy Werner (cf. Gabriel 2005, p. 209ff.; Mergenthaler 2012, p. 60ff.). The developmental psychologist, Emmy Werner, started her long-term study with research into the development conditions and possibilities of 698 children who were born in the 1950s and tracked their development over decades (cf. Werner; Werner & Smith 1982, 2001). About one-third of the children were in a situation of high developmental risk beforehand, because they had been born into chronic poverty, exposed to birth-conditional complications

---

4   See http://www.oxforddictionaries.com/definition/english/resilience (Access: April 18th, 2014).

and grew up in difficult social constellations. However, the developmental risks have not fully determined their behavior. Indeed, the majority of the children with biological, medical or social risk factors developed less to social standards than the children without such risk factors. Contrasting with the second group the children of the first were less healthy, less successful, and more delinquent. On the other hand – and this is equally remarkable – about one-third of the children in situations of high risk did not present any problems, but rather developed successful, stable personalities. Indeed, it is possible to discuss in detail, whether or and why it has been this way, and Emmy Werner did not provide an explicit answer to this. However, she did open up a new perspective and changed focus from the unsuccessful to the successful children. The latter were obviously resilient in terms of resistance against negative initiative conditions. This aspect attracted special attention in psychological research during the period that followed (cf. Wunsch 2013, p. 24ff.).

2. Quite another line and from the psychological research mostly independent traditional line, is the ecological resilience discourse (cf. Brand et al. 2011; Günther 2009, p. 28ff., 117ff.). Furthermore there are meanwhile approximately 2.000 contributions within the English and German language area.[5] Crawford Stanley Holling is hailed as the founding father for the ecological discourse of resilience. He published his epochal essay in 1973 about "Resilience and stability of ecological systems" (Holling 1973). From this early work a book about "adaptive environmental assessment and management" (Holling 1978) arose and also a release about "panarchy" (Gunderson & Holling 2002; see figure 3) and recently a collection about "Foundations of ecological resilience" (Gunderson et al. 2010) were published. In connection to Holling ecological resilience is mostly defined as the "ability of systems to absorb changes of state variables, driving variables and parameters and still persist" (Holling 1973, p. 18). To say it in other words: "Resilience is the capacity of a system to absorb and reorganize while undergoing change in order to retain essentially the same function, structure, identity, and feedback" (Walker et al. 2004). From this definition an important point is already becoming clear: Resilience is a power of resistance within the area of conflict of persistence and change, whereas persistence is in the foreground. Regardless of the changes, the functions, structures and identities of an (eco-)system shall be preserved within such resilient systems. Here

---

5   For the English-speaking discourse cf. http://www.resilliance.org and also http://www.resalliance.org/bibliography/list.php with actual about [05/06/2014] 1.658 entries; the additional German-speaking entries are estimated against the background of specific inquiry.

the power of resistance is referred on the one hand to socially constructed factors and on the other hand to prior ecologic aspects. Nevertheless, the ecological discourse of resilience is predominately focused on physical surroundings. Thus, even if the ecological problems are caused by humans, the notion is still about natural resilience. In this context physical forces or nature itself are regarded as important to keep resilient.
3. Since the turn of the millennium an additional third line has come to the psychological and ecological concepts of resilience, namely the "discourse of vulnerability" (cf. Bankoff 2003). Bankoff had already started in the 1970s. This new perspective urged in the foreground after growing ecological calamities (storms, flooding and earthquakes) and especially since the attack on the World Trade Center on the 11th of September in 2001. Through 9/11 the discourse about security has gained an entirely new frame. As it had previously been security and resistance, especially under the perspective of a potential internal system failure (systems do not work as planned), which had been discussed, it is now another aspect that is put into perspective, namely the vulnerability of systems. Vulnerability refers systems that can be hurt or destroyed through external forces. In contrast to vulnerability resilience means that systems does not get into trouble due to internal reasons (construction faults, wear e.g.), but rather through a specific external attack. Hereby the spectrum of attention shifts almost inevitably from a technical to social and normative aspects. For though technical systems can be vulnerable, vulnerability is not a technical affair, but rather "a complex characteristic produced by a combination of factors derived especially (but not entirely) from class, gender and ethnicity" (Cannon 1994, quoted after Bankhoff 2003, p. 6).

The various traditional lines of resilience discourse refer to diverse benchmarks and conceptions of "ability for resistance," which come together at one point though. It does not matter whether resilience is recognized as psychological, ecological or social, in most cases it is described as an antecedent, an already existing ability. This can be supported and enhanced, but in general it cannot be created entirely new. In fact the research on resilience has changed a lot. At its beginning it was a common assumption, that resilience is somehow "hereditary" (cf. Fröhlich-Gidlhoff & Rönnau-Böse 2014, p. 9), but cannot be arbitrarily produced. At this point a difference between the concepts of prevention and precaution become clear: While (crisis-)prevention focuses on fighting threatening system changes, through preventive arrangements and the elimination of them if possible, resilience is rather reactive or defensive. It can be expressed in another way: The discourse about resilience no longer assumes, that catastrophes can be avoided through preventive planning but rather that negative developments (regardless of all private and governmental promises for safety) can occur at any time. Therefore the ability of keeping resilient today is connected with existing potentials of resistance, which allow a system returning into a normal state – however this state is defined.

2 Between shock and creeping threat – Benchmarks of resilience

The USA National Research Council (2012, p. 18, 33) defines resilience as "the ability to prepare and plan for, absorb, recover from, and more successfully adapt to adverse events". Thus, it is about the ability to parry adverse events, to prepare one's self for them, to take them into account, to bear them, to recover and to adapt oneself for them in an increasingly better way. The USA Research Council in 2012 especially thought about increasing ecological disasters in the USA such as hurricane Betsy (1965), Andrew (1982) or Katrina (2005) or potential earthquakes, especially in California. One also has to think about socially produced ecological disasters, such as the Exxon Valdez tanker accident, which destroyed unique sanctuary for birds and sea otters on Alaska's coast. Last but not least, terrorist attacks play an increasing role. Terrorism gains more and more attention through "9/11". Terrorism likes radiologic weapons, dirty bombs" and the like cause more and more uncertainty (cf. Geiger 2003).

It has to be clear, that Katrina, a potential earthquake in California or a possible volcanic eruption could not have been prevented, especially because these events are not socially produced. That is why resilience or capability of resistance is gaining more and more attention in the public and political perception. If adverse events, for whatever reasons, cannot be definitely avoided, then the ability to react to such circumstances and create normality, has to be fostered – whatever that means in each case.

However, some results show that events like Katrina, disregarding all rhetorical efforts, are unequally distributed and even are hard to support in ex post. Specific population groups are per definition more resilient than others. It just may be true, because they live in better residential neighborhoods. Katrina refers to further characteristics of the resilience's debate, which goes beyond the psychological resilience discourse.

It is always about large-scale damages and these should emerge mostly suddenly or abruptly in general. From the perspective of psychological research on resilience both attributes can be confusing, because resilient children who cope with poor initial situations, do not have something to do with large-scale damages and they do not suffer from abrupt events in most cases, but rather from impairments which creep in. However psychological research for resilience is no longer in the spotlight (even if it dominates specific Google-inquiries). If one searches for what resilience is about, the following statement is more typical: "Resilience thinking [...] anticipates change and understands that major shocks are inevitable in a world that is facing huge challenges like climate change, resource scarcity, biodiversity loss, economic instability, and social unrest."[6]

This wording highlights two things: On the one hand the actual resilience thinking refers to a whole range of phenomena which reaches from climate change over to resource scarcity up to economic and social uncertainty. These uncertainties are noticed as unexpected events in a world that is organized in an uncertain way, where one cannot rely on anything. This perception explicitly disagrees with the planning optimism of the 1960s and 1970s. If one thought back then, scientific progress was meant to eliminate all future problems. In a world that is affected by climate change, growing scarcity of resources, economic crises and growing social inequality, not only are fantasies of doom becoming more and more popular but also the scenarios for stability. At the same time diverse disturbances, regardless of which system they occur in , are increasingly noticed as unexpected (because they have not been anticipated before) and as a shock (due to their extent and abruptness). This empirical funded change of perspective refers to a crisis of the former understanding of scientific progress. Indeed, this lead to a new perspective on scientific progress that does not mean uncertainty could be regulated in general. Furthermore, systems are to be considered as vulnerable, at times disturbing, crises or in terms of violations. Against this backdrop, the question for antecedent resilience potentials becomes more important as well as factors of resilience which are connected to private responsibility. In other words as Charlie Edwards, in his book about the resilient nation states (Edwards 2009, p. 1) next generations rely on "citizen and communities, not the institutions of state".

How do we have to understand the aim of this resistance? On the one hand resilience means that a normal condition, as it has existed before the break, is restored. On the other hand, resilience activities become just necessary, because there is a need for change to exist. The question if and what has to be changed remains: Does return to a normal condition mean that former parameters will be reconstructed again? Or does return to a normal condition mean that the system parameters have to be replaced because of irrefutable changes? These questions remain unanswered. Furthermore resilience means resistance against unexpected challenges as well as survival, because of the need to adapt to a changing environment.

---

6   See http:// www.getresilient.com/whatisresilience [03/26/2014].

Walker et al. (2004) outline in this context "four crucial aspects of resilience," which grow in importance. On the one hand resilience refers to latitude namely to the scope and the capacity of a system. Within this perspective, change is in the spotlight. A system is only able to work under pressure, when it is able to bear new external challenges without losing the ability to recover. Another second aspect of resilience is the resistance, namely the resistance in times of change. While resilience does not exclude change, resistance deals with the aspect of being able to oppose new requirements and remain unchanged in its core features. As a third aspect, Walker et al. highlight the "precariousness," which stands for the uncertainty and the system's degree of exposure. Within this perspective, it deals with the question of where the threshold of the system's instability is and how the threshold could be raised. As a fourth aspect Walker et al. last mentions panarchy – a keyword that Gunderson and Holling (2002) dedicated a whole book to. As a counter-concept to hierarchy, panarchy means a specific viewpoint to the structuring and changing of systems: The resilience of systems has to be considered multidimensional and indeed, in two ways. First, local systems are embedded into subordinated contexts, or as an example "external oppressive politics, invasions, market shifts, or global climate change can trigger local surprises and regime shifts" (Walker et al. 2004). Second, forces of persistence and change can be found in nearly all systems, which could be labeled as "remember" and "revolt". Resilience means that remember and revolt are in balance, whereas Holling et al. (2002) act on the assumption that the concept of panarchy is under the frame of developmental viewpoints, some kind of adaptive cycles, which is shown in the following figure 1.

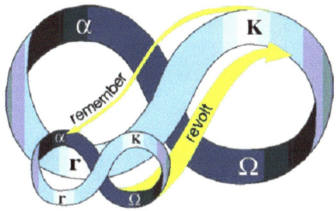

Figure 1 Adaptive Cycle
Source: http://www.resalliance.org/index.php/panarchy

It is a bit of a stretch to explain the adaptive cycle in detail, but what is interesting is that the power of change (revolt) is definitely more distinctive than the moments of persistence (remember). There is an ambivalence behind it, which is not entirely discussed in the previous discussions. Indeed, resilience stands for a defense against changes in principle and the recreation of previous states of normality, but it can also mean that a system has to change itself to survive and that new states of normality have to be found. It is possible to discuss the statement through current examples, such as examples of flood damages. Is it just those resilient people who raise their dikes and encapsulate their homes more and more? Or are people resilient who leave their homes in face of the annual flood damages and built new homes, because they do not want to renovate every year? This question is hard to answer. In general it assumes that resilience does not have to result in the defense of what exists, it could rather refer to an irreversible and changed basic condition, whereas it is hard to draw the line between resistance and adaption in particular.

3 Disaster-Management, resilience cycle and the question about resilience's core

It is possible to differentiate between two directions of the research concerning resilience in general. While the psychological and the economic research on resilience is primarily focused on the question of how a successful handling of previous or creeping handicaps could be ensured, recent social-scientific resilience research is nowadays deals mostly with threatening and sudden events with catastrophic effects that have to be handled in some way. Thus, since the middle of the 20th century there have emerged a variety of approaches to the disaster-research in the USA (Quarantelli 1978, 1998; Meyer 2010). These have been borrowed by the "sociology of catastrophes" and pursued in Germany (cf. Dombrowsky 1989; Clausen 1994; Clausen et al. 2003; Voss 2006). Within the disaster-research there have already been several models put forth for handling catastrophes for over six years. One of the oldest is the disaster-management-cycle which was proposed by John Powell and Jeanette Rayner in 1952 (cf. Coetzee 2009, p. 64ff.).

Powell and Rayner distinguished disaster-handling into eight stages which move from pre-disaster conditions stage (everything is still stable) up to warning stage, threat and impact (event of the disaster) to the point of determining stages inventory stage, rescue phase, remedy stage and recovery phase (handling the disaster). Already in this model, someone implied that catastrophes do not happen fully unexpected, but rather take place somewhat predictably. Again, the handling of catastrophes proceeds in multiple stages, starting with the immediate reaction up to the recovery phase and stabilization. The following illustration is a little bit easier to follow and is more logical. It makes it clear that catastrophes are neither unique nor ultimately unable to be handled:

Figure 2 Disaster Management Cycle[7]

Source: http://www.careermagic.in/2012/02/normal-0-false-false-false-en-us-x-none.html [05/20/2014]

Regarding this, in diverse variants shown and meanwhile even certified model (cf. peck 2008, p. 8ff.), the current ideas of the resilience cycle have been constructed (see figure 3).

---

[7] There are several presentations of the Disaster Management Cycle (in the same or similar form); but this precise presentation to my mind, one of the most demonstrative. Unfortunately its original author is unknown to me.

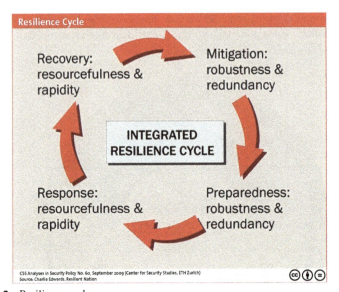

Figure 3 Resilience cycle
Source: Jakubowski 2013, p. 376, after Leismann, Fraunhofer EMI 2012

From a bifocal perspective two things are conspicuous. First, there is not any kind of cutting event anymore. The focus is no longer on the catastrophe, but rather on the resilience cycle, which is a steady desire for better crisis management. By this crises become a permanent phenomenon. Second, the question of the potentials of resistance, as mentioned in the earlier resilience debate, is missed in the presentation of the resilience cycle. In fact, the topic of resilience disappears in some aspects. Thus, there is no independent force of resilience in these cycles. Instead, the handling of catastrophes is reduced to classical disaster models, in which the event catastrophe is faded out.

The change of perspective is only partly convincing, and that is why one has to return to the question of what resilience accounts for in its core. Does it is stand for an antecedent power of effect, or acquirable ability? Authors like Emmy Werner (1977) or Paul Willis (1979) do not agree with this point. While Willis did research on the refusal of lower class youngsters against official requirement of normality, he explained the amusement of resistance and relocated it to class positions. Werner argues differently. Indeed, she sees social reasons why a part of the Kauai's' children have failed. However, the reasons are not explicit in any way and she, with the more successful children, acts on the assumption that resilience is some kind of natural power which is or is not available to the subjects.

This is far too general and not fully satisfactory. The question of resilience responds to the individual and to the social level. Even if, against all social influences, there is some kind of non-explicable natural power, it is different if one is looking at social resilience, or the resistance of social communities. In contrast to the psychological or ecological resilience, social resilience refers to the threat of the particular living conditions, and the reaction is generally non-antecedent potential set by nature, but rather a social achievement or effect of social characteristics of a community. The resistance, for example, against a threat to democratic living conditions does not create itself, but rather has to be practiced, and is only possible against the background of an appropriate democratic practice. Preconditions of "social" resilience would be, in this case, the relationship between law, democracy and, what is mentioned as "civil society" (cf. Adloff 2005, Gosewinkel et. al 2004). Indeed, the basic conditions of civil society (and the resilience that is referred to it) are not clarified in any way. However the fact that social resilience in modern societies is connected to civil society is still undisputed. So far, psychological or ecological resilience debate, do insufficiently discuss the phenomenon of social resilience by means of a social system against internal disturbances and, as well, against adverse environmental influences. These could make themselves noticeable as abrupt and/or creeping events. In addition, at this point, one can differentiate between shock and shifted irritation. Against this background, Adger (2000, p. 347) defines social resilience as "ability of groups or communities to cope with external stresses and disturbances as a result of social, political or environmental change." More specifically it is about the "ability of communities to withstand external shocks to their social infrastructure" (Adger 2000, p. 361).

Social resilience means the ability to tolerate stress and to keep the existing "social infrastructure" alive (cf. Adger 2000, p. 361). The problem, as Adger says, intensifies especially in developed societies which are more likely to be vulnerable to stress, because of their complexity. Indeed, this stress is not a psychological or ecological kind, but rather a social one that should be explained, based on Durkheim, through social factors. As a matter of fact, it is possible to argue this, especially if the suggested linkage of stress and shock is convincing. Indeed, it is hardly disputable that catastrophes, such as the world economic crisis of 1929 or the (incomparably weaker) financial crisis of 1990 have occurred abruptly and cracks have not been expected. These cracks have already been being prepared through structural aberrations over a long period of time. That is why it seems to be legitimate to prepare more powerfully for these structural aberrations then the early resilience debate.

There is again the question remaining, does resilience means that the old infrastructure stays and nothing will change or does resilience refer to learning processes with structural change? The answer often attempts to show that, next to the appropriate discussions, remember" and revolt are mostly mentioned. There are two other keywords which are mentioned, namely "adopt" and "adapt." While "adopt" stands for retaining the old infrastructure and only marginal changes. "Adapt" means the need for and also forced change to the old infrastructure because of new frame conditions. In fact, this is also where the line between persistence and change remains open, because the question can only be decided under empirical viewpoints, not in general.

4 "Simple" versus "reflexive resilience" – Variants of social resilience

From a sociological point of view these results remain not convincing because they do not offer a sufficient answer to the question of whether resilience as ability of resistance exists mainly natural or antecedent. Furthermore, the question needs to be discussed whether the notion of resilience should be regarded as socially constructed socially and by that becomes changeable and constructible. Beyond this it is possible to formulate several other questions about resilience. First of all it needs to be discussed whether it is psychological, ecological or social-scientific research about resilience. Secondly, the question needs to be discussed, how the relationships between antecedent and socially produced or constructible resilience potentials is just rarely discussed. Besides, it is only operated from a simple understanding of resilience potentials in relevant analysis. So there is no practical differentiation between different kinds of resilience concepts. This is much more astonishing as if one could differentiate between "simple" and "reflexive" variants of resilience all the time, but none have done it so far.

In this context I will suggest to highlight simple concepts of resilience that refer to an immediate reaction on large-scale damages. What have to be done if, for example a large-scale power blackout happens, what should be advised reactive to the people concerned (e.g. the accumulation of food provisions and/or the acquisition of emergency backup generators – whereat latter is often not possible in overcrowded areas). In contrast to reactive or simple resilience a concept of "reflexive" resilience can be seen somehow more active or proactive. "Reflexive resilience" is not about post-reactions, but rather about, how the event of a large-scale damage could be prevented. Simple resilience means (by all means of preventive thinking) the reaction on not preventable accidents; whereas "reflexive" resilience ties refers to the thought of preventing uncertainty and risk. Simply resilient in this setting could be all efforts to qualify something, which aims at ensuring the recreation of a power supply in cases of black outs, for example.. "Reflexively resilient" would be, in contrast, all actions to prevent a power outage in advance or trying to reduce energy consumption through specific actions for example in better local anchoring.

This consideration about a selection between simple and "reflexive" resilience may appear unnecessary on first glance, especially since no specific line could be drawn between them. However, in practice, the difference between simple and "reflexive" resilience (even if it is not mentioned) has already existed for a long period of time. This could be studied within the example of the forecasting earthquakes. Chances of earthquakes worldwide are as unequally distributed as earthquake prevention is. Turkey, California, and Japan are considered as high risk places for earthquakes. Indeed, all regions react differently to this kind of threaten. In Turkey, there is hardly any systematical earthquake prevention within the area of Istanbul. Whereas in California one finds more simple resilience. In fact, the building codes there are much more restrict than in Turkey, but in everyday life people there satisfy themselves with so called survival kits. These kits should ensure survival for one- or more days in destroyed regions, which are especially fostered through the growing "prepper" movement.[8] Japan, in contrast, is the most reflexive oriented country. Against the backdrop of recurrent earthquake experiences, there are several prescriptions for earthquake proofed buildings which have been successful, since the damages from the last earthquakes were minor.

What do these examples imply for the difference between simple and reflexive resilience? Firstly, this means social resilience is not an antecedent asset, but rather has to be learned individually or socially. Such learning processes have to be supported for reaching a state which could be referred to as "reflexive resilience". Reflexive resilience" means a power of resistance, which does not fear change and offers reflexive justifiable innovations. Such flexible innovations are potentials of resistance especially for non-preventable crisis situations. Furthermore they are rather increasing.

To be sure, one can argue whether the increase is quantitatively measureable in all cases (such as damages from hurricanes, floods or other natural disasters), or whether there is increase of awareness and sensibility towards crises and natural disasters. In that case, sensibility increases that neither science nor public policy no longer promise that catastrophes can be prevented in the long term. With this in mind the growing resilience discourse actually refers to a changing attitude towards uncertainty. Uncertainty is no longer seen as a decreasing, controllable

---

8   Preppers defines people that want to be prepared in an event of a catastrophe – within the USA there are more than 3 million estimated Preppers. Offers for survival kits can in the meanwhile also be found in Germany's ebay.

problem, as Talcott Parsons affirmed (1980) (cf. Bonß 1995, p. 11f.). Uncertainty and crises seem to be much more of a permanent companion of humanity. From this on uncertainty can be somehow a little bit relativized by scientific research and political means. It is not assumed to eliminate or avoid uncertainty in general. In this extent, as the specific claims decrease, the need for (pre-governmental) resilience grows, whereby the development has to be rated ambivalent. The insights from this new perspective are that more scientific research, governmental competency, and possibilities of strengthening private resistance are needed. However that makes sense only if simple and "reflexive" resilience is supported.

References

Adger, W. N. (2000). Social and ecological resilience: are they related? Progress in Human Geography 24 (3), S. 347-364. Retrieved from https://groups.nceas.ucsb.edu/sustainability-science/2010 weekly-sessions/session-102013-11.01.2010-emergent-properties-of-coupled-human-environment-systems/supplemental-readings-from-cambridge-students/ Adger_2000_Social_ecological_resilience.pdf/view [02/99/2014].

Adloff, F. (2005). Zivilgesellschaft. Theorie und politische Praxis. Frankfurt a. M.: Campus.

Bankoff, G. (2003). Vulnerability as a Measure of Change in Society. International Journal of Mass Emergencies and Disasters 21 (2), S. 5-30.

Bonß, W. (1995). Vom Risiko – Unsicherheit und Ungewißheit in der Moderne. Hamburg: Hamburger Edition.

Brand, F., Hoheisel, D., & Kirchhoff, T. (2011). Der Resilienz-Ansatz auf dem Prüfstand: Herausforderungen, Probleme, Perspektiven. In Bayerische Akademie für Naturschutz und Landschaftspflege (Hrsg.), Landschaftsökologie. Grundlagen, Methoden, Anwendungen (pp. 78-83). Laufen: ANL.

Clausen, L. (1994). Krasser sozialer Wandel. Opladen: Leske + Budrich.

Clausen, L., Geenen, E. M., & Macamo, E. (Hrsg.). (2003). Entsetzliche soziale Prozesse. Münster: Lit.

Coetzee, C. (2009). The development, implementation and transformation of the Disaster Management Cycle. Mini-Dissertation, Nordwest-Universität, Potchefstroom, Südafrika. acds.co.za/uploads/thesis/christocoetzee_m.pdf [04/13/ 2014].

Dombrowsky, W. R. (1989). Katastrophe und Katastrophenschutz. Wiesbaden: Deutscher Universitäts-Verlag.

Edwards, C. (2009). Resilient nation. London: Demos.

Fröhlich-Gildhoff, K., & Rönnau-Böse, M. (2014). Resilienz. München & Basel: Ernst Reinhardt.

Gabriel, T. (2005). Resilienz – Kritik und Perspektiven. Zeitschrift für Pädagogik 51(2), 208-218.

Geiger, G. (2003). Die schmutzige Bombe. Radioaktives Material als Terrorwaffe. SWP-Aktuell 2003/25, 1-8.

Gosewinkel, D., Rucht, D., van den Daele, W., & Kocka, J. (eds). (2004). Zivilgesellschaft – national und transnational. Berlin: edition sigma.

Gunderson, L., & Holling, C. S. (eds.). (2002). Panarchy: understanding transformations in human and natural systems (p 25-62). Washington: Island Press.

Gunderson, L., Allen, C., & Holling, C. S. (eds) (2010). Foundations of ecological resilience. Washington: Island Press.

Günther, E. (2009). Klimawandel und Resilience Management. Interdisziplinäre Konzeption eines entscheidungsorientierten Ansatzes. Wiesbaden: Gabler.

Holling, C. S. (1973). Resilience and stability of ecological systems. Annual Review of Ecology and Systematics 4, 17-23.

Holling, C. S. (Hrsg.). (1978). Adaptive environmental assessment and management. New York: John Wiley.

Jakubowski, P. (2013). Resilienz – eine zusätzliche Denkfigur für gute Stadtentwicklung. Informationen zur Raumentwicklung 2013/4, 371-378. http://www.bbsr.bund.de/BBSR/

DE/Veroeffentlichungen/IzR/2013/4/Inhalt/DL_Jakubowski.pdf?__blob=publicationFile&v=2 [05/04/2014].

Mergenthaler, A. (2012). Gesundheitliche Resilienz. Konzept und Empirie zur Reduzierung gesundheitlicher Ungleichheit im Alter. Wiesbaden: Springer VS.

Meyer, M. A. (2010). The sociology of disaster: The classics, social vulnerability, resilience, environmental migration and risk perception. A reading list. http://disaster.colostate.edu/Data/Sites/1/cdra-research/cdra-readinglists/michelle-readinglist2010-1.pdf [04/13 2014].

National Research Council (2012). Disaster Resilience: A National Imperative. Washington, DC: The National Academies Press.

Parsons, T. (1980). Health, uncertainty and the action structure. In S. Fiddle (eds), Uncertainty. Behavioural and Social Dimensions (pp. 145-163). New York: Praeger.

Peck, T.-G. (2008). The Fish Model of Crisis Management System. Singapur: NUS. www.cshema.org/uploadedFiles/PUBLISHED/Meetings_and_Seminars/Annual_Conference/2008STL/peck.pdf [04/13/ 2014].

Powell, J. W., & Rayner, J. F. (1952). Progress Notes: Disaster Investigation. Chemical Corps Medical Laboratories Contract Report. Maryland: Army Chemical Center.

Quaranteillli, E. L. (1978). Disasters. Theory and research. London & Beverly Hills, CA: Sage.

Quarantelli, E. L. (1998). What is a disaster? Perspectives on the question. London & New York: Routledge.

Voss, M. (2006). Symbolische Formen. Grundlagen und Elemente einer Soziologie der Katastrophe. Bielefeld: transcript.

Walker, B., & Salt, D. (2006). Resilience Thinking. Sustaining Ecosystems and People in a Changing World. Washington: Island Press.

Walker, B., Holling, C. S., Carpenter, S., & Kinzig, A. (2004). Resilience, adaptability and transformability in social-ecological systems. Ecology and Society 9/2, 5. http://www.ecologyandsociety.org/vol9/iss2/art5/ [04/13/2014].

Werner, E. E. (1977). The Children of Kauai. A longitudinal study from the prenatal period to age ten. Honolulu: University of Hawai'i Press.

Werner, E. E., & Smith, R. S. (1982). Vulnerable but invincible: A longitudinal study of resilient children and youth. New York: McGraw Hill.

Werner, E. E., & Smith, R. S. (2001). Journeys from childhood to midlife: Risk, resilience and recovery. Ithaca, NY: Cornell University Press.

Willis, P. E. (1979). Spaß am Widerstand: Gegenkultur in der Arbeiterschule. Frankfurt a. M.: Syndikat.

Wunsch, A. (2013). Mit mehr Selbst zum stabilen Ich! Resilienz als Basis der Persönlichkeitsbildung. Heidelberg: Springer.

Resilience in Catastrophes, Disasters and Emergencies

Socio-scientific Perspectives

Daniel F. Lorenz and Cordula Dittmer

1 Introduction

Resilience is a widely discussed topic in various fields of application. Within the context of socio-scientific disaster research and psychological research on traumatic events, the concept has been used since the late 1970s. Since then, some important and quite remarkable transformations have occurred which have changed the concept, its application, and its scope. With the expansion and transference of this concept into very different contexts, its explanatory potential became increasingly more diffuse to the point where it became nearly devoid of actual content in some application areas. Resilience has become one of the fast traveling notions, which circulates in the meantime as a linguistic passe-partout that can be loaded up with ever changing meanings (Knapp 2001).

Perhaps because the concept has become so blurred, its recent mainstreaming was accompanied by a fundamental critique which describes the resilience concept as a neoliberal approach which normalises disasters and crises, drops any disaster prevention and reduction measures, and likewise leaves the individuals with the sole responsibility to take countermeasures to mitigate disaster loss and damage (Hall & Lamont 2013; Chandler 2013; Kaufmann 2015). Bonß (2015) views both the fact that crisis and/or insecurity are seen as the "normal" development and that negative developments ought not to be prevented, as a programmatic renewal of the resilience concept. This has been likewise accompanied by an observable turning away from prevention strategies and optimism that such occurrences are indeed manageable in the first place (see Endreß & Rampp 2015). The driving point behind this movement is centred about the conundrum of how one can be prepared for that which is per se unable to be prepared for (Blum et. al. 2016). Behind the neoliberal co-option and bias of resilience as a concept for dealing with disasters, there is in fact an orginally scientific phenomenon which is also quite relevant in practice (Hempel & Lorenz 2014). One need only register resilience's entanglement with vulnerability research to see that the social production of disasters as well as the socially influenced affectedness in disasters were indeed discussed in the context of resilience. If resilience itself does not actually focus so much on preventive measures and structural causes of disasters, this is due to the fact that such measures are usually discussed under the umbrella of vulnerability as a complementary concept

We would like to add another dimension to the evolution of the concept regarding its transformative capital, a capacity of agency, and integrative empowerment by focusing on the field of power relations and asymmetric developments. Our main argument is that the potential of the resilience concept in disaster research was its original questioning of predominant ways of thinking and acting in science, disaster management, and politics. The insight that people in disasters are indeed not helpless victims and sole receivers of aid, but rather self-determined, acting, and organizing subjects furnished with specific ways of coping with inner and outer challenges, challenged the logic of existing scientific and sundry systems of thought in addition to challenging political institutions.

Based on the classification of current resilience discourses into distinct categories: e.g. as being respectively oriented in more systematic or more systemic fashion (Voss & Dittmer 2016) or, to put it in other words, as being simpler or more reflexive (Bonß 2015), we argue that both ways of argumentation tend to do away with the genuine critical potential that the resilience concept has had in its historical origins. Systematic or simple approaches deal with clearly identifiable quantitative parameters based on rationalistic assumptions. Though they may be used and can in fact be useful in the context of disaster preparedness and awareness, in disaster response actions and in political discussions about e.g. global disaster risk reduction (DRR), they also necessarily rely on essentialist and simplifying readings of the world. In contrast, systemic or reflexive approaches are focusing on the prevention of disastrous events; they try to understand, frame and contextualise resilience as an embedded capacity of social systems (Voss & Dittmer 2016). Systemic approaches are used particularly in sociology and anthropology, but they inherit the aforementioned danger of the resilience term itself becoming unclear, diffuse, and blurred through its widespread usage and topical mainstreaming.

It is very interesting to note that both strategies are functioning as competing concepts in political decision-making processes. This can be seen when comparing, e.g. the evolution of resilience definitions in Climate Change Adaption Processes in IPCC (2007, 2014) and the global DRR frameworks of Hyogo (2005) and Sendai (2015). Resilience was defined very systemically and comprehensively in the Hyogo Framework as "the capacity of a system, community or society potentially exposed to hazards to adapt, by resisting or changing in order to reach and maintain an acceptable level of functioning and structure. This is determined by the degree to which the social system is capable of organising itself to increase this capacity for learning from past disasters for better future protection and to improve risk reduction measures" (UN/ISDR 2004, p. 4). In looking at the IPCC Fourth Assessment Report (2007) three years later one can witness a transition in meaning for the term "capacity": from its original understanding as a learnable and promotable characteristic, into a genuinely static and ingrained ability found among the reference units from birth. "Resilience is defined as the ability of a social or ecological system to absorb disturbances while retaining the same basic structure and ways of functioning, the capacity for self-organisation, and the capacity to adapt naturally to stress and change." (IPCC 2007, p. 37).

While the Hyogo definition directs its focus on the learning and developmental potentials of social systems regarding future challenges, the IPCC Fourth Assessment Report interprets in a decidedly different direction and focuses on the sustainability of coveted foundational structures. In the most recent succeeding actualisations of both documents, resilience is further extended into the climate change framework: "The capacity of social, economic, and environmental systems to cope with a hazardous event or trend or disturbance, responding or reorganizing in ways that maintain their essential function, identity, and structure, while also maintaining the capacity for adaptation, learning, and transformation" (IPCC 2014, p. 5). This change is accompanied by a narrowing of the term in the Sendai Framework for DRR using the resilience defintopn of UN/ISDR (2009, p.9): "The ability of a system, community or society exposed to hazards to resist, absorb, accommodate to and recover from the effects of a hazard in a timely and efficient manner, including through the preservation and restoration of its essential basic structures and functions".

We argue that both strategies, mainstreaming as well as essentialization, conceal the transformative potential of the resilience concept and inadvertently work to preserve existing power relations without taking into question the underlying structural root causes of vulnerability, resilience and disasters.

Our analysis's work is led by the meta-theoretical assumption that resilience can be understood as a *dispositif* or apparatus. Specifically, the work directs its orientation around the definition of *dispositif/apparatus* from Agamben (2009, pp. 2f.), which itself strongly leans on the work from Foucault: "It is a heterogeneous set that includes virtually anything, linguistic and non-linguistic. Under the same heading: discourses, institutions, buildings, laws, police measures, philosophical propositions, and so on. The apparatus itself is the net work that is established between these elements. […] The apparatus always has a concrete strategic function and is always located in a power relation. [...] As such, it appears at the intersection of power relations and relations of knowledge." This assumption enables us to conduct a reflexive analysis: on the one hand, we can explore the effects and concretions which resilience experiences at various institutional and societal levels, and on the other hand, the term maintains the critical moment (in the dialectical sense) which thematises the strategic and power-related impetus of resilience.

In the first step, we will trace back resilience's usage in socio-scientific disaster research and point to the close connections the resilience concept has with other related concepts with special attention paid to the vulnerability concept. In the second part, we will analyse the development of the original potential offered by resilience with a special focus on its transformative potential, thus focusing on the concept of agency as the referential object.

In the last few sections we will illustrate our arguments and sketch a more complex picture of resilience in socio-scientific disaster research by distinguishing resilience within the different scopes of emergencies, disasters and catastrophes as introduced by Enrico L. Quarantelli (2000). As these damaging events have different characteristics in terms of the impact, the response and help being provided, the potential of recovery, the disruption of fundamental social functions, and most importantly the role of social and cultural interpretative patterns for meaning creating, we will inquire into the implications for the resilience concept respective to the different types of events.

Most of the predominant socio-scientific disaster research literature focuses on resilience in disasters, while the more psychologically inclined research into resilience in emergencies leaves resilience in catastrophes almost untouched. In our view, all three perspectives need to be balanced and correlated in order to help define a meaningful application of resilience in disaster research. We then conclude the article by summing up the legacy of the resilience concept and point to important aspects in the analysis and application of resilience in sociological disaster research and management.

2 Tracing Back Resilience in Disaster Research

2.1 Resilience in Ecology and Social-Ecological Systems

Notwithstanding the term's etymological origin in *resilire* which stretches as far back as Roman antiquity (Alexander 2013), nor to speak of the concept's development in field of psychology in the 1950s (found prominently in Werner 1971) which would later find a renewed popularity in the 1980s (Flach 1988) (which we will later discuss), one can easily say that the contemporary topic of resilience draws first and foremost upon the ecological research of Crawford Stanley Holling. By viewing the interactions of populations, Holling (1973) investigated why some systems collapse in the face of changing environmental conditions, while others persist in spite of constellations having changed. Holling developed his concept of resilience in contrast to previous classical formulations based upon a notion of stability. His research culminated with the idea that non-linear influencing factors of ecosystems dynamically interact and produce a multi-stabile system which does not have merely one equilibrium state, but instead has a multitude of equilibrium states or a so-called steady state equilibrium. "Resilience determines the persistence of relationships within a system and is a measure of the ability of these systems to absorb changes of state variables, driving variables, and parameters and still persist" (Holling 1973, p. 17). In Holling's perspective, a resilient system can be conceived as being of limited stability and subjected to permanent change (Handmer & Dovers 1996). Therefore, resilience here is not to be understood as a system characteristic which acts as a baseline for the fluctuations beyond the equilibrium, rather, it serves to preserve the system in the case of disturbances.

The original empirical and (allegedly) quantitative and descriptive concept was transformed into a qualitative and normative concept without sufficient reflexive consideration accompanying it in the process. Even Holling's paper from 1973 begins with the search for perspectives "for theory and practice" (Holling 1973, p. 2) and ends – albeit in a reserved fashion – with the first considerations regarding the "application" of the resilience notion in active resource management. Thus how it touch upon the related idea to utilise the concept in approaches aiming to control and manage. In this aforementioned move, the concept is necessarily and inherently stretched beyond its original application in ecosystems. This expansion of the resilience concept into social-ecological systems, which Holling also contributed significantly to, is only possible thanks to the axiom which heuristically describes ecosystems in the same manner as social-ecological systems: namely, as adaptive cycles, or accordingly, in the paradigm of complex adaptive systems (Westley et al. 2002; Walker & Cooper 2011). As already implied in the foundational theory of abstract systems which serves as basis for resilience's description (Lindseth 2011), this took a particularly argumentative detour through social-ecological systems until it could then finally and explicitly be postulated for social systems.

Current ecologically oriented research directs its attention to the systemic interaction of social and ecological systems with non-linear feedback loops because, to reference Norgaard (1994), this research firstly assumes a coevolution and interaction of the systems (Zimmerer 1994; Gunderson et al. 1997; Levin et al. 1998; Berkes & Folke 2002; Berkes 2007). This, when combined with the complexity of existing and future environmental problems, has led to the situation in which these problems can no longer by resolved within disciplinary confines (Berkes et al. 2003; Holling et al. 1998; Young et al. 2006). The interaction of social and ecological systems is dealt with upon the basis of such terms as "socio-ecological systems" (SES) (Gallopín 2006) or social-ecological systems (Berkes et al. 2003) whereby the main focus should be directed at the entire system which itself arises through interactions (Berkes 2007). In general, the research initiatives into SES seemingly manage to get by although they lack a specific social systems theory or a societal theoretical approach grounding them (Bürkner 2010; Geenen 2012). Resource utilisation and the maintenance of the relationships between social and ecological systems stand at the centre of this research into SES. Subsequently, disasters play at best a subordinate role alongside other less considered factors such as socio-economic structures, inequality, power relations, poverty, and agency.

2.2 The Detour through Vulnerability Research

Regardless whether one sees resilience as an entirely new paradigm of disaster research as McEntire et al. (2002) view it, or even if one assumes that it occupies a complementary relationship to the concept of vulnerability (Mayana 2006; Voss 2010), one cannot completely comprehend resilience without connecting it to the hitherto existing research into vulnerability.

While vulnerability research represents a break with the preceding dominant natural disaster paradigm and its inherent technocratic solutions therewith (Hewitt 1983; 1997; Bolin & Stanford 1998; Fordham 2004; Hilhorst & Bankoff 2004; Phillips & Fordham 2010), resilience is instead ascribed the role of a critical corrective which is supposed to work against the pathologisation of (potential) disaster victims. Furthermore it should – in every social, economic, and political conditionality of disasters – also point out the capability for agency among the affected or to the structural limitations of their capabilities.

Vulnerability research, which is often seen as an attempt to disappropriate natural disasters of their alleged naturalness (O'Keefe et al. 1976), stretches back into the 1970s and has its roots in the research into poverty and hunger, as well as human ecology (Sen 1982; Chambers & Conway 1991; Watts 1983; Hewitt 1983; Adger 2006). "[V]ulnerability expresses the multi-dimensionality of disasters by focusing attention on the totality of relationships in a given social situation which constitute a condition that [...] produces a disaster." (Oliver-Smith 2004, p. 11) In this sense, vulnerability research investigates the social production of inequality and the "state of powerlessness in the face of a known or unknown hazard" (O'Riordan 1990, p. 295) as a condition of the uneven distribution of damages inflicted by disasters.

The *Risk-Hazard Model* (Burton et al. 1978; 1993), which is also occasionally named the *Natural Hazards Approach*, was one of the first approaches that described vulnerability but nonetheless remained trapped in the previous naturalising paradigm; so much so that it is extremely difficult to draw a dividing line between the two from our present point of view. In this approach vulnerability is primarily described as the exposition of a reference unit vis-à-vis rarely occurring, stationary, and identified hazards. These hazards then form the primary focus of the investigation. As such, political economy, socio-economic conditions, the specific social structures, as well as human behaviour are comparatively granted marginal attention at best and, in the event that social resilience comes to be mentioned, it is done without reference and without a conceptual foundation. Instead, forms of coping are denoted in the sense of adaptation or adjustment and, as before, social structures, power relations, etc. are granted altogether little attention.

In comparison, the *Pressure and Release Model* from Blaike et al. (1994 and Wisner et al. 2003) regards disasters as the result of the interaction between a broadly-termed and non-specific stressor and the vulnerability of social groups. The model identifies so-called roots causes as the societal base conditions for vulnerability, whose economic, demographics, and political processes which are spatially and temporally detached from the manifested risk: these root causes are then accordingly given great significance in the model. Through dynamic pressures root causes are translated into concrete unsafe conditions which, together with a hazard, can result in a disaster. The authors define vulnerability as the devaluation of coping: i.e. that vulnerability means "the characteristics of a person or group and their situation that influence their capacity to anticipate, cope with, resist and recover from the impact of a natural hazard" (Wisner et al. 2003, p. 11). So although the word "resilience" was already used in the first edition in 1994, it nonetheless developed further until 2003 where it seemingly approached the conceptually similar idea of "livelihood and community resilience" which was also just being established at that time. The nine years between the first and second edition evidence a traceable change in resilience's attributed significance. This newer conceptualisation during this period emphasised the ability to withstand shocks and to put adaptation into execution.

The understanding of resilience in socio-scientific disaster research was likewise pivotally influenced by the investigations of Turner et al. (2003) into Coupled Human-Environmental Systems (CHES), which in a certain sense combines ecological resilience with vulnerability against the background of global environmental change. The *Framework for Vulnerability Analysis in Sustainability Science* should, as the name hints at, serve for the analysis of vulnerability. To be specific, the authors of this framework refer to the *Risk-Hazard Model* and the *Pressure and Release Model*. Building upon both of these approaches, Turner at al. (2003, p. 8074) define: "Vulnerability is the degree to which a system, subsystem, or system component is likely to experience harm due to exposure to a hazard, either a perturbation or stress/stressor". Important to note in this definition is that the origin of the hazard affecting the system can be traced to a location either within, or on the outside of a system (Gallopín 2006; Kasperson et. al 2005). The authors here do not remain entrenched in the idea of the violability of the system (its ability to be damaged), rather they complement the framework of resilience by declaring it to be the ability of a system to deal with disturbances as they occur. In doing this, the authors explicitly hark back to the research into coupled social-ecological systems: "resilience enters vulnerability analysis from ecology, where it has evolved in meaning through extended debate and application. The concept has been used to characterise a system's ability to bounce back to a reference state after a disturbance and the capacity of a system to maintain certain structures and functions despite disturbance [...]. Resilience and related concepts influence a variety of interdisciplinary research focused on coupled human–environment systems [...], especially through the key component of 'adaptive capacity', the flexibility of ecosystems, and the ability of social systems to learn in response to disturbances" (Turner et al. 2003, p. 8075). Although the framework does indeed conceptualise resilience as an own independent component, it nonetheless forms one component of the system's vulnerability (Birkmann 2008).

An important point in Adger's work (2000, p. 361) (who extensively worked with the concept of social resilience) is that external stressors can arise "both in the form of environmental variability (such as agricultural pests or the impacts of climatic extremes), as well as in the form of social, economic and political upheaval (associated with the variability of world markets for primary commodities, or with rapid changes in property laws or state interventions)"; i.e. that they can also be caused by other (superordinate) social systems. Resilience is a distinctly relational concept for Adger a concept which stresses both the importance of coordinated system-environment relationships as well the occasional necessity of a radical transformation in the system so as to secure future existence. As Adger's work points out, the word "environment" here doesn't just mean the ecological environment. In viewing social reference units, they are to be understood above all as the basic conditions of the social framework. In such a relational conceptualisation forming the basis, it is irrelevant whether the shock affecting the reference units is either of ecological or social origin. Even that social change internal to the system can sufficiently stress the system if the established structures are incompatible with the environment: "Perturbations are usually assumed to come from outside the system. But this may be an unduly restrictive definition. […] [P]rocesses can give rise to modifications in the functioning or structure of the system triggered by changes in the system's environment […], by internal alterations […], or by the interaction among external and internal processes" (Gallopín 2006, p. 295).

3 The Original Potential of Resilience

Even if vulnerability research has led to an overcoming of the previous technocratic paradigm which naturalised disasters, this new perspective nonetheless came with attached problems and biases of its own. Vulnerability research was criticised for its pathologising of (potential) victims as it specifically emphasised susceptibility and violability to the point where it can illustrate the affected persons as being wholly passive. Hewitt (1997, p. 167) for example writes that, "'vulnerability' may prove to be an unfortunate term. Unlike much of the work it labels, the word emphasises a 'condition' and encourages a sense of societies or 'people' as passive." Furedi's critique (2005, p. 77) goes in a similar direction whereby he understands vulnerability not as a specific concept, but more so as a "cultural metaphor" which is accompanied by a "deference to Fate (sic!)". Furedi sees political consequences stemming from this understanding of the concept as "vulnerability dooms people to the role of helpless victims of circumstances" (Furedi 2005, p. 77). Furthermore, he states that this "call[s] into question people's capacity to assume a measure of control over their affairs" and that it likewise represents a "cultural legitimation for the downsizing of the idea of the active citizen" (Furedi 2005, p. 77).

Greg Bankoff views the vulnerability discourse as being bound to a uniquely western perspective and places it alongside other western discourses that denigrate non-western perspectives like the topicality discourse or the discourse of (under)development. He states: "The discourse of vulnerability, no less and no more than that of topicality or development, belongs to a knowledge system formed from within a dominant Western liberal consciousness and so inevitably reflects the values and principles of that culture" (Bankoff 2001, p. 29). Even if the technocratic natural hazards discourse as a precursor to the vulnerability paradigm allegedly provided for a rise of marginalisation for regions located in the global south, and in spite of the fact that the concept is paternalistically and colonially structured at its core, *both* discourses are nonetheless "variants of the same hegemonic discourse that identifies one and the same parts of the globe as the abode of mainly disadvantaged people who dwell in poorly governed and environmentally degraded spaces. [...] [T]he concept of vulnerability still encourages a sense of societies and people as weak, passive and pathetic, and he compares it to other 'social pathologies like, or derived from poverty, underdevelopment and overpopulation' (Bankoff 2001, p. 29). The quasi-solutions which were produced and legitimised by such a diagnosis allow that those who are (apparently) vulnerable to "become [...] the objects of planning by the various stakeholders in poverty reduction and development" (Delica-Willison & Willison 2004, p. 145). This is compounded by the fact that (western) interventions and intrusions often appear to be the only helpful possibilities available from the common outsider's perspective (Bankoff 2001). Van Loon's (2008) argument follows a similar line of reasoning with special considerations for governmentality practices.

This aforementioned criticism of vulnerability research though should not aid to hide the fact that some authors in vulnerability research have nonetheless allotted potentially affected persons an active and agency-filled role that fulfils a significant reflexive function. This function is given a variety of names in the research literature: coping, capacities, adaptation and/or resilience (O'Keefe et al. 1977; Hewitt 1983; Watts 1983; Burton et al. 1993; Blaikie et al. 1994; Adger 1996; Davis 2004; Oliver-Smith 1996). A prime example can be found in the first and second editions of "At Risk" (Blaikie et al. 1994; Wisner et al. 2003), and then it appears as if more and more alternative terms and concepts were gradually replaced by resilience over the course of time.

"Vulnerability studies have given as much emphasis to people's active capabilities or resilience in relation to dangers as to weakness" (Hewitt 1997, pp. 150f.). In fact, persons that must live with unsafe living conditions, also have identifiable corresponding adaptation strategies (Heijmans 2004). A good juxtaposition of passive vulnerability and active capacities can be found, for example, in the works of Anderson and Woodrow (1989; see Davis 2004). Adger (2006, p. 274) sums up the state of research accordingly in the following manner: "While developing countries are portrayed as 'most vulnerable' there is, at the same time, much evidence, [...] suggesting that communities and countries themselves have significant capacity to adapt latent in local knowledge and experience of coping with variability. The paradox derives from two faces of vulnerability—a state of 'powerlessness and endangerment' [...] and the recognition of the ability [...] to adapt to changing circumstances." Upon a closer inspection of a number of authors one can indeed notice that vulnerability reveals itself as being the external hindrance of coping and resilience as a result of structural conditions. Anthony Oliver-Smith (1996, p. 315) similarly identifies the cause of increasing vulnerability in the "undermining of indigenous adaptations, based on long-term experience in local environments, through direct government policies or political economic forces creating production systems inappropriate to local culture and environmental conditions." On the other hand, Bolin and Standford (1998) view the socially produced lack of adaptation capacity as the cause of vulnerability: a phenomenon which Hewitt (1997, p. 150) terms as "impaired adaptive capabilities". In an even more striking manner, Wisner (2004, p. 189) defines vulnerability specifically as "the blockage, erosion or devaluation of local knowledge and coping practices".

The core meaning of resilience arises out of this same vulnerability context and the specific emphasis on peoples' agency to act in accordance to their constraints. In any case, the common conceptualisations of vulnerability with their inherent pathologisation and victimisation of affected persons made it necessary that the resilience concept step out of the shadow of the vulnerability term and present itself as an independent concept.

Whether one orients oneself according to the rather conservatively conceived "bouncing-back" as the central characteristic of resilience, or if one instead adheres to on a comparatively progressive-processual understanding which views resilience as a learning and adaption process, one is still nevertheless bound by an inherent notion: namely, the notion that there is possibility for action and reactions which, when impaired, causes vulnerability in turn. In order to best understand the argument concerning the usage of agency in the resilience concept, a glance at sociological action theory is well-advised: for example the so-called relational sociology (Emirbayer & Mische 1998). In looking at this theory, one can find definitions of agency that are astoundingly similar to the resilience concept.

> "[T]he temporally constructed engagement by actors of different structural environments—the temporal relational contexts of action—which, through the interplay of habit, imagination, and judgment, both reproduces and transforms those structures in interactive response to the problems posed by changing historical situations" (Emirbayer & Mische 1998, p. 970).

Emirbayer and Mische conceptualise the different components of agency as *iterative, projective* and *practical-evaluative*. The *iterative dimension* refers to "past patterns of thought and action, as routinely incorporated in practical activity, thereby giving stability and order to social universes" (Emirbayer & Mische 1998, p. 973). The second dimension of agency, the *projective element*, "encompasses the imaginative generation by actors of possible future trajectories of action, in which received structures of thought and action may be creatively reconfigured in relation to actors' hopes, fears, and desires for the future" (Emirbayer & Mische 1998, p. 973). The practical-evaluative element "entails the capacity of actors to make practical and normative judgments among alternative possible trajectories of action, in response to the emerging demands, dilemmas, and ambiguities of presently evolving situations" (Emirbayer & Mische 1998, p. 973).

At the same time, it can be said to be equally valid when one analyses the socio-economic context in which the actors are embedded: a highly variable context which provides them with their cultural, linguistic, symbolic, institutional or legal surrounding conditions and societal positioning and which should be grasped relationally (Emirbayer & Goodwin 1996).

Agency refers to a relational perspective; i.e. the interconnectedness of subject and society; the notion that individuals in their formations of how they act are produced by their discourses and that they then produce these discourses in turn (akin to the dialectic of habitus and field from Bourdieu, or the notions of subject and discourse as per Foucault and Butler). The challenge then is to presume the social enabling and social limiting of individual self-determination and agency, and to assume at the same time that the individual self-determination and agency, which individuals ascribe to themselves and others, presuppose processes of social subjectivity formation in socialisation processes (Scherr 2012). With such an understanding agency is, on the one hand, a process of active shaping of one's given circumstances. On the other hand, it is at the same time embedded in social structures which are in turn historically, culturally, and societally framed in a specific manner. These structures provide 'radii of agency' to the actors thus determining who is in the position to act all and who is not, or how specific ways of acting/agency are each symbolically charged, interpreted, and societally acknowledged, here see for example Gayatri Chakravorty Spivak`s famous essay "Can the Subaltern Speak?" (1988) or Pierre Bourdieu's concept of symbolic capital (1991).

As we have demonstrably shown, theoretical and conceptual ideas about agency and resilience greatly overlap one another to the point where one could even exchange one term for another and their respective meanings would not shift. When one traces this understanding back through the various approaches of social scientific disaster research, it often elicits quite interesting research questions and desiderata. It furthermore allows for the reconstruction of the resilience concept's significance as a transformation element in the discourse.

4 Resilience in Catastrophes, Disasters and Emergencies

According to the findings of socio-scientific disaster research (see Quarantelli 1996, 2000, 2006), disasters can analytically be located at a variety of levels. While *catastrophes* come particularly into play at a (cross-)societal level (examples here would be devastating events which encompass entire societies like the 2010 earthquake in Haiti), the range of *disasters* is comparatively less far-reaching. There are only few social scientific approaches for a (cross-)societal conceptualisation of resilience. The *disaster* category is most often made up of localized so-called natural disasters or man-made disasters (violent conflict, civil war, technological and biological accidents, or terrorist attacks). Most of the resilience approaches are touching upon the level of disasters. Scale-wise, an *emergency* has the least range whereby only single persons or groups of persons are affected. Therefore psychology is rich with ideas, approaches, and empirical studies covering the resilience topic above all concerning the mental overcoming of trauma. Although, the fine details of the actual disaster events play a more subordinate role.

In pointing out this difference, we are not only drawing upon a quantitative dimension with a specific look at amount of affected persons, but there is quite critically a qualitative dimension being drawn upon: namely, that events must necessarily result in *different* reactions because disaster management measures of the state are less promising and less helpful in catastrophes and the foundational explanatory and interpretive patterns of everyday life no longer fulfil their orientating function. As such, catastrophes thus provoke questions regarding collective meaning and signify a radical breaking point which nullify the rationality and organisational form of the affected society, and furthermore destroy the social structures and orders therewith (Clausen 2003). The aforementioned classification into three levels – a macro-perspective with global concerns or concerns for societies, a regional meso-perspective, and an individual micro-perspective – acts as an overlay with which we can grasp and conceive resilience while maintaining a particular view toward the various challenges which are associated with individual types of events/occurrences. The assigning and attributing of resilience's prevailing core points into discrete levels serves analytical purposes and should not be understood in a one-dimensional manner. Individual, communal, and (cross-)societal understandings of resilience are to be understood in a complementary manner whereby they are interwoven with one other. In such a manner, the various levels presuppose one another but can nonetheless be analytically differentiated.

4.1 Resilience in Emergencies

In the 1970s, the Anglo-American field of psychological research experienced a far-reaching paradigm shift which then had reverberating effects in Germany in the 1980s (Zander 2008) the field went from a sickness-oriented pathogenetic conception of human beings, to a salutogenetic one. This signified a shift in understanding whereby deficits to be found were no longer the driving focus. Rather, strengths, competencies, and the resources of individuals or groups took centre stage as the conception of human beings became more variable, complex, and thoroughly positive (Bercht 2013). A pioneering study representative of this paradigm shift was the Kauai study (Werner & Smith 2001). The study investigated the "1955 cohort" on the Hawaiian island of Kauai which consisted of 698 children who had been born on the island and came from different social an ethnic groups. The children were comprehensively studied at various intervals starting at the age of 1, then 2, 10, 18, 32, and eventually 40 years of age. This examination paid a special deference to the subjects' psycho-social development. Of the nearly 700 children, more than 200 originated from backgrounds characterised by very troubled social relations in which they endured extreme poverty, violence, or had existences characterised by serious health issues (Werner 2005). Around 70 of these children (nearly 30%) continued into adulthood from their childhood or youth without further problems or complications and developed into functioning and integrated adults who had completed a course of education, had achieved an independent source of income, were not dependent upon social welfare, were not criminal or otherwise known to the law, had led an intact social live, and who had a significantly lower divorce, sickness, and mortality rate in comparison to the other children from the examined cohort. Interestingly enough, the "resilient youngster […] who succeeded against the odds" (Werner 2005, p. 12) displayed a certain moment of agency. This moment of agency is best evidenced by the fact that the aforementioned few children actively shaped their own social environment by means of "establish[ing], early on, a close bond with at least one competent, emotionally stable person who was sensitive to their needs" (Werner 2005, p. 12). The majority of the remaining at-risk children, numbering nearly 120 persons, developed serious adaptation problems during their childhood and youth. These problems however were partially overcome between the ages of 32 and 40, whereby women, more so than men, were able to pull-through and succeed. This study was *the* study responsible for ending the myth that "a child who is a member of a so called 'high-risk' group is fated to become one of life's losers" (Werner 2005, p. 12).

In the meantime, the resilience term has also undergone far-reaching modifications in psychology in addition to having entered the realm of popular science discourse. One can observe a watering down of the concept here as well as it is being increasingly put to use when dealing with everyday conflicts. Fooken (2015) advocates therefore that one should then only speak of resilience if it is about contention with (either manifest or latently existing) damages, dangers, threats, risks, traumas, or aversive, toxic or pathogenic living circumstances and impact factors. Following this prescription, an inquiry into resilience would then correlate to the psychological perspective regarding the question of how and under which conditions can such a positive life context be produced in spite of risk and damage and against all expectations and probability (Fooken 2015). Resilience would accordingly be defined by the concurrence of risk and protective factors which can, in turn, dynamically vary in a context specific and inter/intra-individual manner. Important to note here is that such developmental processes may occur somewhat quicker than under normal conditions, even though they cannot be exepected (when viewed from an outside perspective) (Carver 1998). In such psychological approaches, it is interesting to note how there is a concrete definition of a goal: a goal targeting a specific way of life which then should to be integrated into the analysis of resilience itself. Such a manner of analysis is rarely found in the approaches in vulnerability research. That sought after goal, which might or might not be achieved in the end, is most often explicitly defined in psychological approaches as wellness (Norris 2008), as a sufficiently good life (Fooken 2015), or as general mental health (Zraly et al. 2013). Resilience is seen as a principal factor for negative psychological consequences after a traumatic event (Kimhi 2014). The sense of coherence (SOC) has also become a relevant factor for measuring resilience. The term is generated from a combination of three components: a sense of meaningfulness, comprehensibility, and manageability (Kimhi 2014). These three components refer to the extent to which affected individuals in extreme situations – but also in their everyday life – feel to be in the position where they can attribute meaning to their lives and their actions and/or feel to be in the position where they can actively shape their environment. Even comprehensive and often-tested quantitative items used in measuring resilience and self-efficacy must also necessarily measure the estimated or existing degree of agency. This degree of agency offers the individual the possibility to come out of an apparently hopeless situation, to return to a constitutive position, and to follow a goal leading to the betterment of their current living situation.

There are many studies in psychological resilience research which contemplate the relationship between resilience and health, how sickness is dealt with, and highlight the significance of social networks and communal support. In order to measure these factors, data is collected on individual personality characteristics or at the community level. However, relatively few studies to date have analysed the interactions *between* the various levels. Often, in the field of disaster prevention and coping, psychological resilience tends to instead be themed with regard to the aspect of preparedness/awareness (Paton 2003; Paton et al. 2005).

4.2 Resilience in Disasters

The majority of qualitative and quantitative studies which deal with resilience and disaster in a social scientific manner are engaged with evaluating and strengthening of resilience at the community level (for example Abelev 2009; Aldrich & Meyer 2015; Cohen et.al. 2013; Meyer 2013; Norris et al. 2008; Murphy 2007; Boon et al. 2012; Cutter et al. 2008; Brown & Kulig 1996; Norris & Stevens 2007; Paton 2008; Zautra 2008; Berkes & Ross 2013; Aldrich 2012)[1], at the city level (UN/ISDR 2012; Da Silva & Morera 2014), or at the regional level (Lukesch et al. 2011; Swanstrom 2008; Christopherson et al. 2010).

Many of the existing approaches utilise quantitative standardised methods (for example Cutter et al. 2008; Cutter et al. 2010; Cutter et.al. 2003), but also qualitative approaches in combination with participative processes are able to be identified among others (Alexander 2011; Fazey et. al. 2010). The indices developed from these various approaches define resilience most often in terms of certain capacities which are either already present or must be developed in the future in order to facilitate resistance and robustness in the face of future disasters.

These capacities serve first and foremost to descriptively extend agency's meaning. In this definition, agency encompasses both the adaptive processes (adaptation/transformation) as well as the interpretive processes for events and occurrences (coping). The relationship between adaptive capacity and resilience is hotly contested in the academic debate due to the multitude of prevailing differing concepts: some authors identify resilience with adaptive capacity (Smit & Wandel 2006) while others define the robustness of a system vis-a-vis change as adaptive capacity (Gunderson 2000). On the other hand, others view adaptive capacity as an element of resilience which can both reflect learning processes brought about by change and be made use of in the future (Carpenter et al. 2001). Given the context present here in this work, we promote the understanding of adaptive capacity in the way Walker et al. (2004) described it: as the ability to establish new structural relationships which should then be able to ensure the persistence of the system in case of radical environmental changes, or in the case of emerging incompatible structures

---

1 As an additional analytical level, neighbourhoods have also occasionally shifted into the research focus (Wallace & Wallace 2008; Aldrich 2012; Breton 2001).

within the system itself (Gallopín 2006). These adaptation efforts encompass all the short-term reactive interventions implemented in dealing with disasters as well as those long-term structural changes which aim to prevent future disasters (Brown & Kulig 1996). Folke (2006) refers to both of these versions of adaptive capacity with the terms adaptability and transformability: the former in the case of short-term reactive measures, and the later as the establishment of entirely new system structures. Within adaptability one can differentiate between mitigation – active disaster coping – and recovery – those reconstruction measures after the disaster. Recently there has been an identifiable surge in examinations into reconstruction efforts after disasters (recovery) in connection with resilience: such approaches (for example Aldrich 2012; Vale & Campanella 2005) often appear to use the city as their referential object (Bürkner 2010). Adaptations can be implemented in a goal-oriented and reflexive manner by taking advantage of the available body of knowledge and collected experience (Gunderson 2003; Westley et al. 2002; Gunderson et al. 2002; Young et al. 2006). Nonetheless it has been shown that structural adaptations are not always carried out in this manner and instead often prove to be exercises of trial-and-error (Bohle 2008; Voss 2009; Lindblom 1959).

Many authors (Adger 2000; Norris et al. 2007; Voss 2009; Folke et al. 2003; Berkes 2007; Hagan & Maguire 2007) argue that the level of dependence on specific resources limits adaptive capacity. This is due to the fact that dependence on singular resources connote rigid couplings with the environment and in turn that the environmental change invariably results in systemic stress. According to Folke et al. (2003), resource diversity and variability form the core elements of resilience. Therefore, the first step toward increasing resilience is in fact recognising and examining insecurity as well as the exigent nature of certain transformation processes (Folke et al. 1998; Folke 2006; Michael 1995; Folke et al. 2003; Berkes 2007; Michael 1995; Gunderson 2003; Oliver-Smith 1996). As to what the form and design of these transformation processes should be, the authors highlight the necessity to draw upon various differing sources of knowledge for their design (Berkes 1999; Berkes et al. 2003; Olick & Robbins 1998; Folke et al. 2003). The synthesis or outright complementarity of different forms of knowledge is viewed by authors (Berkes 2007; Berkes et al. 1995, Folke et al. 2003; Voss 2009) as a promising strategy in dealing with insecurity and those rare events for which there is lack of have adequate scientific data. The significance of social capital in adaptive capacity has also been discussed at length in Adger (2000b), Hagan & Maguire (2007), Breton (2001) and Folke (2006). Aldrich (2012, p. 15) argues for example that social capital exhibits a more significant influence in resilient recovery processes after disasters than socio-economic factors, the population density, the extent of damages, or the aid provided.

Coping is understood as the cultural and social "dealing" with collective stress. Simply put, coping strategies ultimately make larger stresses bearable (Voss 2009). Coping capacity therefore provides the system's handling of failed expectations with a continuity of expectations which emerged through the system (Voss 2008; Norris et al. 2008). As a result, coping especially comes to bear in the midst of, or after a disaster. This begs the question then: is the reference unit furnished with the capacity to interpret disastrous events in a sensible manner within their bounded horizon of meaning or via the structures which help delineate the significance of such things? Dombrowsky (1987) responds and clarifies this question in the following manner: The significance of a disaster can be measured by how much "labour" must necessarily be expended in the construction of meaning whilst overcoming it. By ascribing meaning to disaster by means of socially, culturally, or religiously anchored interpretive patterns, it then becomes possible to produce a connection to the interpretive pattern found in everyday life. In contrast to catastrophes, disasters allow for a recourse with already existent interpretative or explanatory patterns. In order to maintain a suitable conceptualisation of resilience in the first place, one must recognise the pronounced significance of cultural boundaries and forms of meaning creating/sense-making (Voss 2008; Voss & Funk 2015). Such approaches that recognise this are often found among predominately in anthropological studies to topics such as how young Inuit make use of cultural narratives for the production of resilience strategies (Wexler et al. 2014). Either that, or they point to culturally specific forms of coping such as a study which investigates the Rwandan term "Kwahinagana". "Kwahinagana" describes the creative process "whereby the self imagines the possibility of something other than the present mode of suffering, even if that possibility is yet undefined, and by doing so generates the durability to continue living" (Zraly et. al 2013, pp. 413f.). In another example Macamo (2003) demonstrates through the example of the flooding in Mozambique in 2000, that death and destruction alone do not constitute a disaster if they are instead grasped as "accompanying symptoms" of an otherwise positively recognised occurrence. Similarly, Voss (2008, p. 53) describes the situation for Indonesia when writing: "For example, the victims of a volcanic eruption are seen as holy beings, which the volcano has called for a wedding party. The possibility of creating meaning in such a way, necessitates a much more complex evaluation of the relationship between potential gains on the one hand [...] and the possibility of losing material valuables (which might be accepted because this loss has a meaning) or even human lives. " In the same vein, certain cultural arrangements with "disasters" can exist so that said "disasters" become ordering elements of the social sphere (Bankoff 1999; 2007).

Beyond meaning creation via cosmologies, every culture harbours within itself forms of dealing with the loss and collapse of collective order creation which can be entirely different from those found in other cultures. While the collapse of collective meaning creation can be viewed as being an integral component of disaster (Weick 1993), meaning creation proves to be a significant precondition for the overcoming of disastrous occurrences (Norris et al. 2007). The legitimacy of political institutions as well as the trust placed in these institutions can have a large influence on whether an occurrence is viewed as a disaster at all (Rodríguez et al. 2006). In addition to this, (social-)psychological research amongst others has come to learn of numerous social meaning creation practices such as mourning rituals, shared narratives, social cohesion and networks, or even certain forms of humour which serve to aid and help individual and collective coping by linking it to the past. Mourning and unification rituals along with collective reorganisation (emergent groups) both during and after disasters require specific circumstances. As such, it is not surprising that communities are the paramount focus of research as they must necessarily already have a certain degree of cohesion as a social foundation before the disaster strikes (Eyre 2006; Aldrich 2012). As shown by Kai T. Erikson (1976) in his study concerning the loss of community after the Buffalo Creek dam failure and subsequent flooding, if collective coping fails, then there will be reciprocal effects on the social sphere.

4.3 Resilience in Catastrophes

The conceptualisation of resilience as a systemic category which indicates general societal conditions necessarily demands a clarification of a multitude of fundamental questions: to start, it needs to be clarified e.g. what is a "normal condition" of societal relations? Or, at which juncture can one say that a "tipping point" has been reached after which a system can no longer cope with a challenge or is no longer capable to change itself? This carries with it the assumption however that a system no longer has the capacity to change itself to meet the prevailing challenges, which itself likewise presupposes an inner essence or a previously existing capability (Bonß 2015). This is challenging to rectify with a relational and genuinely constructive perspective (see also Endreß & Rampp 2015). Similarly, the question of spatial and temporal boundaries is central for the application of the resilience concept. Especially if one grasps resilience in the sense as offered by the agency definition (see also Christmann et al. 2015). Those catastrophes which touch upon entire societies as whole – including their organisational principles and rationality in a Clausenian sense (the 2010 Haiti earthquake) – have yet to be investigated by social scientific approaches which ask the aforementioned questions with regard to the resilience aspect. Primarily owing to the inherent complexity associated with

it, it is no wonder that such an approach has yet to be undertaken. This is because catastrophes, in the sense as proposed by Clausen (1992; 1994; 2003), sustainably disintegrate societies in their entirety. This societal disintegration is accompanied by falsification of society's various interpretative and explanatory patterns, to the point where it can scarcely be said that a collective, that could be resilient, exists anymore. While one can muster up, draw upon, make use of cultural value patterns, action patterns, and rationality patterns for interpretation in a limited fashion during a disaster, this is not the case in catastrophes where such ability is extremely limited or impossible. This is due to the fact that those social structures which enable agency and interpretation in the first place no longer exist as such in such catastrophes. As an "unconditional surrender of collective defence" (Clausen 1992, p. 186), catastrophe represent the opposite of agency. Catastrophes reveal societal structures as ineffectual and powerless in the face of the societal environment: "neither professionalised elites nor power elites, nor other ruling classes, nor clergy are able to cope with disasters, so society breaks up into much smaller networks of actors" (Clausen 1992, p. 186). Agency is heavily compromised and restricted as the three foundational dimensions have been sustainably destroyed. Those "past patterns of thought and action" of the iterative dimension which seemed to have promised stability can no longer act upon and respond to the catastrophe at hand. Rather, these bespoken past patterns are an integral cause of the catastrophe. The second dimension, the projective element, is by definition excluded as a generator for possible futures in catastrophes as catastrophes are characterised by necessity and sheer survival. This is in direct contrast to concepts of freedom and possibility of choice (Clausen 1994; 2003). Finally, the loss of value orientation also means that the practical-evaluative element is no longer present: in catastrophes, those social foundations which enable agency are so sustainably destroyed (Clausen 2003)
that resilience would rather consist in (re)enabling agency through community formation and therefore the (re)establishment of a shared normative basis, a future orientation, etc. To date there has been very little empirical material regarding resilience in catastrophes because, on the one hand, catastrophes are rather rare in comparison to disasters and emergencies and, on the other hand, because developing a suitable research program which could manage to suitably grasp resilience upon the basis of such formative processes is inherently quite complex.

5 The Legacy of Resilience

We see the critical potential of the resilience concept in its original conceived meaning and its modifications in the following light.

The acknowledgment of the populace and its subjects as actors with a certain agency (even) in times of disaster is a fundamental critique of the functions of the modern state, perhaps even obviating the need for predominant aid and disaster management structures offered by the state. It is a challenge to common understandings of development and leads to alternative ways of dealing with uncertainty in a perhaps more decolonial and appreciative way.

Our main argument is that the potential of the resilience concept in disaster research was its questioning of predominant ways of thinking and types of action in science, disaster management, and politics. Since the concept of vulnerability immanently harbours the tendency to consider those affected by disasters as being "deficitary", pathological, and passively suffering, the resilience concept – at least when viewed from a historical perspective – came on to the scene to fulfil a corrective role. This role was to point out the agency among those potentially affected in every systemic/structural and socio-economic production of disaster. The insight that people in disasters are not merely helpless victims and solely receivers of aid, but that they instead are self-determined, acting and organizing subjects with specific ways of coping with inner and outer challenges, defied the logic of both existing scientific and other, dominant systems of thought, as well as political institutions.

Political institutions publically demand the resilience of citizens time and again, but crisis situations as well as disaster management structures have repeatedly shown that political institutions simply do not trust in the agency of the populace. Geenen (2012) contends that the alleged anomic behaviour (panic, disaster, looting, shock/syndrome, and so forth) of the general public during disasters, as it is often expected from the side of government agencies and which seemingly goes against all empirical findings in disaster research (auf der Heide 2004; Schulze et. al 2015) is in fact an attempt to disavow the general population of their agency. This disavowance serves the purpose of (re)attaining symbolic capital for the state vis-à-vis the symbolic devaluation of the general populace. "With the claim of anomie, the police institutions [sensu Rancieré] attempt to legitimise themselves and to hide their own failure. However, this failure becomes even more obvious and also reveals itself as failure, the more resilience unfolds its impact […] among those affected who have become autonomous." (Hempel & Lorenz 2014, p. 54) Disasters radically pose questions concerning interpretive authority, agency, and therefore, systems of domination and authority in general. However, it is not the disaster's acclamation which alone acts as the centrifugal deciding point over sovereignty, rather it is also important to inquire how the factual agency is indeed performatively distributed during a disaster. In short: who is a "rescuer" and who is a "victim" (Hempel & Markwart 2013)? Using the example of the disastrous snows of 1978-9 in northern Germany, Dombrowsky (1981) was able to demonstrably show how government agencies perceive resilience – when understood as the greater population *not* assuming the role of a victim and *instead* taking on a role of active agency above and beyond the state, its capacities, and storyboard – as not being a form of help or aid. Rather, they perceived it more so as a threat. "Resilience [...] can be an accusation against the police institutions [sensu Ranciaré] when spaces of possibility for survival under conditions of neglect, marginalisation and the absence of state protection are created in a self-organizing fashion." (Hempel & Lorenz 2014, pp. 54f.) As exemplarily demonstrated by the self-determined activity of civilians in non-registered/unaffiliated volunteer roles during the Elbe River flooding of 2013, or through various examples in other European countries, the debate and topicality surrounding the changing role of the general population in disasters is still on-going. Currently, if there is an apparent open-mindedness

or an apparent open recognition among management levels for such new forms of volunteer engagement, it seems that this does not imply recognition and trust in the general population's agency and resilience. Rather these seeming advances often more likely appear to be mere attempts at (re)attaining control and containment strategies in the face of a lack of alternatives stemming from the sheer magnitude of informal volunteer engagement. And if this outreach and recognition are indeed not plain outright attempts at regaining total control, they are instead attempts at containment or a redirection.

Against this background, the mainstreaming of resilience can be seen as a strategy to cement power structures, dependencies and attributions that (re)construct the populace and its subjects as helpless and powerless in the face of disaster. As proven by developments in other fields (e.g. gender), the mainstreaming of originally emancipatory concepts can take away their brisance and critical potential (Dittmer 2007). Butler (1997) speaks of the importance to keep emancipatory concepts outside dominant discourses because they are not able to represent things which could be a fundamental threat to their existence. The aim to fight against dominant norms should not be to become part of the mainstream, but rather to upset current regimes of definition (Thürmer-Rohr 2001).

To take resilience seriously as a concept would mean to ask the question concerning the sources of resilience that are not just static adverse of deficient conditions – like this is often the case for conceptualisations of vulnerability – but rather as an instruction to change existing inequalities and power structure. To sum up and complete the use and critique of resilience in disaster research and management, the following aspects have to be integrated into conceptualizing and analysing. Analyses have to be undertaken and a change of hegemonies and power relations (Scandlyn et al. 2010; Peacock & Ragsdale 2012), of discursive inequalities, of political processes that mean exclusion for risk-disposed persons (Voss 2008; Hewitt 1997), as well as analyses and change which target socio-economic inequalities and unequal access to resources and capitals have to be pursued (Obrist et al. 2010; Geenen 2012; Deffner 2007, further developments are to be found in the forthcoming Dittmer et al. 2016). All of the above requires that the power dimension of language as a basis for social life and social order be brought to the forefront, and integrated into the core analysis (Oliver-Smith 2004). In order to make this all possible, it must necessarily come to a general empowerment and informed understandings of participation (Hewitt 1997), but above all a discussion about goals and what exactly a resilient society, community, or individual means. At the same time, the implications of resilience's role as a hegemonic and western knowledge *dispositif* have to be thoroughly inquired into. Similarly, those knowledges and understandings which are all too often devalued for being *"local"* need to be integrated (Hilhorst & Bankoff 2004). To acknowledge the agency and autonomy of subjects and populations on an analytical level would involve the tolerating of "negative" developments that are potentially not in line with Western democratic values: e.g. markets of violence or the so-called IS. On the analytical level, resilience would need to at least, be constructed as a consummately value-free concept for investigating complex processes, whether the observer likes it or not (Voss & Dittmer 2016).

A first expansion of previous efforts which attempts to integrate the above-mentioned aspects was made by supplementing both of the known discussed capacities (adaptive and coping) with a *third* capacity which would be more sensitive to notions of power: this is termed participative capacity. The idea of participative capacity attempts to direct attention to the interpretive power and influential prospects of the reference units regarding those local, regional, and global processes which affect them. "Thus, participative capacity becomes a key category in the circle of disasters: the lower the participative capacity [is], the lower the resonance for critical developments, the lower the prevention activities, the lower the capacity to respond and to adapt and so on [are]." (Voss 2008, p. 52). A contraction of participative capacity limits the various potentials to affect the conditions of life as well as the possibilities to deal and work with change. In this perspective, a reduction of social resilience would mean nothing other than "the blockage, erosion or devaluation of local knowledge and coping practices" (Wisner 2004, p. 189; Anderson & Woodrow 1989) which are caused by unequal participative capacities. From this perspective, the local perspective in the form of local factors of adaptive and coping capacity proves to be an essential starting point for increasing social resilience (Bankoff 2007c; Delica-Willision & Willision 2004; Adger 2010; Heijmans 2004; Bohle 2008). Due to an asymmetric distribution of participative capacity, a number of local structures are poorly appraised, disqualified, and then commodified through external planning (Midgley 1983; Hewitt 1997; Bankoff 2003). According to Delica-Willision and Willision (2004), these interventions in local structures – in addition to the bringing in of external beliefs – often contrarily resulted in an increase in vulnerability rather than its reduction. The uneven distribution of resources (Adger 2000b), the differing strength and scope of available networks (Blaikie et al. 1994; Hurlbert et al. 2006), expert cultures (Clausen 1992), mechanisms of exclusion and inclusion (Cutter et al. 2003), mobility (Adger 2000b), gender identity and status (Oxfam 2005; Krishnaraj 1997), language, as well as property law (Berkes & Folke 1998) and education (Brauner & Dombrowsky 1996) interfere and culminate in the unequal distribution of interpretive power and the participative ability to affect change to the conditions of life.

All of these aforementioned intervening factors could be combined under the domain of Pierre Bourdieu's expanded concept of "capital" (Bourdieu & Wacquant 1992). The concepts of social capital (Scheffer et al. 2002; Bankoff 2007b; Murphy 2007; Aldrich 2012) and cultural capital (Berkes & Folke 1992) are already being used in the discussion surrounding social resilience and questions of adaptation. Nevertheless, the power dimension, which is inherent in Bourdieu's idea of symbolic capital and is likewise found in participative capacity itself, has been largely neglected in the discussion of social resilience till now. In not considering these perspectives, the social conditions of vulnerability and the causal origins of disaster have receded into the background (Cannon et al. 2010).

In spite of all the justified critiques pointing out concerns of open-endedness and diffuse meanings (e.g. Aldunce at al. 2015; Alexander 2013; Sudmeier-Rieux 2015), and in spite of the neoliberal co-opting of resilience, we nonetheless see resilience as a bridging concept which can ignite interdisciplinary and transdisciplinary processes in disaster research and management. Despite the structural conditionality of disasters, resilience is indeed a sensible approach even today. Even when one considers the advances in scientific prediction and technical prevention capabilities, certain occurrences of disasters still cannot be precisely predicated and spatiotemporally affixed. In spite of the effort expended, catastrophic events still occur and manage to surprise in their concrete manifestations. The idea that an earthquake will shake Istanbul is a sufficiently proven certainty according to the current status of research. But when and with which magnitude this exactly will occur, is not. When one thinks of resilience in terms of agency, the role these findings play for the mainstreaming of resilience, remains to be seen and should to be analysed in the future. Furthermore, it ought to be brought under consideration whether the resilience concept is in fact more of a proclamation of uncertainty at this juncture, or whether it offers a category for processing the residual pieces of uncertainty and thus ushering and enabling in participatory role from a previous role of passivity. Perhaps it should at least be considered whether resilience is not the driving factor, but rather if it is just a possible answer for the perceived and more general uncertainty, proneness to crisis, and neoliberalisation of the present age?

References

Abelev, M. S. (2009). Advancing Out of Poverty: Social Class Worldview and Its Relation to Resilience. Journal of Adolescent Research 24(1), 114–141.

Adger, N.W. (2000b). Social and ecological resilience: Are They Related? Progress in Human Geography 24, 347–364.

Adger, N.W. (2006). Vulnerability. Global Environmental Change 16(3), 268–281. DOI: 10.1016/j.gloenvcha.2006.02.006.

Adger, W. N. (1996). Approaches to Vulnerability to Climate Change (CSERGE Working Paper GEC 96-05).

Adger, W. N. (2000a). Indicators of Social and Economic Vulnerability to Climate Change in Vietnam (CSERGE Working Paper GEC, 98-02). Online verfügbar unter http://www.cserge.ac.uk/sites/default/files/gec_1998_02.pdf.

Agamben, G. (2009). What is an Apparatus? And Other Essays. Stanford, California: Stanford University Press.

Aldrich, D. P. (2012). Building Resilience. Social Capital in Post-disaster Recovery. The University of Chicago Press: Chicago.

Aldrich, D. P., & Meyer, M. (2015). Social Capital and Community Resilience. American Behavioral Scientist 59(2), 254-269.

Aldunce, P., Beilin, R., Handmer, J., & Howden, M. (2015). Framing Disaster Resilience. The Implications of the Diverse Concepualisations of "Bouncing Back". Disaster Prevention and Management 23(3), 252–270.

Alexander, D. E. (2013). Resilience and Disaster Risk Reduction: An Etymological Journey. Natural Hazards and Earth System Science 13(11), 2707–2716. Retrieved from http://www.nat-hazards-earth-syst-sci.net/13/2707/2013/nhess-13-2707-2013.pdf [03/25/2015].

Anderson, M. B., & Woodrow, P. J. (1998). Rising from the Ashes. Development Strategies in Times of Disaster. London: IT Publications.

auf der Heide, E. (2004). Common Misconceptions about Disasters: Panic, the "Disaster Syndrome", and Looting. In M. O'Leary (ed.), The First 72 Hours: A Community Approach to Disaster Preparedness (pp. 340-380). Lincoln (Nebraska): Universe Publishing.

Bankoff, G. (1999). A History of Poverty. The Politics of Natural Disasters in the Philippines, 1985-1995. The Pacific Revue 12(3), 381–420.

Bankoff, G. (2003). Cultures of Disaster. Society and Natural Hazards in the Philippines. Routledge, London.

Bankoff, G. (2007a). Comparing Vulnerabilities. Toward Charting a Historical Trajectory of Disasters. Historical Social Research 32(3), 103–114.

Bankoff, G. (2007b). Dangers to Going it Alone. Social Capital and the Origins of Community Resilience in the Philippines. Continuity and Change 22(2), 327–355.

Bankoff, G. (2007c). Living with Risk; Coping with Disasters. Hazard as a Frequent Life Experience in the Philippines. Education about Asia 12(2), 26–29.

Bankoff, G. (2001). Rendering the World Unsafe. 'Vulnerability' as Western Discourse". Disasters 25(1), 19–35.

Bercht, A. L. (2013). Stresserleben, Emotionen und Coping in Guangzhou, China. Mensch-Umwelt-Transaktionen aus geographischer und psychologischer Perspektive. Stuttgart: Steiner.

Berkes ,F., Colding, J., & Folke, C. (2003). Introduction. In F. Berkes, J. Colding & C. Folke (eds), Navigating Social-Ecological Systems. Building Resilience for Complexity and Change (pp. 1–29). Cambridge: Cambridge University Press.

Berkes, F. (1999). Sacred Ecology. New York: Taylor & Francis.

Berkes, F. (2007). Understanding Uncertainty and Reducing Vulnerability: Lessons from Resilience Thinking. Natural Hazards 41(2), 283–295. doi:10.1007/s11069-006-9036-7.

Berkes, F., & Folke, C. (2002). Back to the Future: Ecosystem Dynamics and Local Knowledge. In L. H. Gunderson & C. S. Holling (eds.), Panarchy. Understanding Transformations in Human and Natural Systems (pp. 121–146). Washington: Island Press.

Berkes, F., Folke, C., & Gadgil, M. (1995). Traditional Ecological Knowledge, Biodiversity, Resilience and Sustainability. In C. A. Perrings et al (eds), Biodiversity Conservation. Problems and Policies (pp. 281–299). Kluwer Academic Publishers, Dordrecht.

Berkes, F., & Ross, H. (2013). Community Resilience: Toward an Integrated Approach. Society & Natural Resources: An International Journal, 26(1), 5-20.

Berkes, F, & Folke, C. (1992). A Systems Perspective on the Interrelations between Natural, Human-made and Cultural Capital. Ecological Economics, 5(1), 1–8.

Birkmann, J. (2008). Globaler Umweltwandel, Naturgefahren, Vulnerabilität und Katastrophenresilienz. Notwendigkeit der Perspektivenerweiterung in der Raumplanung. Raumforschung und Raumordnung, 66(1), 5-22.

Blaikie, P. M., Cannon, T., Davis, I., & Wisner, B. (1994). At Risk. Natural Hazards, People's Vulnerability, and Disasters. London: Routledge.

Blum, S., Endreß, M., Kaufmann, S., Rampp, B. (2016). Soziologische Perspektiven. In R. Wink (ed.), Multidisziplinäre Perspektiven der Resilienzforschung. Wiesbaden: Springer (forthcoming).

Bohle, H. G. (2008). Förderung von Resilience als Herausforderung für die Risikowelten von morgen. In C. Felgentreff & T. Glade (eds), Naturrisiken und Sozialkatastrophen, (pp. 435-441). Berlin: Spektrum.

Bolin, R., & Stanford, L. (1998). The Northridge Earthquake: Vulnerability and Disaster. Vulnerability and Disaster. London, New York: Routledge.

Bonß, W. (2015). Karriere und sozialwissenschaftliche Potenziale des Resilienzbegriffs. In M. Endreß & A. Maurer (eds). Resilienz im Sozialen. Theoretische und empirische Analysen (pp. 15–31). Wiesbaden: Springer VS.

Boon, H. J., Cottrell, A., King, D., Stevenson, R.B., & Millar, J. (2012). Bronfenbrenner's Bioecological Theory for Modelling Community Resilience to Natural Disasters. Natural Hazards 60(2), 381–408.

Bourdieu, P., Wacquant, L. (1992). An Invitation to Reflexive Sociology. Chicago: University of Chicago Press.

Bourdieu, P. (1991). Language and Symbolic Power. Harvard: Harvard University Press.

Brauner, C., & Dombrowsky, W. R. (1996). Defizite der Katastrophenvorsorge in Industriegesellschaften am Beispiel Deutschlands. Untersuchungen und Empfehlungen zu methodischen und inhaltlichen Grundsatzfragen.

Breton, M. (2001). Neighbourhood Resiliency. Journal of Community Practice, 9(1), 21-36.

Brown, D., & Kulig, J. C. (1996). The Concept of Resiliency. Theoretical Lessons from Community Research. Health and Canadian Society, 4, 29-52.

Bürkner, H.-J. (2010). Vulnerabilität und Resilienz. Forschungsstand und sozialwissenschaftliche Untersuchungsperspektiven (IRS Working-Paper 43).

Burton, I., Kates, R. W., & White, G. F. (1978). The Environment as Hazard. Hoboken: Guilford Press.
Burton, I., Kates, R. W., & White, Gilbert F. (1993). The Environment as Hazard. 2nd ed. Hoboken: Guilford Press.
Butler, J. (1997). Das Unbehagen der Geschlechter. 6. Aufl., Frankfurt am Main: Suhrkamp.
Cannon, T., & Müller-Mahn, D. (2010). Vulnerability, Resilience and Development Discourses in context of Climate change. Natural Hazards, 55(3), 621-635.
Carpenter, S., Walker, B., Anderies, J.M., & Abel, N. (2001). From Metaphor to Measurement: Resilience of What to What? Ecosystems, 4(8), 765–781.
Carver, C. (1998). Resilience and Thriving: Issues, Models, and Linkages. Journal of Social Issues, 54(2), 245–266.
Chambers, R., & Conway, G. R. (1991). Sustainable Rural Livelihoods: Practical Concepts for the 21st Century. Institute of Development Studies DP.
Chandler, D. (2013). Resilience and the Autotelic Subject: Toward a Critique of the Societalization of Security. International Political Sociology, 7(2), 210–226.
Christmann, G. B., Balgar, K., & Mahlkow, N. (2015). Zur sozialwissenschaftlichen Konzeption von Vulnerabilität und Resilienz. In M. Endreß & A. Maurer (eds), Resilienz im Sozialen. Theoretische und empirische Analysen (pp. 15–31). Wiesbaden: Springer VS.
Christopherson, S., Michie, J., & Tyler, P (2010). Regional Resilience: Theoretical and Empirical Perspectives. Cambridge Journal of Regions, Economy and Society, 3, 3–10. doi:10.1093/cjres/rsq004
Clausen, L. (1992). Social Differentiation and the Long-term Origin of Disasters. Natural Hazards, 6(2), 181–190.
Clausen, L. (1994). Krasser sozialer Wandel. Opladen: Leske und Budrich.
Clausen, L. (2003). Reale Gefahren und katastrophensoziologische Theorien. Soziologischer Rat bei FAKKEL-Licht. In L. Clausen, E. M. Geenen & Elísio Macamo (eds), Entsetzliche soziale Prozesse. Theorie und Empirie der Katastrophen (pp. 51–76). Münster: Lit.
Cohen, O., Leykin, D., Lahad, M., Goldberg, A., & Aharonson-Daniel, L. (2013). The Conjoint Community Resiliency Assessment Measure as a Baseline for Profiling and Predicting Community Resilience for Emergencies. Technological Forecasting and Social Change 80(9), 1732–1741.
Cutter, S. L., Boruff, B. J., & Shirley, W. L. (2003). Social Vulnerability to Environmental Hazards. Social Science Quarterly, 84(2), 242–261.
Cutter, S. L., Burton, C. G., & Emrich, C. T. (2010). Disaster Resilience Indicators for Benchmarking Baseline Conditions. Journal of Homeland Security and Emergency Management 7(1).
Cutter, S., Barnes, L., Berry, M., Burton, C., Evans, E., Tat, E., & Webb, J. (2008). A Place-based Model for Understanding Community Resilience to Natural Disasters. Global Environmental Change, 18(4), 598–606.
Da Silva, J., & Morera, B. (2014). City Resilience Framework. Arup & Rockefeller Foundation. Online: http://publications.arup.com/Publications/C/City_Resilience_Framework.aspx [12/15/2015].
Davis, I. (2004). Progress in Analysis of Social Vulnerability and Capacity. In G. Bankoff, G. Frerks & D. Hilhorst (eds), Mapping Vulnerability. Disasters, Development and People (pp. 128–144). London: Earthscan.

Deffner, V. (2007). Soziale Verwundbarkeit im ‚Risikoraum Favela'- Eine Analyse des sozialen Raumes auf der Grundlage von Bourdieus „Theorie der Praxis". In R. Wehrhahn (ed.), Risiko und Vulnerabilität in Lateinamerika (pp. 207–232). Kiel: Selbstverlag des Geographischen Instituts der Universität Kiel.

Delica-Willison, Z., & Willison, R. (2004). Vulnerability Reduction. A Task for the Vulnerable People Themselves. In G. Bankoff, G. Frerks & D. Hilhorst (eds), Mapping Vulnerability. Disasters, Development and People (pp. 145–158). London: Earthscan.

Dittmer, C. (2007). Gender Mainstreaming in der Entwicklungszusammenarbeit. Eine feministische Kritik. Saarbrücken: VDM Verlag Dr. Müller.

Dittmer, C., Lorenz, D. F., & Voss, M. (2016). Resilience and Vulnerability in the Eye of Pierre Bourdieu. A Theoretical Framework of the Sociology of Disasters (forthcoming)

Dombrowsky, W. R. (1981). Solidaritätsformen während der Schneekatastrophen in Norddeutschland. SIFKU-Informationen, 4(1), 27–38.

Dombrowsky, W. R. (1987). Das Tschernobyl-Syndrom. Katastrophen als verhaltensändernde Ereignisse. In J. Friedrichs (ed.), Deutscher Soziologentag 1986 (pp. 806 ff). Opladen: Westdeutscher Verlag.

Emirbayer, M., & Goodwin, J. (1996). Symbols, Positions, Objects. Toward a New Theory of Revolutions and Collective Action. History and Theory: Studies in the Philosophy of History. Online verfügbar unter http://ssc.wisc.edu/~emirbaye/Mustafa_Emirbayer/ARTICLES_files/symbols,%20positions,%20objects.pdf.

Emirbayer, M., & Mische, A. (1998). What Is Agency? American Journal of Sociology 103(4), 962–1023.

Endreß, M., & Rampp, B. (2015). Resilienz als Perspektive auf gesellschaftliche Prozesse. Auf dem Weg zu einer soziologsichen Theorie. In M. Endreß & A. Maurer (eds), Resilienz im Sozialen. Theoretische und empirische Analysen (pp. 33–55). Wiesbaden: Springer VS.

Erikson, K.T. (1976). Everything in Its Path. Destruction of Community in the Buffalo Creek Flood. Simon and Schuster: New York.

Eyre, A. (2006). Remembering. Community Commemoration After Disaster. In H. Rodríguez, E. L. Quarantelli & R. Dynes (eds), Handbook of Disaster Research (pp. 441–455). Springer: New York.

Fazey, I., Kesby, M., Evely, A., Latham, I., Wagatora, D., & Hagasua, J.-E. (2010). A Three-tiered Approach to Participatory Vulnerability Assessment in the Solomon Islands. Global Environmental Change, 20(4), 713–728.

Flach, F. (1988). Resilience – Discovering a New Strength in Times of Stress. Fawcett Books: NewYork.

Folke, C., Berkes, F., & Colding, J. (1998). Ecological Practices and Social Mechanisms for Building Resilience and Sustainability. In F. Berkes & C. Folke (eds), Social and Ecological Systems. Management Practices and Social Mechanisms for Building Resilience (pp. 414–436). Cambridge: Cambridge University Press.

Folke, C., Colding, J., & Berkes, F. (2003). Synthesis. Building Resilience and Adaptive Capacity in Social-Ecological Systems. In F. Berkes, J. Colding & C. Folke (eds), Navigating Social-Ecological Systems. Building Resilience for Complexity and Change (pp. 352–387). Cambridge: Cambridge University Press.

Folke, C. (2006). Resilience: The Emergence of a Perspective for Social–ecological Systems Analyses. Global Environmental Change, 16(3), 253–267. DOI: 10.1016/j.gloenvcha.2006.04.002.

Fooken, I. (2016). Psychologische Aspekte der Resilienzforschung. In R. Wink (ed): Multidisziplinäre Perspektiven der Resilienzforschung. Wiesbaden: Springer.

Fordham, M. (2004). Gendering Vulnerability Analysis. Towards a More Nuanced Approach. In G. Bankoff, G. Frerks & D. Hilhorst (eds), Mapping Vulnerability. Disasters, Development and People (pp. 174–182). London: Earthscan.

Furedi, F. (2005). Politics of Fear. London: Continuum.

Gallopín, G. C. (2006). Linkages between Vulnerability, Resilience, and Adaptive Capacity. Global Environmental Change, 16(3), 293–303. DOI: 10.1016/j.gloenvcha.2006.02.004.

Geenen, E. M. (2012). Gesellschaftliche Verfügung über Kapitalien und Vulnerabilität in konzeptioneller Perspektive. In A. Berlejung (ed.), Disaster and relief management. Katastrophen und ihre Bewaeltigung (pp. 41–65). Tübingen: Mohr Siebeck.

Gunderson, L. H. (2003). Interactions between Social Resilience and Ecological Crises. In F. Berkes, J. Colding & C. Folke (eds), Navigating Social-Ecological Systems. Building Resilience for Complexity and Change (pp. 33–52). Cambridge: Cambridge University Press.

Gunderson, L. H., Holling, C. S., & Peterson, G. D. (2002). Surprises and Sustainability: Cycles of Renewal in the Everglades. In L.H. Gunderson & C. S. Holling (eds), Panarchy. Understanding Transformations in Human and Natural Systems (pp. 315–332). Washington: Island Press.

Gunderson, L. H., Holling, C. S., Pritchard, L., & Peterson, G. D. (1997). Resilience in Ecosystems, Institutions and Societies (Beijer International Institute of Ecological Economics Discussion Paper 95), Stockholm.

Gunderson, L. H. (2000). Ecological Resilience—In Theory and Application. Annual Review of Ecology and Systematics, 31 1), 425–439. DOI: 10.1146/annurev.ecolsys.31.1.425.

Hagan, P., & Maguire, B. (2007). Disasters and Communities. Understanding Social Resilience. The Australian Journal of Emergency Management, 22(2), 16–20.

Hall, P. A., & Lamont, M. (eds) (2013). Social Resilience in the Neoliberal Era. Cambridge: Cambridge University. Press.

Handmer, J. W., & Dovers, S. R. (1996). A Typology of Resilience. Rethinking Institutions for Sustainable Development. Organization & Environment, 9(4), 482–511. DOI: 10.1177/108602669600900403.

Heijmans, A. (2004). From Vulnerability to Empowerment. In Greg Bankoff, Georg Frerks und Dorothea Hilhorst (eds), Mapping Vulnerability. Disasters, Development and People. London: Earthscan, 115–127.

Hempel, L., & Lorenz, Daniel F. (2014). Resilience as an Eelement of a Sociology of Expression. Behemoth, 7(2), 26–72.

Hempel, L., & Markwart, T. (2013). Einleitung. Ein Streit über die Katastrophe. In L. Hempel, M. Bartels & T. Markwart (eds), Aufbruch ins Unversicherbare. Zum Katastrophendiskurs der Gegenwart (pp. 7-27). Bielefeld: transcript.

Hewitt, K. (1983). The Idea of Calamity in a Technocratic Age. In Kenneth Hewitt (ed), Interpretations of Calamity from the Viewpoint of Human Ecology (pp. 1–32). Boston: Allen & Unwin.

Hewitt, K. (1997). Regions of Risk. A Geographical Introduction to Disasters. Hoboken: Taylor and Francis.

Hilhorst, D., & Bankoff, G. (2004). Introduction. Mapping Vulnerability. In G. Bankoff, G. Frerks & D. Hilhorst (eds), Mapping Vulnerability. Disasters, Development and People (pp. 1–9). London: Earthscan.

Holling, C. S. (1973). Resilience and Stability of Ecological Systems. Annual Review of Ecology and Systematics, 4(1), 1–23. DOI: 10.1146/annurev.es.04.110173.000245.

Holling, C. S., Berkes, F., & Folke, C. (1998). Science, Sustainability and Resource Management. In F. Berkes & C. Folke (ed.), Social and Ecological Systems. Management Practices and Social Mechanisms for Building Resilience (pp. 342–362). Cambridge: Cambridge University Press.

Hurlbert, J. S., Beggs, J. J., & Haines, V.A. (2006). Bridges over Troubled Waters. What are the optimal Networks for Katrina's Victims? http://understandingkatrina.ssrc.org/Hurlbert_Beggs_Haines/IPCC 2007: Contribution of Working Group II to the Fourth Assessment Report of the Intergovernmental Panel on Climate Change "Impacts, Adaption and Vulnerability". Cambridge: Cambridge University Press.

IPCC (2014). Working Group II Report "Climate Change 2014: Impacts, Adaptation, and Vulnerability". Cambridge University Press.

Kasperson, J. X., Kasperson, R.E., Turner, B.L., Schiller, A., & Hsiel, W.H. (2005). Vulnerability to Global Environmental Change. In J.X. Kasperson & R.E. Kasperson (ed.), Social Contours of Risk, Vol. II (pp. 245–285). London: Earthscan.

Kaufmann, S. (2015). Resilienz als Sicherheitsprogramm. um Janusgesicht eines Leitkonzepts. In M. Endreß & A. Maurer (eds.), Resilienz im Sozialen. Theoretische und empirische Analysen (pp. 295–312). Wiesbaden: Springer VS.

Kimhi, S. (2014). Levels of Resilience: Associations Among Individual, Community, and National Resilience. Journal of Health Psychology, 3, 1-7. Journal of health psychology, 3, 1-7.

Knapp, G.-A. (2001). Grundlagenkritik und stille Post. Zur Debatte um einen Bedeutungsverlust der Kategorie „Geschlecht". In B. Heintz (ed.), Geschlechtersoziologie (pp. 54-74). Wiesbaden: VS-Verlag.

Krishnaraj, M. (1997). Gender Issues in Disaster Management. The Latur Earthquake. Gender, Technology and Development, 1(3), 395–411. DOI: 10.1177/097185249700100304.

Levin, S., Barrett, S., Aniyar, S., Baumol, W., Bliss, C., Bolin, B., Dasgupta, P., Ehrlich, P., Folke, C., Gren, I.M., Holling, C.S., Jansson, A.M., Jansson, B.O., Mäler, K.G., Martin, D., Perrings, C., & Sheshinski, E. (1998). Resilience in Natural and Socio-Economic systems. Environment and Development Economics, 3, 222–235.

Leykin, D., Lahad, M., Cohen, O., Goldberg, A., & Aharonson-Daniel, L. (2013). Conjoint Community Resiliency Assessment Measure-28/10 Items (CCRAM28 and CCRAM10). A Self-report Tool for Assessing Community Resilience. American Journal of Community Psychology, 52(3), 313-323.

Lindblom, Charles E. (1959). The Science of 'Muddling Through'. Public Administration Review, 19, 79–88.

Lindseth, B. (2011). The Pre-History of Resilience in Ecological Research, Limn 1.

Luckesch R., Payer H., & Winkler-Rieder W. (2011). Wie gehen Regionen mit Krisen um? Eine explorative Studie über die Resilienz von Regionen, ÖAR Regionalberatung, Fehring.

Macamo, E. (2003). Nach der Katastrophe ist die Katastrophe. Die 2000er Überschwemmung in der dörflichen Wahrnehmung in Mosambik. In L. Clausen, E. Geenen & E. Macamo (eds.), Entsetzliche soziale Prozesse. Theorie und Empirie der Katastrophen (pp. 167–184). Münster: Lit Verlag

Manyena, S. B. (2006). The Concept of Resilience Revisited. Disasters, 30(4), 433–450.

McEntire, D., Fuller, C., Johnsten, C.W., & Weber, R. (2002). A Comparison of Disaster Paradigms: The Search for a Holistic Policy Guide. Public Administration Review, 62(3), 267–281.

Meyer, Michelle Annette (2013). Social capital and collective efficacy for disaster resilience: Connecting individuals with communities and vulnerability with resilience in hurricane-prone communities in Florida. Dissertation. Online available http://disaster.colostate.edu/Data/Sites/1/cdra-research/cdra-thesesanddissertations/meyer_michelle.pdf.

Michael, D. N. (1995). Barriers and Bridges to Learning in Turbulent Human Ecology. In L. H. Gunderson, C.S. Holling & S.S. Light (eds), Barriers and Bridges to the Renewal of Ecological Systems and Institutions (pp. 461–485). New York: Columbia University Press.

Midgley, J. (1983). Professional Imperialism. Social Work in the Third World. London: Heinemann.

Murphy, Brenda L. (2007). Locating Social Capital in Resilient Community-Level Emergency Management. Natural Hazards, 41, 297–315. doi:10.1007/s11069-006-9036-6

Norgaard, R. B. (1994). Development Betrayed: The End of Progress and a Coevolutionary Revisioning of the Future. London: Routledge.

Norris, F. H., & Stevens, S. P. (2007). Community Resilience and the Principles of Mass Trauma Intervention. Psychiatry, 70(4), 320–328.

Norris, F. H., & Stevens, S. P., Pfefferbaum, B., Wyche, K. F., & Pfefferbaum, R. L. (2008). Community Resilience as a Metaphor, Theory, Set of Capacities, and Strategy for Disaster Readiness. American Journal of Community Psychology, 41(1-2), 127–150.

O'Keefe, P., Westgate, K., & Wisner B (1976). Taking the Naturalness out of Natural Disasters. Nature 260.

O'Keefe, P., Wisner, B., & Baird, A. (1977) Kenyan Underdevelopment: A Case Study of Proletarianisation. In P. O'Keefe, P. & B. Wisner (eds), Landuse and Development (pp. 216-228). London: International African Institute.

Obrist, B., Pfeiffer, C., & Henley, R. (2010). Multi-layered social resilience: A new approach in mitigation research. Progress in Development Studies, 10, 283–293.

Olick, J. K., & Robbins, J. (1998). Social Memory Studies. From "Collective Memory" to the Historical Sociology of Mnemonic Practices. Annual Review of Sociology, 24(1), 105–140. DOI: 10.1146/annurev.soc.24.1.105.

Oliver-Smith, A. (1996). Anthropological Research on Hazards and Disasters. Annual Revue of Antropology, 25, 303–328.

Oliver-Smith, A. (2004). Theorizing Vulnerability in a Globalized World. A Political Ecology Perspektive. In G. Bankoff, G. Frerks & D. Hilhorst (eds), Mapping Vulnerability. Disasters, Development and People (pp. 10–24). London: Earthscan.

O'Riordan, T. (1990). Hazard and Risk in the Modern World. Political Models for Programm Design. In J. Handmer & E. Penning-Rowsell (eds), Hazards and the Communication of Risk (pp. 293–302). Brookfield, VT.

Oxfam (2005) The Tsunami's Impact on Women. http://www.oxfam.org.uk/what_we_do/issues/conflict_disasters/downloads/bn_tsunami_women.pdf.
Paton, D. (2003). Disaster Preparedness: A Social-cognitive Perspective. Disaster Prevention and Management, 12(3), 210–216. doi: 10.1108/09653560310480686
Paton, D. (2008). Community Resilience: Integrating Individual, Community and Societal Perspectives. In K. Gow & D. Paton (eds), The Phoenix of Natural Disasters: Community Resilience (pp. 13–31). New York: Nova Science Publishers.
Paton, D., Smith, L., & Johnston, D. (2005). When Good Intentions Turn Bad: Promoting Natural Hazard Preparedness. The Australian Journal of Emergency Management, 20(1), 25–30.
Peacock, W., & Ragsdale, G. (2012). Social Systems, Ecological Networks and Disaster. In W. Peacock, H. Galddwin & B. H. Morrow (eds), Hurricane Andrew. Ethnicity, Gender and the Sociology of Disasters (pp. 20-35). Hoboken: Taylor and Francis.
Phillips, B. D., & Fordham, M. (2010). Introduction. In D. Brenda D., D. S. K. Phillips, A. F. Thomas & L. Blinn-Pike (eds), Social Vulnerability to Disasters (pp. 1–23). Boca Raton, Fla: CRC Press.
Quarantelli, E. L. (1996). Just as a Disaster is Not Simply a Big Accident, so a Catastrophe Is Not Just a Bigger Disaster. The ASPEP Journal, 68-71.
Quarantelli, E. L. (2000). Emergencies, Disasters and Catastrophes Are Different Phenomena (Disaster Research Center Preliminary Paper 304).
Quarantelli, E. L. (2006). Catastrophes are Different from Disasters: Implications for Crisis Planning and Managing drawn from Katrina. In Understanding Katrina: Perspectives from the Social Sciences. Social Science Research Council. http://understandingkatrina.ssrc.org/Quarantelli/.
Rodríguez, H., Díaz, W., & Santos, J.M. (2006). Communicating Risk and Uncertainty. Science, Technology and Disasters at the Crossroads. In H. Rodríguez, E.L. Quarantelli & R. Dynes (eds.), Handbook of Disaster Research (pp. 476–488). New York: Springer.
Scandlyn, J., Simon, C. N., Thomas, D. S.K., & Brett, J. (2010). Theoretical Framing of Worldviews, Values, and Structural Dimensions of Disaster. In B. D. Phillips, D. S.K. Thomas, A. Fothergill & L. Blinn-Pike (Hg.). Social Vulnerability to Disasters (pp. 27–49). Boca Raton, Fla: CRC Press.
Scheffer, M., Westley, F., Brock, W.A. et al (2002). Dynamic Interaction of Societies and Ecosystems – Linking Theories form Ecology, Economy, and Sociology. In L.H. Gunderson & C. S. Holling (eds), Panarchy. Understanding Transformations in Human and Natural Systems (pp. 195–240). Washington: Island Press.
Scherr, A. (2012). Soziale Bedingungen von Agency. Soziologische Eingrenzungen einer sozialtheoretisch nicht auflösbaren Paradoxie. In S. Bethmann, C. Helfferich, H. Hoffmann & D. Niermann (eds), Agency. Qualitative Rekonstruktionen und gesellschaftstheoretische Bezüge von Handlungsmächtigkeit (pp. 99–121). Weinheim und Basel: Beltz Juventa.
Schulze, K., Lorenz, D.F., Wenzel, B., & Voss, M. (2015). Disaster Myths and their Relevance for Warning Systems. The 12th International Conference on Information Systems for Crisis Response and Management. http://iscram2015.uia.no/wp-content/uploads/2015/05/4-4.pdf.
Sen, A. (2010). Poverty and Famines. An Essay on Entitlement and Deprivation. Oxford: Oxford University Press.

Smit, B., & Wandel, J. (2006). Adaptation, Adaptive Capacity and Vulnerability. Global Environmental Change, 16(3), 282–292. DOI: 10.1016/j.gloenvcha.2006.03.008.

Spivak, G. C. (1988). Can the Subaltern Speak? In C. Nelson & L. Grossberg (eds). Marxism and the Interpretation of Culture, Chicago: University of Illionois Press.

Sudmeier-Rieux, K. (2015). Resilience – An Emerging Paradigm of Danger or of Hope? Disaster Prevention and Management, 23(1), 67–80.

Swanstrom, T. (2008). Regional Resilience: A Critical Examination of the Ecological Framework. Berkeley, CA : University of California.

Thürmer-Rohr, C. (2001). Gleiche unter Gleichen? Kritische Fragen zu Geschlechterdemokratie und Gender Mainstreaming. Forum Wissenschaft, 2, 34-37.

Turner, B. L., Kasperson, R. E., Matson, P. A., McCarthy, J. J., Corell, R., & Christensen, Lindsey (2003). A Framework for Vulnerability Analysis in Sustainability Science. Proceedings of the National Academy of Sciences of the United States of America 100 (14), 8074–8079. DOI: 10.1073/pnas.1231335100.

UN/ISDR (2004). Hyogo Framework for Action 2005-2015. Building the Resilience of Nations and Communities to Disasters Genf, UNISDR.

UN/ISDR (2009). 2009 UNISDR Terminology on Disaster Risk Reduction, Geneva, May 2009 (http://www.unisdr.org/we/inform/terminology).

UNISDR (2012). Making Cities Resilient. Report 2012. Genf, UNISDR.

Vale, L. J., & Campanella, T. J. (2005). The Resilient City. How Modern Cities Recover from Disaster. New York: Oxford University Press.

van Loon, J. (2008). Governmentality and the Subpolitics of Teenage Sexual Risk Behaviour. In A. R. Petersen & I. Wilkinson (eds), Health, Risk and Vulnerability (pp. 48–65). London, New York: Routledge.

Voss, M. (2008). The Vulnerable Can't Speak. An Integrative Vulnerability Approach to Disaster and Climate Change Research. Behemoth, 1(3).

Voss, M. (2009). Vulnerabilität. In C. Hammerl (ed.), Naturkatastrophen. Rezeption – Bewältigung – Verarbeitung (pp. 103–121). Innsbruck: Studien-Verlag.

Voss, M., & Dittmer, C. (2016). Resilienz aus katastrophensoziologischer Perspektive. In R. Wink (ed.), Multidisziplinäre Perspektiven der Resilienzforschung. Wiesbaden: Springer (forthcoming).

Voss, M., & Funk, L. (2015). Participative Vulnerability and Resilience Assesment and the Example of the Tao People (Taiwan). In F. Krüger (ed.), Cultures and disasters. Understanding cultural framings in disaster risk reduction (pp. 255-276). New York, NY: Routledge.

Voss, M., & Wagner, K. (2010). Learning from (Small) Disasters. Natural Hazards, 55(3), 657–669. DOI: 10.1007/s11069-010-9498-5.

Walker, J., & Cooper, M. (2011). Genealogies of Resilience: From Systems Ecology to the Political Economy of Crisis Adaptation. Security Dialogue, 42(2), 143-160.

Wallace, D., & Wallace, R. (2008). Urban Systems during Disasters: Factors for Resilience. Ecology and Society, 13(1).

Watts, M. (1983). On the Poverty of Theory: Natural Hazards Research in Context. In K. Hewitt (ed.), Interpretations of Calamity from the Viewpoint of Human Ecology (pp. 229–262). Boston: Allen & Unwin.

Weick, K. E. (1993). The Collapse of Sensemaking in Organizations. The Mann Gulch Disaster. Administration Science Quarterly, 38, 628–652.

Werner, E. (1971). The Children of Kauai. A Longitudinal Study from the Prenatal Period to Age Ten. Honolulu: University of Hawaii Press.
Werner, E. (2005). Resilience and Recovery: Findings from the Kauai Longitudinal Study. Research, Policy, and Practice in Children's Mental Health, 19, 11-14.
Werner, E., & Smith, R. S. (2001). Journeys from Childhood to Midlife. Risk, Resilience, and Recovery. Ithaca, N.Y: Cornell University Press.
Westley, F., Carpenter, S.R., & Brock, W.A. (2002). Why Systems of People and Nature Are Not Just Social and Ecological Systems. In L.H. Gunderson & C.S. Holling (Hg.), Panarchy. Understanding Transformations in Human and Natural Systems (pp. 103–120). Washington: Island Press.
Wisner, B. (2004). Assessment of Capability and Vulnerability. In G. Bankoff, G. Frerks & D. Hilhorst (eds), Mapping Vulnerability. Disasters, Development and People (pp. 183–193). London: Earthscan.
Wisner, B., Blaikie, P., & Cannon, T. (2003). At Risk. Natural Hazards, People's Vulnerability and Disasters. 2. ed. London: Routledge.
Young, O. R., Berkhout, F., Gallopin, G. C., Janssen, M. A., Ostrom, E., & van der Leeuw, S. (2006). The Globalization of Socio-ecological Systems. An Agenda for Scientific Research. Global Environmental Change, 16(3), 304–316. DOI: 10.1016/j.gloenvcha.2006.03.004.
Zander, M. (2008). Armes Kind – starkes Kind? Die Chance der Resilienz. Wiesbaden: VS Verlag.
Zautra, A., Hall, J., & Murray, K. (2008). Community Development, and Community Resilience: An Integrative Approach. Community Development, 39, 130–147.
Zimmerer, K.S. (1994). Human Geography and the New Ecology: The Prospect and Promise of Integration. Annals of the Association of American Geographers, 84, 108–125.
Zraly, M., Rubin, S. E., & Mukamana, D. (2013). Motherhood and Resilience among Rwandan Genocide-Rape Survivors. Ethos, 41(4), 411–439.

Part II
RESILIENCE IN THE ECONOMIC SPHERE: THEORETICAL AND EMPIRICAL EVIDENCE

Resilient Financial Systems: Methodological and Theoretical Challenges of Post-Crisis Reform

Renate Mayntz

1 Introduction: The question

When, in 2007, a real estate bubble burst in the US, banks – not only American banks – were threatened by failure, and had to be saved from bankruptcy by political intervention. Apparently banks had lacked resilience. As the crisis spread, investment funds, the stock market, and eventually insurance companies became implicated and suffered losses. Having succeeded to prevent the looming "meltdown" of the global financial system, governments set about to re-constitute its stability through regulatory reforms. The case of the financial crisis, and the reform efforts it triggered, thus provide a welcome opportunity to study resilience: what it means, what it depends on, and whether it can be achieved by institutional engineering.

Resilience is a topic that has not been treated very frequently in social research and theory. Contemporary social theory is much concerned with social change – change at the level of societies and at the level of organizations, technological change, and cultural change. The belief that in history as in evolution change is progress may have been shaken; but in a world in constant search of growth and a higher standard of living, there is still the tacit assumption that change normally means change for the better. In this context, resilience, easily confounded with resistance, can have a negative connotation. Efforts have been made to distinguish resistance, that can spell the inability to cope with a challenge and adapt to change, from resilience (see for instance Douven et al. 2012), a concept that has recently assumed a highly positive connotation, especially in connection with economic policy and financial market reform. Though Moschella and Tsingou (2013, 200) use the term resilience when actually talking about the resistance of European countries with different economic and financial systems to measures of regulatory reform that would require substantial change, resilience is generally attributed to an economy that is capable to return, after a shock such as the recent financial crisis, relatively quickly to pre-crisis growth. In this sense, the OECD has recently discussed the features of "resilient economies", but also more generally of "resilient institutions" and even "resilient societies" (Scheidegger 2014).

Originally, resilience meant a property of physical material, such as rubber or a steel spring. According to Webster's New World Dictionary (1966, 1238), resilience is "1. …the ability to bounce or spring back into shape, position etc. after being pressed or stretched; elasticity. 2. the ability to recover strength…". Resilience thus originally refers to the maintenance of physical form, but it has come to be seen as a property not only of material, but also of biological and social phenomena. In biology, the related concept of homeostasis is familiarly used; homeostasis is the tendency of an organism to keep internal conditions like body temperature constant, regardless of changes in environment. In sociology, resilience came to be understood as a property of social entities able to maintain the status quo after a contingent, external disturbance.

In a dynamically evolving social world, the survival of a specific formal organization, political regime, or social group depends on their ability to adapt, to change some structural and operational elements in order to survive over time. Resilience must therefore be given a dynamic meaning, for example the ability to cope with disturbances by "adapting" to change in external circumstances. But if something must change in order to persist, what is it that must be kept constant so that we can speak of persistence? Social scientists have long struggled to distinguish between change *in* a system, and change *of* a system. A political regime, corporation or local community can change without loosing its identity. Rather than venturing into the mire of ontological considerations, "identity" can be treated in the nominalist tradition as a matter of definition. Resilience can be defined as the capability of a social unit to maintain its identity through changes in its structure and operation. Obviously, the identity of a family has a different basis from the identity of a political regime; in a functionally differentiated social system, the identity of a social part rests in its function, just as the identity of a medical doctor rests in the exercise of specific professional skills. A resilient social unit in a dynamically evolving social system characterized by division of labour is capable to continue performing its function in spite of disturbances, even if this requires adaptive changes in its structure and mode of operation. Will this understanding of resilience help to explain what happened in the recent financial crisis, and what the success of financial market reforms depends on?

Before engaging in case analysis, we must sharpen our main analytical tool, the concept of resilience. Resilience does not refer simply to "reproduction". Even without external disturbances, the maintenance of a given social practice or structure over time requires constant acts of affirmation: reproduction implies repetition, compliant behaviour, the re-enactment of customs. In the case of resilience, the disturbance of the status quo, of a given form is assumed by definition to come from the outside, to be exogenous rather than endogenous. This would distinguish resilience from persistence in the face of threats arising internally – threats like rebellion against a political regime, strikes in a corporation, mutiny disabling an army in war. Tensions (or contradictions, in Marxist terminology) that inhere in a given social form can produce endogenous disturbances. Resilience is conceptually tied to external disturbances. But whether we conceive of disturbances as endogenous or exogenous, in both cases it is assumed that we are dealing with a bounded entity that can be analysed as a social system. There are many kinds of social systems – organizations like General Electric, the German health system, or whole societies like the French Republic. Applied to different kinds of social system, the meaning of resilience can vary, but in any case resilience can only be attributed to social entities that have the character of a system; it makes no sense to ask whether a given demographic structure, or income distribution is resilient. Resilience inheres in the structure and mode of operation of bounded social entities.

2 Resilience and political intervention

Living systems – surviving organisms – presumably possess adaptive resilience as a result of evolution, i.e. variation and selection. To what extent this also holds for social systems is answered differently by different theories. Parsons' functionalist systems theory has often been said to assume an inbuilt tendency towards equilibrium in social systems. An inbuilt tendency to safeguard the continuous functioning of a system is also assumed in economic theories that take markets to be spontaneously self-regulating; Eugene Fama's "efficient market theory" (familiarly called EMT) is a case in point (Fama 1970). Critics of equilibrium theories point out that in actually existing, "historical" social systems, the achievement of final stasis or what amounts to an "end of history" is illusory. In a functionally differentiated social system, the sub-systems tend to emancipate themselves, moving from service to domination and transforming into an end what for the embracing macro-system is only a means. Functionally differentiated social systems would thus be inherently instable.[1] In this case to maintain the performance of the tasks assigned to different institutions in a society is a permanent challenge. The function to safeguard, if not improve the performance of sub-systems on which the well-being of the system members depends is attributed to the political-administrative sub-system. Political intervention is called for if self-equilibrating forces fail to make a functional subsystem, in particular the economy, perform well. Assumptions about the equilibrating or conflictive nature of social systems underlie the choice between laissez-faire and political activism.

Political intervention into complex functional systems in order to safeguard their performance and prevent the creation of negative externalities is a recognized task in many policy fields. This holds for transport, for energy supply, and for food production, and at the time of the Bretton Woods agreements and of the financial crises of the 1970ies it also held for the functioning of financial markets. But in the 1980ies, impressed by Eugene Fama's efficient market theory, the financial industry urged, and economists argued that financial markets should be deregulated. Policy-makers complied. The global financial crisis, triggered by defaults on the US subprime mortgage market and expanding globally, surprised both economists and policy-makers who had believed that financial markets were self-regulating. The transformation of classical commercial banks into transnational financial institutions, the ascendance of large institutional investors, and the construction and use of new financial instruments meant continuous change, but changes in the financial system appeared to be adaptive, and in support of the functions it fulfils for the real economy, private households, and investors. The realization that the multi-level financial system did not perform its function as expected came as a shock. The financial system, it seemed, had become autonomous, self-serving, and out of control (Mayntz 2014), thus proving theories correct that expect functional sub-systems, if left to their own devices, to try and escape their servant character and to become master.

The (unexpected) crisis was quickly explained as consequence of deficits in the regulation of financial markets that had evidently been incapable of self-regulation, so that banks now needed to be saved by politicians with tax-payer money. The political response to the crisis were reform plans intended to change, through regulation, those features of the then existing financial system held to be responsible for the crisis. The aim of the reforms was generally said to be "financial stability". Already before the recent crisis, the goal of financial stability ranked high in the mandate given to international institutions concerned with monitoring

---

[1] If power, the search for dominance and the rejection of subservience is a universal motive, stratified and segmentally differentiated systems are likewise inherently instable.

financial markets; the Financial Stability Forum FSF, founded in 1999, and the G20, a forum for the meeting of finance ministers and governors of central banks also institutionalized in 1999, are examples. Today, the successor to the FSF, the Financial Stability Board FSB, is the main coordinator of international reform efforts. Since 2002, the International Monetary Fund IMF publishes annually a "Global Financial Stability Report". The meaning of "financial stability" is rarely spelled out (see, however, Schinasi 2004). Nor is the reference point of financial stability always specified: is it banks, the financial system, or even the "financialized" economy? At a minimum, "financial stability" means that banks do not go bankrupt; more ambitiously understood it means the continuous fulfilment of the functions attributed to the financial system in relation to the real economy, to private households, and to investors – stability not of form but of function. Thus understood, financial stability, the term that was and still is used most commonly, comes close to meaning resilience. The post-crisis reforms impose changes on a subsystem that had failed to perform its function as expected.

3 Political intervention and knowledge

Effective political intervention presupposes not only a defined goal-state of intervention, but also sufficient knowledge of the object of intervention to be able to identify variables that can be manipulated politically, and that are crucial in producing the relevant effect. Attempts to gain systematic knowledge of the structure and functioning of the economy or of a given social sector have in fact always been connected to political efforts to steer socio-economic processes. This was evident already in early attempts to construct national accounts. From its beginning with William Petty in the 17th century, the development of national accounting in England has been closely related to political efforts to intervene in the economy. Before 1900 individual scholars attempted to construct national accounts; in the course of the 20th century the state assumed this task, parallel to the development of a concerted economic policy (Zorn 2009). The close link between the promotion of scientific research and attempts at political steering is today visible in many fields, including climate change, energy provision and public health.

When governments and experts, in shocked response to the financial crisis, demanded far-reaching regulatory reforms, it was quickly seen that the knowledge needed for effective intervention was lacking. As long as neo-liberal thinking dominated in the major Western polities, the felt need of having detailed data about the actions and transactions of financial institutions and about the state of different financial markets had been low. Now it became evident that knowledge about important details of the structure and functioning of the financial system had been insufficient. Supervisory authorities apparently had been unable to recognize the dangers inherent in the use of new financial instruments, the shift in the balance between commercial banking and investment banking, and the consequence of increasing international competition for the risk appetite of banks. Knowledge was lacking especially about what happens in the so-called shadow banking sector that accounts for an estimated 20-30% of the global financial system. It was generally admitted that the activities in the shadow banking sector contributed to the development of the financial crisis – but this was more guess work than certain knowledge. Even basic information about the incidence, the number and the size of different shadow banking institutions such as money market funds, hedge funds, and private equity funds, and about activities such as repo-funding and the use of commercial paper was lacking. In April 2012 the ECB flatly stated that "an in-depth assessment of the activities of shadow banking and of the interconnection with the regulated banking sector" presupposes significant improvement in the availability of data (ECB 2012, 4).

When the financial crisis became manifest in 2008, politicians and experts alike called for a radical and comprehensive reform of the financial system. But a comprehensive reform of the financial system does not simply need "more data", it requires knowledge of a specific kind. The financial crisis, that started with the default of an initially limited number of American mortgage takers and had spread globally, called attention to the systemic nature of risk in modern financial systems. Financial market regulation had been largely micro-prudential, with rules addressing specific categories of market participants, in particular licensed banks. Recognizing the systemic nature of risk, new agencies have been established for the timely identification of such risk; examples are the European Systemic Risk Board, the American Financial Stability Oversight Council, and the British Financial Stability Committee. Political scientists speak of a "macro-prudential ideational shift" (Baker 2013) as the possibly most significant change in financial market regulation. This shift calls for a special kind of knowledge, not information on individual banks but knowledge of the structure and operation of financial systems. Systemic risks do not only threaten a system's persistence, as vividly expressed in the talk about an impending melt-down of the international financial system; they are not caused by external forces, but inhere in the properties, the structure and operations of the system itself.

The identification of systemic risks faces daunting difficulties, both practically and theoretically. In the empirical social sciences, quantitative and qualitative research methods are familiarly distinguished. In the hot debate about their relative advantages and disadvantages, quantitative research is often equated with survey type research. In survey research, variables such as income, strength of an attitude, or number of children per woman are used to measure properties of the elements in a population; the result are distributions and correlations. Statistical regression provides knowledge about the relationship between different factors (independent variables) and a relevant effect (i.e. specific values of a dependent variable). Systems, however, are characterized by a multitude of causal relations (not mere correlations!) between heterogeneous parts. In research that is called qualitative, these causal relationships are described discursively, but they can be formalized in a model relating a set of variables in a non-linear way. The interactions within a system generate (emergent) effects at the macro-level of the system, or what Lazarsfeld and Menzel (1993, 177) have called "global properties" of social collectivities, in distinction to analytical properties that are based on data about each member.[2]

Properties of a socio-economic macro-system such as its resilience, productivity, innovativeness, or stability are "global" properties in the language of Lazarsfeld and Menzel; they result from a combination of several distinct and interacting factors or processes. To intervene effectively into the operation of a complex socio-economic system in order to achieve its growth, innovativeness, or resilience, it is imperative to have detailed knowledge of the institutions that are its parts, their action propensities (or dispositions), their relations and interactions, and their transactions with actors in its environment. Relevant causal linkages do not only include direct interactions, as when bank A receives a credit from bank B, but also indirect causal linkages that are difficult to recognize ex ante. While direct financial relations of indebtedness can be established quantitatively with relative ease, this is much more difficult in the case of indirect causal links; in the form of unsuspected domino effects, such links have played a major role in the global expansion of the American subprime mortgage crisis. Having invested in the same kind of financial product, the risks of banks became closely correlated, so that the fire sale of this kind of asset by bank A devalued the assets held by bank B, compelling it to sell the now undervalued asset in turn in order to maintain its regulatory capital, and so on for banks C, D, etc. To gain empirical knowledge in the form of a causal model of a complex social system is more demanding than getting knowledge of distributional properties of large populations.

---

2 "Global" properties can be called "emergent", as Lazarsfeld and Menzel indicate (ibid.); they are generated by the behavior of the system elements, but they are of a different category, they are "more than the sum" of some property of the elements, or "members" of a system. Emergent properties cannot be reduced statistically to measured properties of system elements, members of a "collective" (see Mayntz 2011).

4 The resilience of banks

In the debate surrounding recent financial reform efforts, the complexity of the financial system has often been noted as an obstacle to speedy and effective intervention. The globally extended, multi-level financial system is highly differentiated internally. Banks operating on the basis of a licence, and accordingly regulated, were the relatively best understood part of this system. Banks are formally constituted organizations, and even if modern financial holdings may appear complex and their boundary ambiguous,[3] it seems possible to understand their functioning sufficiently to know what their resilience depends on. In fact, while "financial stability" was most often presented as the goal of financial market reform, the European Union in its plans for a European Banking Union explicitly aims to make banks resilient. The European Banking Union introduces among other things a centralized supervision of European banks, and rules for timely resolution to avoid future taxpayer bail-outs of failing banks (Quaglia 2014, 170-177). Preceded by the critical assessment of their balance sheets by the European Central Bank 128 European banks were subjected to a stress test, in order "to assess the resilience of financial institutions to adverse market developments" (EBA 2014, 7). Banks that fail the stress test will have to be restructured, recapitalized, or in the worst case dissolved. The stress test has been initiated by the newly established European Banking Authority EBA, in co operation with the (likewise new) European Risk Board ESRB. The stress test… is designed to provide competent authorities with a consistent and comparable methodology to allow them to undertake a rigorous assessment of banks' resilience under stress…" (ibid.). By the end of October 2014 the test was concluded, and the results published; 25 of the participating banks did not meet the criteria that had been established for passing the test (European Central Bank 2014, 10).

The stress test has been conducted on a bank-by-bank basis; the banks subjected to the stress test were to collect data about themselves and their operation, following the methodology described in over 60 pages of detailed data gathering instructions (see EBA 2014). A closer look at the document is a sobering experience, giving scholars who tend to speak in rather general terms about banks a feel for the hundreds of structural, operational and transactional details that make up a concrete instance. It is instructive to look in detail at this document because it contains an implicit definition of what constitutes resilience. You can also derive

---

3 For instance so-called special purpose vehicles have often not been included in a bank's balance sheet; see Thiemann 2013.

from it a model of the conditions on which the resilience of banks depends that are embedded in, and in interaction with, a wider economic and political environment.

Solvency is the core property to be maintained, the main reference point of resilience and the major dependent variable in the causal model. Solvency stands for the ability of a bank to meet its obligations, it is a basic condition of performance. A solvent bank is able to fulfil its tasks: to guard deposits, process payments, pay interest on debt incurred, and provide credit for firms and private borrowers. A solvency crisis brought Lehman Bros. down. Solvency is assumed to depend on the amount of bank capital (private equity). The stress test provides "statistical benchmarks for the key risk parameters", and shows how a given external shock will impact upon them. Risk parameters are those features of a bank that determine its solvency, such as the interest income of a bank, and the quality of its loans. "The EU-wide stress test is primarily focused on the assessment of the impact of risk drivers on the solvency of banks" (EBA 2014, 11). The shocks, or external disturbances to be assumed, refer to two types of risk, credit risk and market risk. Credit risk means the risk of default – of sovereign, institutional and private borrowers; market risk refers to risks stemming from changes of market prices of different kinds of assets, including counterparty credit risk. The impact of specified external "shocks", i.e. specific changes in default rates and in market prices of assets, is assessed in terms of Common Equity Tier 1 capital – as defined by the rules of the Basel Committee on Banking Supervision BCBS (see BCBS 2010). Roughly speaking, Common Equity Tier 1 capital consists of assets of the highest quality, equal to the lowest risk of diminishing in market value; it is the most "liquid" part of a bank's own portfolio, liquid meaning capital that is judged to be freely available for payment. Liquid capital includes cash reserves and securities up to their risk-assessed value. In the baseline scenario, that is as of December 31, 2013, Common Equity Tier 1 capital has to be at least 8% of a banks' balance; in the "adverse scenario", that is when market risk and credit risk have reached certain previously established values, the core capital has still to be 5.5%.

The European Union stress test is based on a well specified model of resilience; it states what counts as resilience (continued performance in spite of environmental challenges), what it depends on (solvency), what solvency depends on (the "risk parameters"), and what impacts negatively on these (credit risk and market risk). To assess the impact of given external events on bank capital presupposes highly sophisticated mathematical models, models that cannot but operate with assumptions. The calculation of risk – default risks and market risks – is known to be troubled by uncertainty. The most important assumption underlying the stress test may be that a bank remains solvent under adverse external conditions if its core (or regulatory) capital is 5.5% of its balance sheet. This assumption has been seriously doubted (e.g. Hellwig 2010). It has also been argued that higher private equity (bank capital) will not insulate banks against the effect of bubbles; bubbles cannot be prevented by regulation, they call for interest rate interventions (BIS 2014). Even in a seemingly clear-cut case as the resilience of banks, it is obviously challenging to get a grip on the phenomenon.

5 Resilience as "financial soundness"

The stress test of the European Union aims only at licensed and regulated banks, that is on a specific category of formal organizations. This limitation makes the construction of a model of resilience feasible. Banks are subject to supervision, and obliged to collect and disclose information. If critical risk parameters are known and information is sufficient, this information can guide intervention by supervisory authorities. But the resilience of the financial system does not rest only on the existence of individually resilient banks. Is it possible to speak also of the resilience of a financial system that includes much more than regulated banks?

When the systemic nature of the financial crisis was recognized and it became evident that information about the state of the financial system at large was insufficient, international institutions attempted to improve data collection about relevant aspects of the financial system. In 2009, FSB and IMF started what became the Data Gaps Initiative (FSB/IMF 2009). Improved data collection meant both increased coverage of relevant features of the international financial system, and the standardization of data to be collected by the responsible national authorities. The financial crisis, it was stated, "…exposed a significant lack of information as well as data gaps on key financial sector vulnerabilities relevant for financial stability analysis … enhancing data for financial stability will contribute to developing a more robust macro-prudential policy…" (ibid., 9-10).

The Data Gaps Initiative consists of 20 specific recommendations that were endorsed by the G-20. The recommendations deal with three substantive areas: the build-up of risk in the financial sector, cross-border financial linkages, and the vulnerability of domestic economies to shocks (FSB/IMF 2013, 7). The recommendations explicitly concerned with the build-up of risk demand collection of data on concentration in the financial sector, the size of the maturity mismatch (i.e. the practice of financing long term credits by short term borrowing), the amount of leverage (debt financing), and the extent of shifting risks by the use of credit default swaps. These factors have widely been recognized as causes contributing to bank failure. The recommendations concerning cross-border linkages between different financial institutions seek information specifically on global systemically important banks (G-SIBs), and on cross-border streams of derivatives and foreign currencies. The systemic importance of G-SIBs had forced governments to "bail them out" with taxpayer money when they threatened to fail. In the build-up to the crisis, the trade in derivatives, especially the trade in the new type of structured securities constructed out of hundreds of sub-prime mortgages had increased steeply; developed by banks, these securities were not held by them, but sold to investors, including other banks, making them extremely vulnerable to sudden changes in the value of these securities. In the course of the crisis, currency speculation against the Euro had caused serious problems. The recommendations concerned with the vulnerability of domestic economies call for data on public sector debt and on real estate prices. Developments in the national economy such as a real estate bubble and soaring government debts can be shocks to the financial system; the model underlying the European stress test thus includes important sources of external disturbance.

The Data Gaps Initiative does not spell out assumptions about causal relationships between the factors on which data are being sought; it is an exercise in data collection, not a theoretical enterprise. Financial stability, the underlying goal of data collection, is not officially defined, but clearly understood in a functional sense. In an IMF Working paper of 2004 it is stated that "... financial stability can be thought of in terms of the finance system's ability: (a) to facilitate both an efficient allocation of economic resources – both spatially and especially intertemporal – and the effectiveness of other economic processes (such as wealth accumulation, economic growth, and ultimately social prosperity); (b) to assess, price, allocate, and manage financial risk; and (c) to maintain its ability to perform these key functions – even when affected by external shocks or by a build-up of imbalances – primarily through self-correcting mechanisms." (Shinas 2004, 8) Resilience, then, is included in the notion of financial stability. In reality, however, investors, speculators, private households, business firms and government have different interests, and make different and partly incompatible demands on the financial system. The post-crisis literature is full of contradictory assessments of specific structural features of the finance industry, such as the combination of commercial and investment banking in one institution, and of financial practices such as securitization, and repo-financing. There can be conflicts between the systemic function ascribed to the financial system, and the demands made on it by different actors.

The Data Gaps Initiative of 2009 builds on earlier efforts to construct "Financial Soundness Indicators" (FSI). In response to the financial market crises of the late 1990ies, the IMF started more than ten years ago to develop indicators of "financial soundness". In June of 2001, the IMF Executive Board endorsed the first list of FSI; they are considered to be tools "to assess the strengths and vulnerabilities of the financial system" (http://fsi.imf.org/). Over the years, the IMF, in steady contact with an increasing number of countries, developed the FSI further, adapting them to domestic statistical reporting systems. The "soundness indicators" themselves are statistical measures; FSI can be calculated for a domestic, a regional, and even the global financial system. But FSI are more than an exercise in data collection: They claim by their very name to be indicators of a system property, or a "global" property in the language of Lazarsfeld and Menzel. Financial soundness can be taken to include resilience: resilience is, after all, a precondition of health. We look, however, in vain for a definition of financial soundness in the official documents describing the 20 FSI in detail. Authors discussing FSI also seem at a loss; San Jose and Georgiu (2009, 277) for instance simply state that FSI are "aggregate measures of the current financial health and soundness of the financial institutions in a country and of their corporate and household counterparties".

After the financial crisis of 2008, the FSI became incorporated into the Data Gaps Initiative. There is, therefore, some overlap between the data needed for the construction of FSI, and the data demanded by the Data Gaps Initiative. Of the 40 FSI, 25 refer to deposit taking institutions – banks and financial institutions performing similar functions. Unsurprisingly, we find indicators in this group that are also used in European stress testing. Thus, Tier 1 (risk-assessed) capital and "nonperforming loans" figure prominently among the core indicators of financial soundness of deposit taking institutions; other core indicators refer to liquidity, and bank income. It is also recognized that banks do not only take deposits and give loans, but engage also in trading, both for clients and for themselves; thus one of the indicators asks for the share of "deposit takers" income from financial market activities, including currency trading of their total income. The remaining 15 FSI refer to clients of financial institutions – other financial as well as non-financial corporations, and private households – and to markets with which they interact closely, such as the market for securities, and the real estate market. The data requirements are ambitious, and often expressed as ratios; for private households, for instance, not only income and indebtedness are to be measured, but also their indebtedness in relation to GNP, and the relation of household income to debt servicing.

The assessment of "financial soundness", at the domestic and even more at a global level, is both a practical and a theoretical challenge.[4] It is obviously quite demanding to collect all the data needed for the construction of FSI – and to do so in

---

4   There are other measuring enterprises that are even more ambitious than the attempt to construct Financial Soundness Indicators. For years, the Bertelsmann Stiftung has been developing and publishing "Sustainable Governance Indicators" that claim to

an internationally standardized manner. The public authorities charged with data collection face serious limits, not least with respect to the shadow banking sector. Since 2011, the FSB tries to collect in the framework of a "mapping exercise" from the member countries of the G20 data that provide needed information about the activities in the shadow banking sector. Other international organizations likewise try to obtain better knowledge; thus IOSCO is collecting data from hedge funds managers and advisors about the markets in which they operate, including their trading activities, leverage, funding, and counterparty information (IOSCO 2013) – data that obviously do not exist. But the crucial challenge is not the collection of data, it is theoretical: FSI provide information on components of financial systems easily recognizable as relevant to its soundness, however defined, but without a causal model of their interrelation it is impossible to say anything about the values these variables should have in a sound financial system.

6 Analysis

Though the FSI have not been derived from an explicit theory, it is possible to recognize the outlines of an analytical model underlying their construction. A model of resilience, defined as capability of a social unit to remain viable (maintain its identity) in the face of external disturbances, should answer three questions: What is the social unit that is or is not resilient (object)? What is the property to be maintained in the face of external disturbances (object property – dependent variable)? What does resilience depend on (factors, independent variables)? Financial Soundness Indicators, and even the Data Gaps Initiative, imply tentative responses to these questions.

The object in question is the "financial sector" or "financial system", not "financial markets", "the economy", or even "society". The core of the financial system consists of financial institutions. The FSI explicitly address "deposit taking institutions", which nominally excludes most of the shadow banking sector, investment funds, and even investment banks as they do not take deposits. The financial system underlying FSI is thus rather narrowly bounded. To a certain extent, the boundary that constitutes a system, distinguishing it from what counts as its environment, is a matter of definition. If functional interdependencies would be a criterion of inclusion, the shadow banking sector, investment funds, exchanges, and even rating agencies could be considered as parts of a financial system. Markets,

---

display the sustainability of all 41 states of the OECD and the EU. See Bertelsmann 2014.

in contrast, straddle the system/environment boundary and would not be wholly included in a financial system defined by institutions.

Social systems defined by their function are not only characterized by the nature of their parts, but equally by their pattern of interaction with specific sectors in their environment; these interactions are a crucial part of what constitutes stability or soundness. The Data Gaps Initiative quite appropriately seeks information also about the domestic economy in which a financial industry is embedded; FSI similarly refer not only to deposit taking institutions, but also to client sectors (depositors and debtors), and to the markets where disturbances to the financial system originate, i.e. real estate and securities. Corresponding to the focus of FSI on deposit taking institutions, the relevant environment is here likewise conceived selectively; significantly, supervisors and political regulators are not considered, and the indicators that refer to nonfinancial corporations as clients are tailored to firms in the real economy and could be applied to municipalities or governments only with difficulty. The boundary defining a system, and those parts of the environment considered to be relevant, are related.

Turning to the meaning of resilience, the property to be maintained if a financial system is resilient is most clearly defined in the European stress test. The solvency of a bank that enables it to fulfill its financial obligations and give credit is a straightforward, measurable criterion. But the resilience of a financial system, even if as narrowly circumscribed as by the FSI, does not depend on the solvency of single banks; according to economic theory, the bankruptcy of a bank may even be a healthy reaction of the larger system. But it is difficult to formulate a single measurable criterion of resilience for a comprehensively conceived financial system – the financial system as it has in fact been addressed by recent regulatory reforms. It is, then, for a very good reason that the term resilience is used only in relation to individual banks, while the more diffuse terms stability and soundness are used in the Data Gaps Initiative and by Financial Soundness Indicators.

The clearer the criterion of resilience is defined, the easier it becomes to identify the factors on which it depends. The resilience of formal organizations like banks, defined by their solvency (or survival), can be linked to specific properties, such as a certain quota of Tier 1 capital (private equity). But if the fulfillment of a set of specific functions within a larger system is taken as reference point, resilience can hardly be linked to a single measurable criterion. If resilience is to be attributed to something as differentiated and loosely bounded as the global financial system, it becomes difficult to formulate what exactly is supposed to be maintained in the face of disturbances. As we move from banks to the global financial system, it becomes increasingly difficult to conceive of resilience in a way suitable for empirical research.

The meaning of resilience is a matter of definition. When it comes to explaining resilience (or the lack of it), the crucial challenge is knowledge about causal relations. Which of the interacting variables, or combination(s) of indicator values, permit to assess a given financial system as "sound"? To answer this question requires knowledge of the relationships between the variables measured by different FSI, and of their joint impact on soundness, how ever defined. The aggregation of the value of many different indicators to the verdict "financial system X is sound" (or stable, or resilient) is only possible on the basis of an elaborate theory, a causal model that specifies the relationships between all relevant variables. Such a theory does not exist at the moment. FSI and the Data Gaps Initiative do identify relevant factors: Concentration in the financial sector, the financing of bank activities by debt, and the shifting of risk by bundling credits and insuring and selling them, were involved in the build-up of risk in the financial system, making it vulnerable even to a relatively small shock such as the bursting of the sub-prime bubble. But FSI and the Data Gaps Initiative say nothing about the causal relationships between the factors they identify, or what values different variables should have if stability or financial soundness is to obtain, let alone what the "self-corrective mechanisms" mentioned by Schinasi (2004, 8) would be.

If a financial system lacks resilience, it is vulnerable; vulnerability is the opposite of resilience. If a system – a bank, business firm, political regime, or social sub-system – is vulnerable, it is at risk of succumbing to an external disturbance. "Systemic risk" means the risk of failure that inheres in the make-up of a system, its structure and mode of operation. Systemic risk is endogenous. As resilience is built into a system, so is its counterpart, vulnerability or the risk of failure. The financial crisis of 2008 was triggered by a relatively minor external disturbance – increasing defaults in the US housing market – impacting on a financial system that had become vulnerable. The financial crisis thus had endogenous and exogenous causes: System failure follows from the <u>interaction</u> of internal and external causes.

The financial system of the early Twenty-first Century had become vulnerable due to internal changes over the preceding decades – changes such as the rise of globally important financial institutions, a growing shadow banking sector, and a rising level of debt financing. The boundaries between the different sectors of the financial system eroded with the growth of large financial holdings engaging in banking, trading, and insurance activities. Interdependencies between banks had grown together with a flourishing interbank market. The tendency of financial institutions to invest in the same kind of structured securities led first to herding and subsequently to domino effects. The combination of, and interdependencies between these processes made the financial system vulnerable to even a minor disturbance. To minimize systemic risk should be the overriding goal of a financial reform that cannot eliminate environmental threats to a financial system.

It may appear ironic that the structural and operational changes that made the financial system vulnerable were the result of adaptive responses to changes in its environment. As I have argued elsewhere (Mayntz 2014), those changes in the international financial system that made it vulnerable to a limited domestic disturbance like the American subprime crisis resulted from responses of financial institutions and financial entrepreneurs to opportunities arising in the environment, and to specific demands of potential investors. De-regulation paved the way for the rise of new categories of financial institutions like money market funds, hedge funds, and private equity funds. Increasing competition in the financial industry heightened the risk appetite of bankers. De-regulation and advances in information technology made possible the development of complex derivatives that later turned out to be "toxic". Their growing use, and the related expansion of investment banking, responded to the so-called savings glut, and the demand of newly important corporate investors for profitable investment possibilities. The innovations and changes that took place since the 1980ies were largely evaluated as positive, manifesting the resilience of the financial industry in a dynamic environment. In fact they made the financial system vulnerable: Systemic risk ironically was the result of adaptive resilience. As is true of pathological learning, adaptive responses to environmental change that appear to represent resilience can be dysfunctional.

Since a well-functioning and resilient financial system is the aim of the reforms that started in 2008 we may ask what the preceding analysis means for the chance of successful political intervention. In principle, it is possible to shape something deliberately to be resilient. Resilience is built into many technical systems. The CEOs of a corporation can adopt strategies to make sure that the organization remains viable. In the case of a bank they can manipulate lending behavior and interest rates, and avoid maturity mismatch. An effectively problem-solving political intervention in society presupposes the will and the capacity to intervene, and the knowledge needed to decide how and where. Early calls for a radical and comprehensive reform were soon met by resistance from the financial industry, and the fear of governments to harm economic growth. Political competence for intervening in a market economy is limited. Lack of information about the prevailing situation, and lack of causal understanding, militated further against forceful intervention. Political intervention should be able to anticipate the interdependencies that may thwart the desired result of a given regulatory intervention, or even produce a counter-intuitive effect. But a comprehensive theory, a dynamic model of the financial system as a system did not exist. Available knowledge and up-to date information were fragmented, reflecting the internal differentiation of the financial system. The supervisory structure, with its separate supervisory agencies for banks, securities, and insurance, was similarly fragmented. The same holds again for regulatory agencies, especially at higher political levels. In the European Union, different agencies deal with banks, securities, and insurance. At the international level, the Basel Committee BCBS deals with banks, the International Organization of Securities Commissions IOSCO deals with securities, and the International Association of Insurance Supervisors IAIS with insurance. The reform plans of these agencies address different parts of the financial system. Fragmented knowledge and fragmented capacities made the development of a "master plan" from which individual reform measures could be derived impossible. Financial system reform today consists of separate reforms: A reform of (regulated) banks, a reform of the trade in derivatives, a reform of rating agencies etc. Reform inevitably is piecemeal, and remains experimental.

Whether a functional sub-system of society, let alone something like the global financial system, could be intentionally fashioned to be resilient must remain an open question. Banks can be organized to withstand external disturbances. But as we know from experiments with planned economies, deliberate political guidance of societal subsystems is difficult even where it is constitutionally permitted. This, however, is not only a question of steering capacity. Does resilience, defined as a property of social systems, presuppose intentionality, or can it also be emergent? Maybe resilience is a concept that can be meaningfully applied only to clearly bounded and formally organized social units.

References

Baker, A. (2013). The New Political Economy of the Macroprudential Ideational Shift. New Political Economy, 18(1), 112-139.
Bertelsmann Stiftung (2014), Policy Performance and Governance Capacities in the OECD and EU. Sustainable Governance Indicators 2014. Bertelsmann.
BCBS (2010). Basel III: A Global Regulatory Framework for More Resilient Banks and Banking Systems. Basel: BIS.
BIS (2014). 84th BIS Annual Report, 2013/2014. Brussels, 29 June 2014.
EBA (2014). Methodological note EU-wide Stress Test. European Banking Authority, 29 April 2014, Brussels.
European Central Bank (2012). Shadow Banking in the European Area – An Overview. Occasional Paper Series 133, Frankfurt/ M.
European Central Bank (2014). Aggregate Report on the Comprehensive Assessment. October 2014, Frankfurt/ M.
Douven, W. et al. (2012). Resistance versus resilience approaches in road planning and design in delta areas: Mekong floodplains in Cambodia and Vietnam. Journal of Environmental Planning and Management, 55(10), 1289-1310.
Fama, E.F. (1970). Efficient Capital Markets: A Review of Theory and Empirical Work. Journal of Finance, 25(2), 383-417.
FSB/IMF (2009). The Financial Crisis and Information Gaps. Report to the G-20 Finance Ministers and Central Bank Governors. Basel.
FSB/IMF (2013). The Financial Crisis and Information Gaps. Fourth Progress Report on the Implementation of the G-20 Data Gaps Initiative. Basel.
Hellwig, M. (2010). Capital Regulation after the Crisis: Business as Usual? Max Planck Institute for Research on Collective Goods, Bonn, Preprint 2010-31.
IOSCO (2013). Report on the second IOSCO hedge fund survey. Madrid.
Lazarsfeld, P., & H. Menzel (1993). On the Relations between Individual and Collective Properties. In R. Boudon (ed.), Paul F. Lazarsfeld on Social Research and its Language (pp. 172-189). Chicago: University of Chicago Press.
Mayntz, R. (2011). Emergenz in Philosophie und Sozialtheorie. In: J. Greve & A. Schnabel (eds), Emergenz. Zur Analyse und Erklärung komplexer Strukturen (pp. 156-186). Frankfurt/M.: Suhrkamp.
Mayntz, R. (2014). Die Finanzmarktkrise im Licht einer Theorie funktioneller Differenzierung. KZfSS, 66(1), 1-19.
Moschella, M., & Tsingou, E. (2013). Great expectations, slow transformations. incremental change in post-crisis regulation. ECPR Press.
Quaglia, L. (2014). The European Union & Global Financial Regulation. Oxford University Press.
San Jose, A., & Georgiou, A. (2009). Financial soundness indicators (FISs): framework and implementation. IFC Bulletin 31, Measuring financial innovation and its impact. Basel, BIS, 277-282.
Scheidegger, E. (2014). Die Schweiz ist widerstandsfähig –aber wie lange noch? „Resilienz" gegen Schocks als neues Element einer guten Wirtschaftspolitik. Neue Zürcher Zeitung, 09.09.2014, 10.

Schinasi, G.J. (2004). Defining Financial Stability. IMF Working Paper WP/04/187, International Monetary Fund.
Thiemann, M. (2013). In the Shadow of Basel: How Competitive Politics Bred the Crisis. FEPS Working Paper, 1-43.
Webster's New World Dictionary of the American Language (1966). Cleveland/ New York, New World Publishing Company.
Zorn, H. (2009). Recounting the Beans. The Statistical Construction of Fiscal Reality. Dissertation, University of Cologne.

In Search of the Golden Factor: Conceptualizing Resilience in the Framework of New Economic Sociology by Focusing 'Loyalty'

Andrea Maurer

1 The classical view: in search of resilient individuals or systems

Resilience originally meant the trait of individuals or of ecosystems to overcome threatening circumstances.[1] In the case of humans, it states an individual's ability to reach normal development after difficult life events like material poverty, war or social anomy. Resilience appears in reaching normal biography and successful social integration.[2] That ability to deal with threatening events and therefore restore stability is currently gaining approval in the social sciences. Business studies are already questioning why some companies handle market shocks better than others (e.g., Boin & van Eeten 2013, p. 430). In sociology, in the science of history and political science (Endreß & Maurer, 2015; Hall & Lamont, 2013), as well as in interdisciplinary research, scientists have recently started looking for and doing research on *social factors* of resilience. Specific social factors such as fairness, trust, and loyalty become important in times of coping with threatening and unexpected

---

[1] The idea of conducting research on social factors like loyalty, as a factor for resilience within economy can be dated back to earlier confrontations with Albert Hirschman's writings and that of new economic sociologists and socio-economists (Maurer, 2006, 2012). This paper is part of a wider research project on social resilience.

[2] It is remarkable that even in early psychological writings – though, without theorizing it – the contribution of social relations has been recognized (see Werner, 1977).

social events, especially in sociology. So far, rising interest has led social scientists to search for golden factors, which support groups, organizations, regions, societies or social systems when dealing with disruptive processes and which restore normality. In this light, what *normality* means, depends on the theoretical background and covers mutual expectations, social integration and functionality.

2 New theoretical considerations: social resilience

Currently, the sociological research into factors of resilience is increasing but with almost no reference to theoretical concepts, theories or models. It remains unclear what disruption means and also the normal state remains theoretically undetermined. Therefore, what is needed are means to design (sociological) theories and models which help to describe what disruption refers to and what restoration then means in social life. After that, factors which help regain normality or stability can be identified. Only with a clear theoretical reference can one look for social factors which keep social groups, institutions, organizations, and the like resilient. An important topic for sociologists is the collapse of social action systems due to a loss of mutual expectations. In accordance with this, social factors which stop processes of undermining social expectations gain importance.

2.1 Sociological research on resilience

Different theoretical programs can be used in the treatment of social factors of resilient. First, they help to identify relevant social factors of resilience by describing the main logic and characteristics of social action systems, such as social groups, markets, organizations, networks, regions and society have to be defined. Second, they provide precise arguments why those specific social factors support the restoration of that particular social action system. Third, the emergence and function logic of various social factors can be identified according to their general ability to keep particular social action systems resilient. All theories need a conception of a state of normality and a notion of what disruption or threatening of existence means to this normal state. Sociological research on resilience can refer to different notions of normality, such as action systems based on stable mutual expectations or subsystems providing particular functions for the overall system. Events like war, terrorist attacks, bankruptcy, inflation or deflation, economic crises and so on have to be translated into a loss of mutual expectation because of a decline of benefits or a failure of functionality which trigger further events and processes which in turn threaten central elements or functions of a social system at the end.

The specific point in sociological resilience research is that by the means of sociological terms, theories and models, particular resilient units can be defined as confronted by various kind of disruptive events. When these definitions are made, precise theses can be given which state why particular social factors enable the resilient unit to deal with the described disruptive threats and thereby have a higher chance of restoring a normal state, because those factors can stop the driving process. Based on the classics (Durkheim, 1938; Weber, 1978), explanations can be offered which show how what social factors support individuals (see section 2.2) by regaining mutual social expectations. The basic thesis says that some social action systems have particular social factors, the so called *golden factors* such as trust, loyalty and morality which keep the system resilient. If there is an increase of disruptive processes foreseen due to characteristics of modern, western society resilience research also gains a societal perspective. For example, if processes of marketization, the spread of neo-liberalism and capitalism or secularization and individualization are named for increasing threats and risks resilience research gets connected to society diagnoses (s. Bonß in this collection). The follow-up question is, if and how particular societies, organizations or social groups can handle threatening events like environmental disasters, migration, economic crises, the dissolution of social communities/networks or the overload of social relationships. Research on resilience earns societal relevance through empirical observation of the increase of fast process dynamics in society and in the economy, which are often equated with marketization and capitalism or indirectly connected processes of globalization and individualization (Hall & Lamont, 2013). Disruption, collapses, and unexpected events are increasingly derived from the social construction of economy in modern society and thus become a topic of sociology.

2.2 Action-based explanations: linking social actors to social factors

Action based explanations explain resilience by giving causal arguments for why an observed disruption could be stopped by actors due to social factors. Especially, action based explanations determine how individuals can stop such disruptive processes because of their social embeddedness. In this context, resilience is to be regarded from a sociological point of view. It is specifically the search for social factors which assist the actors who are involved to capture these processes and restore stability or normality. Therefore, the notion of resilience needs to be combined with sociological theories which describe why and how social factors influence individual and social actions. These theoretical concepts can be used for different empirical fields like markets, firms, social groups, social movements, and so on. The connecting question is about the handling of disruptive events and especially those factors which help initiate restoration processes and social stability or normality. Social resilience gains a new research perspective through the search for such social factors which support actors by dealing with disruption and thereby restore social action systems.

There has been a shift, within sociology, towards the treatment of social action and the discussion of social action problems, like conflict solving, cooperation and coordination through social institutions. This is generally done in the framework of action-based explanations (Alexander, Giesen, Münch, & Smelser, 1987; Lindenberg, Coleman, & Nowak, 1986). As in the early social theories from Adam Smith, Thomas Hobbes, John Locke and others, *problematic situations* are conceptualized from an individual point of view based on empirically informed models of social action (Maurer, 2016). Successful restoration of social institutions during or after disruptive processes is explained by both individual's intentions and the dominant social factors in the sited situational context. While the emergence and maintenance of stable social expectations is regarded, especially in classic sociology, as the central problem of social action because of contingency (Weber, 1978), new approaches such as multi-level explanations, mechanism approach, chaos theory and new institutionalism work specifically with the assumption of uncertainty or risk (Bonß, 2015). According to these theoretical backgrounds, endogenous and exogenous processes of disruptive processes, like social change, anomy or crises can be captured as unpredictable dynamics. Different models as threshold models, tipping points, cascade effects, linear addition and institution theory are used (J. S. Coleman, 1990; Schmid, 2015) for the description of the process sequences. Such models of disruptive events and existence threats can refer to a variety of action systems and their central characteristics. This means that not only is the threat of stable mutual expectations and therewith, stable social order, made a subject of discussion, but also sudden catastrophes, risk and economic crises. For this reason, it depends on the theoretical contouring of the central aspects of the social action system in review, as to what disruptive events or processes function as existential threats. Furthermore, this means that in order to search within a theoretical conception for social factors of resilience, one has to design a functional relation between such social factors and the general logic or characteristics of that particular action system. Such theses can be described by highly abstract models, as well as middle range concepts or case studies help (Hedström, Swedberg, & Udéhn, 1998; Maurer, 2009; Mayntz, 2002).

In newer multilevel research programs (Hedström & Bearman, 2009), positive effects of social factors in different social contexts are captured, based on a general explanatory logic which uses action theories as a micro foundation (J. S. Coleman, 1986; Granovetter, 1990; Hedström & Swedberg, 1998).[3] Within the framework of action based sociological explanations different elaboration proposals can be made which mark different degrees of difficulty. Thus, subsequent to the understanding-explanatory sociology from Max Weber (Weber, 1949) social expectations are central for social action and order. In contrast to that, rational choice approaches and a number of middle range theories developed by Norbert Elias, Albert Hirschman, Mancur Olson and others, specify the general problem of mutual expectations by specific models of social interdependency. This helps reveal problem constellations such as conflict solving or cooperation and specific solutions in return. In other words, whether small groups, networks, markets or hierarchy help actors when problem solving, depends on the problems of action. Representatives of the new debate of mechanism-based explanations have developed agent-based models. These models particularly focus on the complex interplay between social contexts and action -orientations, -motivations and –abilities for explaining the dynamic of social processes (Hedström & Swedberg, 1998).[4] Actual representatives of action-based explanations in new economic sociology and mechanism approach share the assumption of discovering problems of social action which are realistically described. They all assume that other people influence individual's motives and action either by preference building (Elster, 1998; Granovetter, 1990) or by social expectation building (Burt, 1982; Hedström & Swedberg, 1998). Due to the actor model and the described problem of social action, social factors can be systematically revealed which help overcome the particular problems of social action (J. S. Coleman, 1990; Granovetter, 1990).

In Weber's tradition, socially institutionalized action contexts and especially legitimate order and organization are regarded as the basis for highly stable and rational mutual expectations (Kalberg, 1994). This is how Weber explains the formation of social structure and the tremendous formal rationality, in the sense of high predictability, in the modern western world (Weber, 2009). Max Weber gathered that individual and social actions get highly means-end rational and predictable in the modern western world. He understood this from the interplay of religious ideas

---

3 This is due to the assumption that individuals act intentionally and therefore try to improve their social contexts by establishing and using social mechanisms or institutions which help overcome problems of social action, like challenging situations (see for this general assumption Popper, 1999).

4 Harder abstract models work with a fixed action principle and solely deduce the effects of single social factors. More realistic explanations consider the interplay between individual and social factors. The first principle – the use of an abstract and deductive strong action principle – marks a tight rational choice approach (Maurer, 2016).

of protestant sects and the rational nation state, rational sciences, arts and administration. From the increase of rational action and of self-control in modern western societies, Weber deduces the emergence of formal rational institutions, like markets, firms, and accounting which make life and social order highly rational. The analysis of social institutions as foundations for mutual expectation and social stability is found in new institutionalism as well as in new economic sociology (P. J. DiMaggio, 1998; Nee, 2005; Nee & Swedberg, 2008). Different approaches have dealt with the emergence, function logics, and social effects of institutions in recent social sciences (P. J. DiMaggio, 1998). The emergence of institutions as well as their social effects are explained with regard to interests as well as values (Fligstein, 1996; Greif, 2005; Nee & Ingram, 2005). Thus, social institutions can be explained through self-interested actions, as well as value-oriented or habitual actions against the background of social action problems which reach orientation, as well as conflicts and collective action. This also implies that different institutions can be compared in their function logics, as well as in their social effect for generating loyalty, trust, reputation, leadership and organization which may reduce uncertainty or increase resilience.

In contrast to institution theories which highlight institutionalized expectations, economic sociologists focus on formal structural patterns of social relationships and their effects on the social level. For example, Mark Granovetter shows that in multiple equilibra central actors in networks define further developments and institutional patterns (Granovetter & McGuire, 1998). James Coleman, Mark Granovetter, and several others have discovered the speed at which news travels and the available information in an action system from formal patterns of social embeddedness (J. Coleman, 1988; J. S. Coleman, 1985). Ronald Burt specifically explains the ability of innovative and creative actions with brokers who connect different networks and though that, help to spread and generate new ideas (Burt, 2004). In current sociological research, network structures and social institutions are analysed as golden factors which display, in light of specific problem situations, specific effects at the social level. This means, particular institutions can be analysed as mechanisms which help individuals in different social contexts, to overcome problems of social action. In general, loose and weak ties are deemed to be beneficial for information and knowledge problems, close-tight groups are beneficial for problems of control, leadership and formal positions of cooperation. (Maurer, 2016).[5]

---

5   In mechanism approach, it is explained how particular problems of social action like cooperation and coordination are dealt with by socially connected actors (Hedström & Bearman, 2009; Hedström & Swedberg, 1998). For this purpose agent based models

Multilevel action based explanations of social phenomena allow for defining precise theses about when and how action of individuals lead to particular social effects. Variant analyses of action problems and those social factors which help overcome them have resulted over the years (Hedström & Swedberg, 1998; Lindenberg et al., 1986; Nee & Ingram, 2005). Action-based models concisely ask for social factors which help individuals handle different problems of social action. Thus, theoretical statements can be expressed and be empirically checked as to how social and individual factors reduce uncertainty and thereby restore mutual expectations and reduce uncertainty in general. In new economic sociology, as well as in sociological institution program middle range theories are build up that analyse typical problems of social action. For resilience research such work assumes a considerable importance because all problems of social action can be transferred into an ongoing process of disruption of social expectations that possibly leads to collapse. Therefore, the search for social factors which work against disruptive processes can be done in the framework of multilevel explanations by using the described theoretical and methodological guidance.

3 Resilience in the framework of new economic sociology

New economic sociology did not spend attention on *disruptive existence-threatening events* until now. That seems to have changed a little bit since the beginning of the 21st century, especially in light of the international economic and financial crises. Economic crises or rather the collapse of economic systems are permanent subject of discussion (see also Mayntz and Nessel in this volume).

3.1 Loyalty as social factor

In the framework of new economic sociology, *disruption* in economic spheres can be translated into a loss of *mutual expectations*. This means *a loss* of total and unforeseen social orientation, coordination, or cooperation. The question then is, what social factors help individuals, firms, markets, regions, and economic systems

---

and simulations are used to explain unexpected social processes as the upcoming of bestsellers, fashions, panics etc. (Hedström & Ylikoski, 2010). Thus it is not about identifying helpful single factors, but rather about unexpected processes which are explained by specific interplays between individuals' motives or abilities and social factors (Hedström, 2005).

regain confidence in social expectations. Theoretical concepts in new economic sociology say that social factors such as personal relationships, network patterns, or institutional settings help enforce social expectations through particular mechanisms, like control, information or learning. In more complex models, additional processes of social expectation building through imitation, adaptation, or loyalty are used. The model of exit, voice, and loyalty (Hirschman, 1970) specifically states that in reaction to a decline of functionality rational individuals choose between exit and voice. In other words, individuals calculate benefits from staying and engaging in or leaving firms, markets, and regions and choose the action which provides the highest utility. However, sometimes some of them also follow socio-culturally defined feelings of commitment without a direct link to calculated short-term benefits. Thus, action systems with a high level of socio-cultural defined loyalty should have a greater chance of restoring normality after disruptive events for more relevant actors stay due to social bonds. This is to be expected because the more important members stay and try to rebuild social expectations by choosing voice instead of exit. The empirically informed assumption of loyalty makes the exit and voice models more complex. The empirical assumption of loyalty helps to enrich the model. If in social contexts particular members are loyal, they can stop the decline and rebuild social expectations. The first step is not driven by calculating benefits but by the social factor of loyalty which function unlinked to direct or short-term benefits. Thus, from this point forward, sociology needs to establish empirically informed theses about when and why particular social relationships, institutions or structures lead to an increase or decrease of loyalty and thereby hinder or trigger the process of disruption. The model is more realistic because it not only takes short-term benefits into account but also long-term social-cultural motives, which depend on social embeddedness. The specific ability to restore stability after disruptive events is thus explained by socially defined motives or bonds of social commitment. Its particular effect is that social-cultural embeddedness explains a higher degree of voice in the very first moment, when benefits are not to be expected. Loyalty, can help overcome economic shocks or crises because relevant actors stay and contribute to the restoration and thereby send social signals and increase benefits of social coordination or cooperation when needed most..

3.2   Social resilience factors in economy: an overview

During the last thirty years in the framework of new economic sociology, models have been designed which show how specific social factors, like the formal structure of social networks or particular social institutions help reduce uncertainty in general (Granovetter, 1990). From this idea one can develop further models which provide arguments why particular social factors help restore stability in the case of disruption, by redefining social expectations. In a short overview it is shown what effects of social networks and institutions are outlined in new economic sociology in general. Based on this, *loyalty* is discussed as a social factor of resilience in the economic sphere, in more detail (see section 3.3).

The general idea is to reconstruct and develop middle range theories which explain how and why economically oriented action systems are able to handle disruptive processes better than other systems, because of their specific social construction (Boudon, 1979, 1991; Mayntz, 2004; Merton, 1967). This means reformulating theses about how the well-discussed social factors in economic sociology, namely networks and institutions (Maurer, 2012), contribute to the restoration of mutual expectations during or after shocks which are interpreted as existence-threatening. This could be done, at first, through a more precise description of the situational contexts and the disruptive process. Then, expected benefits, as well as values and habits can be described from the viewpoint of actors. In this manner, social networks or institutions can be translated into both individual and social action. Secondly, regarding specific empirical situations, extensions of the action model can be made by introducing the assumption that some actors make their decisions based on calculations and others attached by bonds of loyalty. Then, one can work with models of social action which show, how positive feedback loops emerge from loyal actors and their action patterns. In addition, one can consider that loyal actors not only increase expected benefits but also the loyalty of other members through social imitation (Maurer, 2016).[6] The power of sociological models would then be, to deduce the initial ignition of loyalty from social factors and then encourage empirical studies. For this purpose, studies need to be created which theoretically show, which social forms of networks, markets or company structures, regional networks or economic systems create socio-cultural loyalty. It is the identification of such social factors which, in light of disruptive processes are able to recreate loyalty and therefore make action systems more resilient.

To date, economic sociologists have reconstructed mechanisms and integrated in models which reduce uncertainty, without having to specify problem-contents or degrees (Granovetter, 1990). Thus, it is shown that network structure can improve information flow as well as trust building. Therefore, the present models about the

---

[6] An alternative would be to look at general theories, like transaction cost or principal agent theories that also provide theses about when and why particular social factors – mostly institutions like hierarchies, markets, or trust help to build mutual expectations by using control mechanisms (J. S. Coleman, 1985; Williamson, 1994).

effects of different social factors have to be made more specific and be expanded. For research on resilience it is important to represent the effects of social factors which restore social expectations in case of disruption and existence-threatening facets. With this in mind, factors and their effects have to be shown which characterise the resilience of action systems.

The central models of the new economic sociology describe different modes of action and social forms for networks and institutions.

1. Weak ties improve the level of information, because individuals have more contacts and less redundant information (Granovetter, 1982). Whereas strong ties in small groups create trust and offer control (J. S. Coleman, 1994) and brokers improve innovation and creativity (Burt, 2004).
2. Formal and informal rules frame economic action and, as long as they have empirical validity, they contribute to the solution of various social problems by reinforcing social expectations. Institutions make individual and social actions predictable and help to make social life more rational (Weber, 1978). Institutions are reflected in social order and characterize markets, firms, economic regions or systems (P. DiMaggio, 1994; Sabel, 1989; Saxenian, 1994).
3. The coordination effects of competition (market), centralized control (organisation) and imagination and patterns of thinking (culture) are being comparably discussed against the background of voting and control problems (J. S. Coleman, 1990; Williamson, 1985). Often the Neo-classic postulate is being criticised by the universal advantageousness of market-voting and the impact of social coordination-mechanisms of group beliefs or hierarchical control is being highlighted (Cox, Broadbridge, & Raikes, 2014; Hirschman, 1986; Ostrom, 1990).
4. In addition to that, in recent times, the effects of social-cultural patterns for economy have been recognised and captured (Swedberg, 1998). Economic historians (Denzau & North, 1994), as well as sociologists and social-economists have recently introduced the effects of socio-cultural basics of economic actions within modern societies again. The specific functionality of socio-cultural patterns in the economy is seen in the ability to frame egotistic purely interest-oriented actions (Fukuyama, 1996; Hirschman, 1970; Swedberg, 2007). Therefore, the works of Albert Hirschman could be important, because he stands for the claim of the realistic extension of action models by empirical theses. What Hirschman leaves open is a theory about the development and empirical validity of social-cultural patterns. Only then situations can be defined theoretically, in which social-cultural patterns can unfold their effects and overlap interests.

New economic sociology normally works with middle range theories. As these theories do not use standardized action theories, an integrative micro fundamental is missing, from which the models could be improved or connected. A solution is provided for this in connection to Max Weber. Thus, the effective interplay between different action orientations and motives can be concretised with the help of empirical theses. Thus, a particular importance belongs to the relation of the different action orientations. One must identify how and when rational calculation is not important. In this way, the special mode of action of social-cultural patterns of interpretation can be seen as a cause for economic relevant action, which is separated from direct, situational, cost-benefit considerations. Max Weber, himself, described the protestant entrepreneur or skilled worker as a human searching for salvation (1978; 2009). However, religious ideas unfold their effects only when they go along with individual's interests and social institutions. For this reason, it can be argued that social-cultural attitudes can lead to social commitment which binds particular actors, without direct or short-term benefits. The meaning of social-cultural commitment or *loyalty* is specifically seen within precarious moments such as, when facing disruptive events, catastrophes or economic crises. Loyalty starts up benefits through social cooperation and coordination again (Etzioni, 1988; Fukuyama, 1996).

3.3 Loyalty: a socio-cultural factor within economy

As is described above, a central element of new economic sociology is the work with more realistic models which offer precise theses about the effects of social factors in economic spheres (Granovetter, 1990). Therefore, most of economic sociologists avoid rational-choice theory as well as concept of habitus. In fact, they rely on Max Weber and Albert Hirschman by starting with the assumption of rational-intentional action but enrich them when they lack empirical proof. This means that the action model needs to be enlarged with empirical knowledge for example saying that and how other individuals influence motives and preferences (Maurer, 2016). The advantages of this type of model-building are those highly abstract and deductively strong models of action can be used when started with and enriched by empirical evidence when needed. Such enriched complex models allow to consider various interplays of social situations and individuals as well as surprising processes. In particular, the relationship between interests and ideas can be taken into account to explain social phenomenon. In concrete terms, this means using empirically informed theses, at the time and to the extent to which shared cognitive or normative belief systems or calculating benefits are the driving factors for individuals. The disadvantage is that the specifically revealed and examined effects of social factors, like networks or institutions are restricted to particular situations. A compromise is to begin with the assumption of intentional-rational action and to explain the effects of social networks or institutions through benefit arguments. Extensions can be made with respect to the empirical context. This can be done by using theoretically guided information about the extent and effects of socio-cultural factors, like loyalty, on individuals in a concrete social situation. Therefore, research on resilience needs to formulate concepts on when and why loyalty can be expected (section 3.3.1). Thus, empirically specified theses about loyalty as a source of resilience *in the economy* can be set up and the corresponding effects can be pointed out (section 3.3.2). How this can be done is illustrated by exemplary empirical data regarding social resilience in the economic region of Baden-Wuerttemberg after 2008 (section 3.3.3).

3.3.1 Loyalty as a social-cultural resource in a performance decrease

At this point, the model *of exit, voice, and loyalty* by Albert Hirschman (1970) is suitable for the sociological resilience research, because it directly refers to processes which threaten benefits through the performance failure of an action system, such as organizations or societies.[7] From the viewpoint of intentional-rational actors, the collapse of benefits either motivates them to leave the system (exit) or to contribute to their own recovery by voice.[8] Resilience research focuses on those factors which hinder the collapse by preventing or limiting exit. If there is a social factor which impedes exit, then the chances of restoration increase. Furthermore, the expected effects can influence other factors and trigger multiple effects of restoration for example less exit means an increasing voice.

The general problem of performance collapse can be transformed into multiple forms of economic crises; e.g. that of markets, companies, regions or economic systems like the EU. Concrete indicators include a massive decrease of the provision of demanded commodities or services, which extend from the market dissolution over insolvency up to the impoverishment (decreasing gross national product) of regions and societies. Rational-intentional actors will then decide between exiting the market, company or region and the effort needed for reconstruction due,

---

[7] For the critical reconstruction of the model of exit, voice, and loyalty see Barry 1974 and Maurer 2006.

[8] If the failure is caused by an endogenous development or through an exogenous shock can be blanked out at this place.

in light of expected recovery benefits. The heuristic viewpoint is to represent the concrete revenues for markets, companies, regions or economic systems and the relevant expectations of the actors for both options regarding the socio-economic situation. Thus, the so called bridge hypotheses help describe and expand (1) revenues and costs (2) and also the likelihood with which they are expected by the actors in particular situations. That is what makes the use of this model applicable, not only for economic spheres, but also for social fields.[9]

The effect mechanism of exit and voice is basically within the relation between the amount and expectation of benefits for both possible actions. When facing performance collapse or disruption, the situation is specifically characterised through the overall collapse of the expectations for any benefits. For this reason, it has to be said that those factors show a high effect of resilience, which contribute to a positive strengthening of *success expectations* and/or new *benefits*. The main thesis would then be that the decline can be hindered when performance relevant actors stay. Then not only expectations of direct benefits from the actions of relevant actors rise but also expected benefits from social commitment. This has to be declared by searching for situational factors, which specifically offer incentives for high-performance actors to stay and contribute to voice which function independently from direct or short-term revenues.

The particularity of the *hydraulic model* (Hirschman 1970) is that both forms of action: exit and voice, have contrary effects and influence each other negatively. If, in the case of disruptive events, high-performance actors leave, then the potential of voice is decreasing due to their exit but also due to the fact that others take this as a signal of decline. These interdependencies launch a downward trend that is difficult to interrupt. Vice versa, observable voice of important members can favour performance recreation by working as signal and by increasing benefits. Since both action forms are deduced from rational calculation of revenues, the spotlight is firstly on the search for *social reasons*, which make exit or voice more profitable for individuals. For example, if there is empirical evidence for essential actors staying during and shortly after crises, it can be argued that this works as an intervening variable, which stops the downward trend independently from direct revenues.[10]

---

9   Albert Hirschman (1970) developed the model from his personal experiences in developing countries like Nigeria and even expanded it to explain the decline of the former DDR. The model found another area of usage in company- and personnel research (Williamson, 1974).

10 That will allow, to take changes of expectation through social action of others into account and to use for example threshold models that explain an abrupt collapse as a

The introduction of a socio-culturally characterized bond of loyalty on the side of the actors is such an intervening variable. Its effect can be seen in that the pure and short-term benefit calculation is interrupted. This needs to be concluded from the social context factors. Only if particular social factors give evidence of social-culturally defined loyalty by specific actors there is good reason for regaining normality. This means nothing other than the social contexts keep the social action system resilient by motivating relevant actors to stay and thereby interrupt exit oft other actors.

In this sense, loyalty refers to the idea of "captain is the last to leave the ship". It is easy to see this is a normative postulate embedded in the fibre of some professions in particular socio-cultural contexts, such as researchers or politicians (Weber, 2004). It is above all the precarious situations, where revenues could hardly be expected, when loyalty is most important for loyal actors can change the downward trend by providing (a) short-term coordination effects, (b) long-term expectations of benefits, and (c) strengthen social standards of commitment in small groups like professions (Greif, 1994; Hirschman, 1970). If first steps of coordination succeed, because of the social-cultural bond of a few strong actors, then from the positive interplay of social-cultural bond and realised benefits, recovery can be declared which functions through the overall improved possibility of success. Companies, sectors, regions and groups, which have minimum loyalty from their important members, because of their given social context, could also, when facing disruptive, existence-threatening events and processes, still gain performance capacity, breaking through the downward trend and in the mid-term could cause a more positive interaction between interests and value binding (Weber, 2009). Adam Smith already described this as the "invisible hand explanation" (Smith, 1982), because such processes are self-enforcing. Of course, the process and the interplay can be specified by diverse assumptions. In the case of loyalty, symbolical signals and real benefits from the loyalty of important actors reinforce each other and can lead to restoration step by step due to a change of social expectations.

Thus, loyalty helps explain the successful handling of disruptive events through social factors. The technique of explanation, which even Max Weber (2009) used, tracks the idea that an action orientation which deviates from a rational mode can be explained by concrete situational factors and thereby a specific power of effect can be unfolded. That corresponds to the claim of new economic sociology in which sociological and economic models have to be made realistically and the material and ideal aspects have to be taken into account within those expla-

---

result of the exit of many. The concrete dynamics are shaped by the specific interplay between increasing migration and parallel decreasing critics.

nations. Although, explanations start with simple assumptions, they need to be created more realistically, if they do not apply empirically. So, in a first step at the performance collapse or disruptive event, the presented rational alternatives of action, exit and voice must be used. However, this simple model can be expanded with the notion of loyalty given in some economic enterprises, regions or systems. Loyalty, is introduced by Hirschman for empirical justification and explains the break through and stopping of collapses mostly at the beginning when benefits are highly uncertain (Maurer, 2016). In the exit and voice-model loyalty there is an intermediate variable: if there are loyal members who do not calculate short-term benefits in the case of a decline or disruption, a restoration can be expected through a reduction of exit. The loyalty of important members can stop the dynamic interplay of increasing exit and decreasing voice because they help to restore success and work as social signals. This is why loyalty helps, especially during and shortly after disruptive events, because precarious points can be overcome, even though short-term benefits are not to be expected. However important members send signals and put benefits in reach again. Hirschman does not mention which social contexts make loyalty expectable and does not offer theoretical arguments about why loyalty is to be expected. This also explains why the concept of loyalty is mostly used in concrete empirical contexts for example in personnel research. In new economic sociology and resilience research, the concept of loyalty needs to be improved at this time.[11] What is needed are theoretically based theses about which social factors support why loyalty in order to make loyalty a concept for sociological research on resilience.

3.3.2 Loyalty in the framework of new economic sociology

The empirical observation is central for new economic sociological resilience research so that some enterprises or economic regions are found to be more resilient than others in light of the shock after the 2008 economic crisis (Kujath 2000; Bristow 2010; European Commission 2014). As was illustrated above, loyalty can be defined as a social-cultural bond to a region or enterprise that works without regard for any direct, situation specific, benefit calculations. The observed resilient effect of loyalty is the highest chance for high-performance members to stay and contribute to the recreation through voice. Loyalty should be very effective in the case of an economic performance decrease, because economic actors normally have alternatives and easier ways of leaving. So, enterprises, markets or regions,

---

11 This is because in the fundamental work of Hirschman (1970) loyalty remains a "black box" (Maurer, 2006).

where loyalty is empirically effective, should show higher standards of investment, labour force and contracts, patents even in light of disruptive events.

Thus, loyal entrepreneurs, managers and members of the work council for example, unfold important signal effect by positively influencing the evaluation of success of others and by setting standards of action at close range. It is important that the first action and the success in the light of collapses hold out the prospect of expectable revenues again. The effect mechanism of loyalty is premised on the fact that some important actors, even in crises will not leave and by staying sending social signals and realising cooperation and coordination benefits. Then the position of the specific company or region improves and even provides better conditions for going further. More and more actors can be won over, even if they act purely out of interest calculation. The collapse is stopped through the interplay of the presented effects. As a result there should be less insolvency, more occupations, higher volumes of sale, and more innovations.

The first indications of loyalty on the part of essential actors can be found in the frequently justified effects of a membership in small groups based on social experiences, like families, religious sects or social communities (J. S. Coleman, 1985; Fukuyama, 1996; Swedberg, 2007; Weber, 2009). Small groups within economy, which offer social status, acknowledgement or reputation could, even in times of decreases, bind especially important individuals. It is the social capital of small strong-knitted groups, such as entrepreneurial families, professional clubs and/or religious communities, which, even in light of existence threatening events, motivate others to stay and perform in favour of the action system, even without direct material consideration (Smith, 1982).

The analysis of strongly-knitted groups or professions links sociological studies with research on resilience. By deducing the emergence of social bonds or commitment from previous interactions by mechanisms of learning and control sociology can explain why loyalty relations could exist for longer periods of time, even if there is no obvious benefit. The specific social capital of small groups with strong and direct personal relations is loyalty, which is free from immediate benefit calculations and which creates bonds through social and long-term benefits. If companies or regions have such islands of direct interaction, a higher bond of loyalty can be considered. On an executive level, this could be established through common team experiences, through family businesses, elite universities, professional organizations or clusters (Padgett, 2001; Portes, 1995). Science, entrepreneur or managerial associations and their small local groups carry particular concepts of how to behave as a "good captain," especially in crises. This can be also the result of small-scale structures in regions or corporations, in which specific ideas of how to act when facing crises are passed on from generation to generation. The "protestant Swabian master craftsman" can be considered as an ideal type of such patterns. The model corresponds to the pattern of a captain, who invests up to his last bit of money to rescue the company in political or economic crises (Berghoff, 1997). This primary socially defined loyalty launches a process of reconstruction of social patterns of expectation, which are mainly based on social signals but which point to benefits in the long run. Such signals are more effective, the more important the particular actors are and the more important the action system is. They work by describing objective chances of future success but also through subjective interpretations.

3.3.3 Social resilience factors in the economic region of Baden-Wuerttemberg after 2008

Social bonds of loyalty which are effective even in crises are to be expected in strongly knitted social relations. So, local clusters, family networks, professionally or ethically based groups enable positive interactions and experiences which build (or reinforce) loyalty that can be stored or transported in local settings for generations. If there are any disruptive events or shocks, such social factors can activate loyalty and thereby increase social resilience in the economic sphere. This means that due to such factors, processes of economic recovering in terms of GDP or revenues (see for recent data Statistisches Landesamt Baden-Württemberg 2016) should be empirically observable. The criteria for social resilience are observable processes in which even existence threatening events, which can be labelled as a breakdown of stock markets, insolvencies, deflation and inflation or market collapse, are successfully conducted. In reference to companies, markets, economic regions and economic systems, expressions of resilience would be the classic socio-economic indicators such as GDP, employment, patents, turnover. The thesis to be proven is that the better performance in terms of investments, foundations and occupation can be understood as an effect of a higher degree of loyalty. This means to understand turnovers, the gross national product and especially the socio-cultural patterns of relevant actors give proof for loyalty as hint for social resilience in economic spheres. Thus, the resilience research can use the appropriate and continual socio-economic data which is raised by the statistical state and federal offices and the Federal Labour Office. These are available on the national and international level for companies, regions and national economies. Furthermore, sociological research on resilience should be able to supplement these with its own empirical data.

Resilient companies, regions and national economies should show during and after disruptive events, like the economic and financial crisis in 2008-9: 1) a better occupational situation (full-time employment, insurable employments, fluctuations); 2) faster and more extensive growth rates (GDP, number of companies, higher revenues); and 3) better expectations of future success (innovation, start-ups, cluster building).

One of the economic regions in Europe which overcame the crisis in a successive way is Baden-Wuerttemberg.[12] It can be empirically shown that the values for the gross domestic product, the quota for occupations and investments, within and directly after the crisis, were always above average in Baden-Wuerttemberg (ESPON, 2014).

Figure 1 Baden-Wuerttemberg with its administrative districts
Source: http://www.badische-seiten.de/baden-wuerttemberg/regierungsbezirke.php [retrieved on 01/07/2016]

Clusters were and are typical within the local are in Baden-Wuerttemberg[13], especially through small companies. At the beginning of the 21st century, Baden-Wuert-

---

12 In Europe even the "third Italy" and the region around Gothenburg turned out to be resilient, because of specific social factors (Sabel, 1989; Zeitlin, 2007).
13 After an administrative reform in 1973, Baden-Wuerttemberg has been divided into 4 administrative regions with each 3 regions (s. fig. 1). Just the region Rhein-Neckar

temberg has to be characterized as a region with regional clusters which are defined by small and medium-sized companies in connection with a highly professional workforce, innovative entrepreneurs and specific cultural patterns of knowledge and loyalty.[14] The quick and extensive resilience in the face of the economic crisis from 2008-9 can be deduced from the socially structured and traditionally organized manufacturing industries in Baden-Wuerttemberg.[15] It becomes clear that Baden-Wuerttemberg, falling back on the classical socio-economic data has recovered more extensive and faster from the shock in 2008-9 in its economic performance, then the other European countries as well as other regions in Germany (BW has to be understood as state, with its own social identity and structures.) In contrast to a short drop in the absolute numbers of the companies within the manufacturing industry in 2008 per -4.52 % and 2009 per -0.79 %, was already counteracted in 2010 (+ 0.68), in 2011 (+ 0.21 %) and after that has been progressively increasing since 2012 (+ 1.68 %, 2013 = + 0.02 %). A similar self-increasing reconstruction of the economic performance can be also seen in the absolute numbers of employed people, which was still decreasing in 2008 and 2009 in the times of crisis (2008 = - 4.52 % and 2009 = - 0.74 %), but then increased continuously from 2010 to 2014 (2010 = 3.23 %, 2011 = 4.97 % and 2012 = 0.90 %).

The meaning of the local bonds of entrepreneurs and employees also manifests itself in collective agreements and the development of payment. After a short and severe drop of pay of − 10.8 % in 2008, it again increased continuously and above average level in comparison with other regions until 2014: 2010 = + 3.45 %, 2011 = + 4.97, 2012 = 3.4 %, 2013 = 3.75 % (Statistisches Landesamt Baden-Württemberg 2015, figures 25-35; Neff 2015). The manufacturing industry in Baden-Wuerttemberg reacted during and after the crisis, on the one hand with personnel reduction and on the other hand with higher pay and binding collective agreements, whereby

---

    makes an exception in reference to machine-makers-tradition (Ministerium für Finanzen und Wirtschaft Baden-Württemberg, 2015b). The term region could thereby mean different things. Here it is used in terms of a social-geographical unit with specific factors and for small units within the administrative region of Baden-Wuertemberg.

14 This is besides regional exceptions and based mostly on metal processing with its implemented professional standards. Till now there is a high and successful result in the registration of patents (Ministerium für Finanzen und Wirtschaft Baden-Württemberg, 2015a).

15 The long tradition of Baden-Wuerttemberg in the manufacturing industry and especially in the metal engineering industry is in the social-historical and- scientific literature well verified (see for example Berghoff, 1997). Furthermore, the leading function of collective agreements in the metal engineering industry in Southern Baden is still clear since for a long time (Müller-Jentsch, 1997).

some essential people could be held in Baden-Wuerttemberg and collective agreements could be saved.

The effect of strong social relations between especially small and medium-sized companies (5 to 500 employees), which emerge from specific regional-local structures, makes even differentiated resilience analysis possible which helps in observing the effects of cluster formations and social-structural peculiarities in small regions. So, it is possible for Neff (2015) to investigate the four administrative districts Freiburg, Karlsruhe, Stuttgart and Tuebingen and their three regions in a first case study, regarding particular economic factors of resilience. The regions differentiate mainly in regard to their meaning of the manufacturing industry. Baden-Wuerttemberg is particularly characterized by regions with city centres as Stuttgart and Karlsruhe. After 2008 the region Heilbronn-Franken kept resilience best. In general, the administrative districts with their regions in Baden-Wuerttemberg showed better resilience, especially those which had more manufacturing industries and more traditional-classic mechanical engineering. In contrast, automobile industry and electronic industry did not have an effect on resilience (Neff 2015, p. 72-3). This can be seen specifically in the different scope and the time that companies or entrepreneurs needed to invest or to produce new innovations after the crisis again. Innovation grow fast and very successful in the administrative district of Stuttgart and its regions. Even investments which exceed the level of the year of crisis 2008, have been made (Neff 2015, p. 71).

Available socio-economic data from these secondary analyses show that the essential companies and employees from the manufacturing industry and especially from the steel industry could manage the crisis 2008-9 much better. First indications show that Baden-Wuerttemberg could use advantages from its characteristic, local, strong social relationships. The economic region of Baden-Wuerttemberg is especially characterised by long-term experiences and collective bargaining between employers and employees. Local based and passed on knowledge in the industry is also typical for most regions. Specific and traditionally anchored as well as socially transported experience and knowledge supported particular economic actions, for example the maintenance of the location, the holding of qualified manpower and reciprocal social relations during crises. If and how the actions of loyal entrepreneurs, managers, members of the work council, trade unions or associations had an effect as signals of crisis management cannot be figured from this data, but need more empirical research. Therefore, additional quantitative and qualitative data collection is necessary, which directly demands the meaning and effect of loyalty with a special focus on firm owners, highly qualified employees and members of the work council within different clusters and regions. Additionally, differences between different local orders have to be examined: modern metropolitan regions like Stuttgart, middle centres with modernised tradition like Karlsruhe or Heilbronn and city outskirts for example the Main-Tauber- or Rhine-Neckar-area regarding their effect on loyalty.

3.4 Social resilience in economy

A sociological analysis of social resilience factors puts the bonds of loyalty for clusters, local-traditional regions or modern metropolitan regions in the spotlight. Loyalty can be regarded as social factor which helps to face disruptive events independent from direct short-term benefits and generates social signals as well as social effects. Again, this is important to motivate other actors to such actions by setting standards and by making benefits expectable. A self-reinforcing recovery process is launched which can be supported or thwarted by other factors.

Modelled after the works of Max Weber and Albert Hirschman and complemented through insights and models of new economic sociology, loyalty can be defined as a social resource of resilience. Most of all, the effects of loyalty as a social factor of resilience can be stated precisely and explained in the form of a self-enforcing process. Sociologists then need to give theoretical theses, as well as empirical evidence for loyalty in particular social contexts. This can be done either by concepts of strong-knit groups based on former experience (reputation system, social signals, commitment), as well as by concepts of socially constructed institutions such as professional ethic, shared model of local identity or typical conventions. In order to provide empirical evidence for loyalty, secondary analysis of the available socio-economic data, questionnaires as well as semi-structured interviews can be used. Today, comprehensive analyses of social resilience factors, like loyalty, require additional quantitative-qualitative data.

4 Conclusions

So far, the resilience research usually deals with ad-hoc-hypotheses and often explains, retrospectively, why and how action systems differ with regard on their abilities to launch resilient processes. However, empirical data for special factors of resilience by companies and economic regions can be given. Without using theoretical concepts about the special effects of particular social-cultural factors, the research on resilience will not improve.

In order to close the research gap, some well-known concepts from new economic sociology have been reconstructed. It has been argued in a critical expansion to the model of exit, voice and loyalty of Albert Hirschman that social-culturally defined bonds of loyalty are particularly helpful in the face of disruptive events. It was discovered that bonds of loyalty can trigger regenerative actions of essential members in crises because the member-bonds function free from short-term benefits. This kind of socially defined action modus can create a self-reinforcing process of reconstruction through two effects. Firstly, it can motivate and enable others to do the same by defining standards in small groups. This also signals revenues by social cooperation (trade unions, clusters) and coordination (institutions such as reputation, trust, ethics) which make benefits in the future expectable again. In addition to the original model of Albert Hirschman and regarding concepts of new economic sociology social-cultural bonds of loyalty are explained and empirically identified for small groups or clusters either based on former experience or on institutionalized models of "staying" in the event of crises. For this the specific concept of "the captain is the last to leave the ship" is helpful. In this process, the thesis has been formulated that a resilient process is put into action sooner, faster and in a more comprehensive manner within economic contexts which are characterised by small groups bound by long-lasting relations. Such contexts of action foster a particular motivation to stay and act for improvement, especially in moments of crisis. The actions which can be deduced from that, especially those of high-performance members, provide good reasons for other individuals to stay even with a threat to existence. This is firstly because firm owners, entrepreneurs, managers, members of the work council and master craftsmen send social signals that they believe in the action system. It is secondly because they can generate coordination and cooperation effects which provide further benefits. Thirdly, in time of uncertainty and a loss of social orientation these members set modes of action which can function as role models. From this on a dynamic model, one can mark the positive effects and loops starting by loyal members. This not only allows for the identification of specific situational factors, but also for deeper insights into the steps of recovery.

With the example of the quite resilient economic region of Baden-Wuerttemberg in the crisis of 2008-9, it can be shown, initially that the classic socio-economic data actually represents this process. Furthermore, it has been shown that Baden-Wurttemberg is characterised not only by clusters, small and medium-sized firms but also by a specific social-cultural tradition in mechanical engineering and appropriate ways to transport local ideas. To comprehensively analyse the effect of social-cultural loyalty in the meantime, some further original data should have been given importance, which specifically examines the process of the estimation of success and expectation of the actors.

The expected revenue of theoretically based sociological resilience research is to analyse the actions and effects which are launched by specific social-cultural factors and thereby to present increasingly precise theses about why some social factors gain resilient effects. Only then will resilience research be able to offer practical design proposals, because only then will resilience factors be theoretically labelled and their action effectives become clear. It is shown, that the social factors which help most in recovering after disruption provide good reasons to the individual actors to stick to the action system without directly calculating expected benefits. By doing so, empirically informed hypotheses can be defined about what kind of social factors help to overcome disruptive processes within particular economic spheres in cases of disruption or crisis.

References

Alexander, J. C., Giesen, B., Münch, R., & Smelser, N. J. (eds). (1987). The Micro-Macro Link. Berkeley: University of California Press.

Berghoff, H. (1997). Zwischen Kleinstadt und Weltmarkt. Hohner und die Harmonika 1857-1961. Paderborn: Ferdinand Schöningh.

Bonß, W. (2015). Karriere und sozialwissenschaftliche Potentiale des Resilienzbegriffs. In M. Endreß & A. Maurer (eds), Resilienz im Sozialen. Theoretische und empirische Analysen (pp. 15-31). Wiesbaden: Springer VS.

Boudon, R. (1979). Generating Models as a Research Strategy. In P. H. Rossi (ed.), Qualitative and Quantitative Social Research. Papers in Honor of Paul F. Lazarsfeld (pp. 51-64). New York: The Free Press.

Boudon, R. (1991). What Middle Range Theories are. Contemporary Sociology, 20, 519-522.

Burt, R. S. (1982). Toward a Structural Theory of Action. New York: Academic Press.

Burt, R. S. (2004). Structural Holes and Good Ideas. American Journal of Sociology, 110(2), 349-399.

Coleman, J. S. (1985). Introducing Social Structure into Economic Analysis. American Economic Review, 74(2), 84-88.

Coleman, J. S. (1986). Microfoundations and Macrosocial Theory. General Discussion. In S. Lindenberg, J. S. Coleman & S. Nowak (eds), Approaches to Social Theory (pp. 345-363). New York: University of California Press.

Coleman, J. S. (1988). Social Capital in the Creation of Human Capital. American Journal of Sociology, 94, 95-120.

Coleman, J. S. (1990). Foundations of Social Theory. Cambridge, MA: Belknap Press.

Coleman, J. S. (1994). A Rational Choice Perspective on Economic Sociology. In N. J. Smelser & R. Swedberg (eds), The Handbook of Economic Sociology (pp. 166-180). Princeton: Princeton University Press.

Cox, R., Broadbridge, A., & Raikes, L. (2014). Building Economic Resilience? An Analysis of Local Partnerships' Plans. Newcastle.

Denzau, A. T., & North, D. C. (1994). Shared Mental Models. Ideologies and Institutions. Kyklos, 47, 3-31.

DiMaggio, P. (1994). Culture and Economy. In N. Smelser & R. Swedberg (eds), The Handbook of Economic Sociology (pp. 27-57). Princeton: Princeton University Press.

DiMaggio, P. J. (1998). The New Institutionalisms: Avenues of Collaboration. Journal of Institutional and Theoretical Economics, 154, 696-705.

Durkheim, E. (1938). The Rules of Sociological Method. Frz. Orig. 1895. New York: Free Press.

Elster, J. (1998). A Plea for Mechanisms. In P. Hedström & R. Swedberg (eds), Social Mechanisms. An Analytical Approach to Social Theory (pp. 45-73). Cambridge: Cambridge University Press.

Endreß, M., & Maurer, A. (eds) (2015). Resilienz im Sozialen. Theoretische und empirische Analysen. Wiesbaden: Springer VS.

ESPON (2014). Economic Crisis and the Resilience of Regions. In: Territorial Dynamics in Europe. Retrieved from http://www.espon.eu/export/sites/default/Documents/Publications/TerritorialObservations/TO12_October2014/ESPON_Territorial-Observation_12-Crisis-Resilience.pdf [07/02/2016].

Etzioni, A. (1988). The Moral Dimension. Toward a New Economics. New York: The Free Press.
Fligstein, N. (1996). Markets as Politics. A Political-Cultural Approach to Market Institutions. American Sociological Review, 61, 656-673.
Fukuyama, F. (1996). Trust. The Social Virtues And The Creation of Prosperity. New York: Free Press.
Granovetter, M. (1973). The Strength of Weak Ties. American Journal of Sociology, 78(6), 1360-1380.
Granovetter, M. (1982). The Strength of Weak Ties. A Network Theory Revisited. In P. V. Marsden & N. Lin (eds), Social Structure and Network Analysis (pp. 105-130). Beverly Hills: Sage.
Granovetter, M. (1990). The Old and the New Economic Sociology. A History and an Agenda. In R. Friedland & A. F. Robertson (eds), Beyond The Marketplace. Rethinking Economy and Society (pp. 89-112). New York: Aldine de Gruyter.
Granovetter, M., & McGuire, P. (1998). The Making of an Industry. Electricity in the United States. In M. Callon (ed.), The Laws of the Markets (pp. 147-173). Oxford: Blackwell.
Greif, A. (1994). Cultural Beliefs and the Organization of Society: A Historical and Theoretical Reflection on Collectivist and Individualist Societies. Journal of Political Economy, 102(5), 912-950.
Greif, A. (2005). Institutions and the Path to Modern Economy. Lessons from Medieval Trade. Cambridge: Cambridge University Press.
Hall, P. A., & Lamont, M. (eds) (2013). Social Resilience in the Neoliberal Era. Cambridge: Cambridge Univ. Press.
Hedström, P. (2005). Dissecting the Social. On the Principles of Analytical Sociology. Cambridge: Cambridge University Press.
Hedström, P., & Bearman, P. (eds.) (2009). The Oxford Handbook of Analytical Sociology. Oxford: Oxford University Press.
Hedström, P., & Swedberg, R. (eds) (1998). Social Mechanisms. An Analytical Approach to Social Theory. Cambridge: Cambridge University Press.
Hedström, P., Swedberg, R., & Udéhn, L. (1998). Popper's Situational Analysis in Contemporary Sociology. Philosophy of the Social Sciences, 28, 339-364.
Hedström, P., & Ylikoski, P. (2010). Causal Mechanisms in the Social Sciences. Annual Review of Sociology, 36, 49-67.
Hirschman, A. (1970). Exit, Voice, and Loyalty: Responses to Decline in Firms, Organizations, and States. Cambridge: Harvard University Press.
Hirschman, A. (1986). Rival Views of Market Society and Other Recent Essays. New York: Viking Press.
Kalberg, S. (1994). Max Weber's Comparative-Historical Sociology. Chicago: University of Chicago Press.
Lindenberg, S., Coleman, J. S., & Nowak, S. (eds) (1986). Approaches to Social Theory. New York: Russell Sage Foundation.
Maurer, A. (2006). Albert Hirschman: Grenzüberschreitungen zwischen Soziologie und Ökonomie? In I. Pies & M. Leschke (eds), Albert Hirschmans grenzüberschreitende Ökonomik (pp. 67-85). Tübingen: J.C.B. Mohr (Paul Siebeck).
Maurer, A. (2009). Authority – A social coordination mechanism: A contribution to the explanation and analysis of social mechanisms. In P. Graeff & G. Mehlkop (eds), Capitalism, Democracy and the Prevention of War and Poverty (pp. 185-201). London and New York: Routledge.

Maurer, A. (2012). 'Social Embeddedness' Viewed from an Institutional Perspective. Revision of a Core Principle of New Economic Sociology with Special Regard to Max Weber Polish Sociological Review, 180(4), 1231-1413.

Maurer, A. (2016). Social mechanisms as special cases of explanatory sociology: Notes toward systemizing and expanding mechanism-based explanation within sociology. Analyse & Kritik. Journal of Social Theory, 1 [forthcoming].

Mayntz, R. (2004). Mechanisms in the Analysis of Micro-Macro-Phenomena. Philosophy of the Social Sciences, 34, 237-259.

Mayntz, R. (ed.) (2002). Akteure – Mechanismen – Modelle. Zur Theoriefähigkeit makrosozialer Ansätze. Frankfurt/M.: Campus.

Merton, R. K. (1967). On Theoretical Sociology. Five Essays, Old and New. New York: The Free Press.

Ministerium für Finanzen und Wirtschaft Baden-Württemberg (2015a). Clusterportal Baden-Württemberg. http://clusterportal-bw.de.

Ministerium für Finanzen und Wirtschaft Baden-Württemberg (2015b). Regionaler Clusteratlas Baden-Württemberg 2015. http://mfw.baden-württemberg.de.

Müller-Jentsch, W. (1997). Soziologie der industriellen Beziehungen. Eine Einführung. Frankfurt/M.: Campus.

Nee, V. (2005). The New Institutionalisms in Economics and Sociology. In N. J. Smelser & R. Swedberg (eds), The Handbook of Economic Sociology. 2nd edition (pp. 49-74). Princeton: Princeton University Press.

Nee, V., & Ingram, R. (2005). Embeddedness and Beyond. Institutions, Exchange, and Social Structure. In N. Smelser & R. Swedberg (eds), Handbook of Economic Sociology (pp. 86-111). Princeton and Oxford: Princeton UP.

Nee, V., & Swedberg, R. (2008). Economic Sociology and New Institutional Economics. In C. Ménard & M. Shirley (eds), Handbook of New Institutional Economics (pp. 789-811). Berlin und Heidelberg.

Neff, A. (2015). Die ökonomische Resilienz des verarbeitenden Gewerbes in den Regionen Baden-Württembergs. Master Thesis. Institute of Sociology. University of Trier. Trier.

Ostrom, E. (1990). Governing the Commons. The Evolution of Institutions for Collective Action. Cambridge: Cambridge University Press.

Padgett, J. (2001). Organizational Genesis, Identity, and Control: The Transformation of Banking in Renaissance Florence. In J. E. Rauch & A. Casella (eds), Networks and Markets (pp. 211-257). New York: Russell Sage Foundation.

Popper, K. (1999). All Life is Problem Solving. Oxford: Routledge

Portes, A. (1995). The Economic Sociology of Immigration: Essays on Networks, Ethnicity, and Entrepreneurship. New York: Russell Sage.

Sabel, C. (1989). Flexible Specialisation and the Re-emergence of Regional Economies. In P. Hirst & J. Zeitlin (eds), Reversing Industrial Decline? (pp. 17-70). Oxford: Berg.

Saxenian, A. (1994). Regional Advantage: Culture and Competition in Silicon Valley and Route 128. Cambridge, MA: Harvard University Press.

Schmid, M. (2015). Disruptiver Wandel und das Problem der Resilienz. In M. Endreß & A. Maurer (eds), Resilienz im Sozialen. Theoretische und empirische Analysen (pp. 57-87). Wiesbaden: Springer VS.

Smith, A. (1982). An Inquiry into the Nature and Causes of the Wealth of Nations. R.H. Campbell & Andrew S. Skinner (eds), vol. I-II. London and New York: Routledge.

Swedberg, R. (1998). Max Weber and the Idea of Economic Sociology. Princeton: Princeton University Press.
Swedberg, R. (2007). Tocqueville and the Spirit of American Capitalism. In V. Nee & R. Swedberg (eds), On Capitalism (pp. 42-70). Stanford: Stanford UP.
Statistisches Landesamt Baden-Württemberg (2016). Konjunkturdaten, Entwicklung und Trends. Konjunkturbericht Baden-Württemberg. Retrieved from http://www.konjunktur-bw.de/entwicklung-und-trends/konjunkturdaten/?ed_fromYear=1995&ed_toYear=2015&ed_seriesId=1 [01/26/2016].
Weber, M. (1949). Essays in the Methodology of the Social Sciences. Trans. and ed. by E. A. Shils & H. A. Finch. New York: Free Press.
Weber, M. (1978). Economy and Society. An Outline of Interpretive Sociology. Orig. publ. in German 1922. Berkeley: University of California Press.
Weber, M. (2004). The Vocation Lectures. Indianapolis: Hackett Publishing Company.
Weber, M. (2009). The Protestant Ethic And The Spirit Of Capitalism. The Talcott Parsons Translation. A Norton Critical Edition. Ed. by Richard Swedberg. New York and London: Norton.
Werner, E. (1977). The Children of Kauai. A longitudinal study form the prenatal period to age ten. Hawai: Universtiy of Hawai'i Press.
Williamson, O. E. (1974). Exit and Voice: Some Implications for the Study of the Modern Corporation. Social Science Information, 13(1), 61-72.
Williamson, O. E. (1985). The Economic Institutions of Capitalism. Firms, Markets, Relational Contracting. New York: Free Press.
Williamson, O. E. (1994). Transaction Cost Economics and Organizational Theory. In N. J. Smelser & R. Swedberg (eds), The Handbook of Economic Sociology (pp. 77-107). Princeton: Princeton University Press.
Zeitlin, J. (2007). Industrial Districts And Regional Clusters. In G. Jones & J. Zeitlin (eds), The Oxford Handbook of Business History (pp. 219-243). Oxford: Oxford University Press.

Consumer Organisations and the Social Resilience of Markets

Sebastian Nessel

1 Introduction

Abundant studies in new economic sociology have shown that the constitution and functioning of markets is based on stable expectations (e.g. Fligstein 2001; Granovetter 1985; White 1981). Only when consumers and firms can expect to regularly realize income and consumption benefits, they will participate in voluntary market exchange. However, uncertainty about the appropriateness of decisions to realize income and consumption benefits is ubiquitous in markets. Uncertainty in market exchange stems from the contingent nature of social interaction, the difficulty to anticipate and forecast the future as well as from the changing nature of markets. For example, technological innovation and change in market's social environment permanently challenge firms' and consumers' routine action. Furthermore, various social groups, e.g. consumer organisations or social movements, permanently seek to modify markets, and hence the conditions for companies and consumers to act and plan.

In this article I argue that markets can only reproduce over time if consumers and firms take up challenges to their routine actions and adjust their expectations accordingly. Consumers and firms need to develop skills to cope with change in markets as well as change in market's environment to overcome uncertainties and to form stable expectations. I call these skills the social resilience of market actors.[1] In this article,

---

1   See Lorenz (in this volume) on the concept of social resilience and the difference between the usage of the concept in social science and natural science.

I examine how consumer organisations influence the social resilience of consumers and firms. Consumer organisations provide an outstanding but yet neglected topic in sociology to study the social resilience and vulnerability of markets. I show that their strategies can both strengthen and weaken the expectations of firms and consumers regarding their routine market action. To demonstrate the impact of consumer organisations on the resilience and vulnerability of markets, this paper is structured in three sections. In the first section, markets are characterized as social structures. The reproduction of markets as social structures is based on stable expectations of consumers and firms regarding anticipated market outcomes. Starting with insights from economic sociology, the first section shows that these market expectations are stabilized by structural, institutional and cultural factors which are called social embeddedness. In the second section of the paper, selected consumer organisations in Germany are analyzed. I argue that consumer organisations contribute to the social embeddedness of markets. I take an actor-centered viewpoint that shows, that each consumer organisation applies different strategies to influence the social structures of markets, and the decisions of firms and consumers. Different strategies of consumer organisations have either stabilizing or destabilizing effects on markets, and hence contribute to the social resilience or, accordingly, the vulnerability of markets. Legal and political efforts to change established market rules as well as public campaigns challenge routine ways of doing things in markets. In contrast, information about the quality of goods and services helps actors to anticipate market outcomes, thus stabilizing their expectations. In the last section of the paper, different strategies of consumer organisations are compared and related to the impact they have on the resilience and vulnerability of markets. I argue that companies may cooperate with consumer organisations in order to increase their resilience against external environmental influences. Similarly, consumer education and consumer information may stabilize the expectations of consumers regarding the quality of goods and services as well as their ability to cope with technological and social change in markets. In contrast, political and legal strategies can increase the vulnerability of businesses and consumers by questioning the suitability of their routine market strategies. Finally, the vulnerability and resilience of consumers and businesses at the level of the actor is linked to the stability and change of markets in general.

2 Markets as Social Structures

Markets can be defined as social arenas where actors voluntary exchange resources. In contrast to other forms of exchange, market exchange is characterized by competition. Before resources change hands, that is before market exchange is realized, consumers and firms compete to enter into concrete social relations with others. Competition between actors precedes exchange. Hence, in market competition, sellers and buyers regularly and voluntarily choose among a range of offers by exchanging partners (e.g. Swedberg 1994, p. 271). Market participants take one another into account and orient their actions and expectations towards concrete and potential offers. It is precisely this permanent mutual orientation of actors that defines the social structure of markets. However, the reproduction of markets is not limited to the mutual orientation of *market actors*. As is shown in the next section, consumers and firms take a *wide range of actors* into account, including politicians, consumer organisations and other social groups, to form stable expectations about potential exchange partners and offers.

The reproduction of markets is inextricably linked to the existence of stable expectations. Economic sociology takes the fragile nature of expectations as the starting point for the analysis of markets. Three theoretical considerations characterize the fragile nature of expectations. As Marc Granovetter (1985) argues, self-interest of atomized actors does not guarantee the stable expectations necessary to reproduce markets. By radicalizing the Hobbesian argument, he suggests that anonymous exchange partners must assume that the other side misleads them, or is in some way duplicitous. He identifies a lack of trust as a threat to the stability of market exchange. The stability of expectations is fundamentally called into question by two other theoretical concepts: The concept of double contingency and the concept of uncertainty. Uncertainty refers to difficulties in anticipating appropriate market strategies ex ante. Uncertainty stems from the potential openness of the future and the cognitive limitations of market actors (bounded rationality, e.g. Beckert 1996). Parsons (see Beckert 1996) formulated the concept of double contingency to highlight the fragility of expectations. To form stable expectations about market strategies actors must take others into account, and anticipate their market behavior. The uncertainty of market decisions, thus, not only stems from what actors do no know about their *own* optimal strategies, but because actors know that *others* also have freedom of choice. All three mentioned concepts – trust, uncertainty, and double contingency – theoretically question the stability of market expectations. Lack of trust, uncertainty and double contingency, thus, are factors that threat the stability of markets. They are vulnerability factors for individual market participants, and entire markets.

Studies in economic sociology identify a number of factors that favor stable expectations and constitute the reproduction of markets. Three social macrostructures can reduce uncertainty, and contribute to trust in markets: structural, institutional and cultural elements (social embeddedness). These elements of social embeddedness constitute and regulate markets by stabilizing the expectations of consumers and firms. In this respect, they are resilience factors of markets. However, as I show in the next section, a change of the structural, institutional and cultural environment of markets confuses actors' routine expectations, and hence can threaten the stability of markets.

In economic sociology, the structural embeddedness of markets is mainly associated with sociological network analysis (Podolny 2001; Zukin and DiMaggio 1991). As Joel Podolny (2001) has suggested, two perspectives of social network analysis can be distinguished: a structural and a phenomenological perspective. In structural approaches, formal structures of social networks cause economic decisions. In my analysis, a central insight of the structural approach is that information from social relations also contributes to trust building in markets. Information from network contacts can be used by consumers to reduce uncertainty regarding the quality of goods (Karpik 2010), or to find appropriate offerings (e.g. jobs, Granovetter 1974). In contrast, the phenomenological network approach construes networks as webs of meaning (Fuhse 2009; White 2000). Network relations are conceived of as prisms or lenses through which consumers and firms can interpret the market and the behavior of other market participants. Following Harrison White, actors interpret their market position by watching their competitors (White 1981, 2000; see also Mützel 2010). The interpretation of competitors' signals – for example, press releases or other "stories" (Mützel 2010) – are important sources of information for companies to orient themselves to each other, and thereby to occupy distinct market positions. According to White, each market position is associated with a distinguishable set of strategies. In his view, the function of networks is not only to generate trust but, above all, to helping firms occupy distinct market niches, and thus to avoid direct competition. White follows that each niche indicates a specific market strategy, and thus facilitates to coordinate firms and suppliers (White 1981, 2000). A network relation indicates subsequent decisions of action and contributes to the social order of markets.

White limits his argument about mutual observation to the sellers' side, and to production markets. In a recent study, Mützel (2010) also justifies this restriction in consumer markets arguing that companies face difficulties when interpreting consumer preferences. White and Mützel both assume that consumer preferences are "discontinuous" and "hard to estimate". They claim that firms observe other firms in a market segment to receive more accurate information in order to set production strategies. In the following I take up Whites original argument and extend it. I argue that companies do not only watch other companies to reduce uncertainty about adequate market strategies, but they also observe a variety of other actors. This is true in all markets, both consumer and production markets. The subsequent sections show show that firms observe consumer organisations to anticipate institutional, cultural and technological changes in order to develop appropriate strategies of action.

Another macrostructure that stabilizes the expectations of firms and consumers towards market outcomes is institutional rules. Institutional approaches analyze formal rules such as laws and property rights as well as informal rules such as cognitive scripts or conventions (DiMaggio and Powell 1983; Fligstein 2001). Formal and informal rules are seen as templates for action. Institutions stabilize market expectations and help actors to choose appropriate strategies even in situations of uncertainty. Such a perspective on institutions is also found in the New Institutional Economics, though economic and sociological approaches differ in some respects (Nee 2005). The source of formal market rules is political decision-making. Laws and other regulations are formulated and enforced by national states, supranational entities (EU) and international organisations (IMF, World Bank, WTO). Given the legal enforcement of states, formal rules are binding for all market participants since non-compliance is sanctioned by law (DiMaggio and Powell 1983; Fligstein 2001). Formal rules reduce uncertainty at different levels of markets. First, legal requirements set a mandatory minimum criterion that defines the quality of goods and services, e.g technical safety criteria or warranty rights. Second, formal rules influence the expectations of market participants about what actions others might take by sanctioning certain market practices (e.g price fixing, insider trading). Third, formal rules regulate competition by defining who can participate in markets and by setting the rules of competition (e.g. for mergers and acquisitions).

In practice, however, formal market rules are frequently bypassed, for example by illegal price fixing or through the action of cartels (Nessel 2012a). Fundamental for my following argument is that non-compliance with legal regulations is a central element of uncertainty in markets, and the vulnerability of market expectations. There are several reasons for non-compliance with formal rules, for example overlapping or unclear laws, or unintended legal violations. Consumers frequently struggle with bypassed warranty and contract rights by firms. Furthermore, there is uncertainty on the consumer side regarding their legal claims against firms. I will illustrate this arguments more closely in the next section, taking consumer complaints to consumer advocates as an example. It should be noted that uncertainty regarding the changing nature of political or legal frameworks that embed markets also threatens firms' and investors' expectations. If firms and investors are uncertain about future political regulations, investment in market segments will not occur or subtracted from them. This can lead to a decline of individual firms, as well as entire market segments. In many instances, formal rules stabilize actors' expectations (Bourdieu 2005; Fligstein 2001). Nevertheless, formal rules are not always to prevent crises in markets. The recent financial crisis has shown this apparently.

In addition to formal rules, informal rules exist in markets. Studies in new economic sociology – in particular the sociological neo-institutionalism and the field approaches of Bourdieu and Fligstein – focus on local rules in market fields to trace stable expectations. Though there are different views within sociological neo-institutionalism (Nee 2005), its main idea is to focus on institutions as cultural patterns "that provide not only legal and normative frameworks, but, above all, cognitive orientations for market participants" (Engels 2011, p. 116). To examine the effect of informal rules, the field concept is usually deployed as a unit of analysis (Beckert 2010). Following Fligstein (2001, p. 48), the goal of action in market fields is to build a system of stable relations (see also Bourdieu 2005). According to Fligstein, market fields become stable over time when firms establish stable relations within their company as well as in relation to their competitors. Notably, social relationships between firms and other actors of the corporate environment are not further discussed in field approaches (for an exception see DiMaggio and Powell 1983, who at least take the influence of consultants into account).

Finally, new economic sociology investigates the cultural embeddedness of markets as a third macro structure to stabilize firms' and consumers' expectations (Zelizer 1983; Zukin and DiMaggio 1990). In this paper, cultural embeddedness is understood as relevant set of societal norms and values. At the analytical level it can be assumed that national societies are built upon a more or less common consensus about norms and values grounded in socialization and habituation (Lüde and Scheve 2012). These macrosocial values and norms are superior to informal rules in local market fields. As does the concept of political embeddedness, the concept of cultural embeddedness refers to macro level phenomena. And similar to field-specific rules, cultural norms and values act as cognitive mind-maps that provide consumers and firms with orientations and frameworks for action. However, unlike (informal) field specific rules, cultural norms do not originate from interaction among market participants. Instead, they are part of a broader set of societies culture-specific values that are relevant in all markets (Zukin and DiMaggio 1990).

Like other forms of embeddedness, cultural embeddedness has a constitutive and a regulative effect on market expectations (Zukin and DiMaggio 1990). Its constitutive effect influences normative and moral ideas that guide economic motivations (Bourdieu 2005), the legitimation of market products (Zelizer 1983), and market competition (Engels 2011). Its regulatory effect influences concrete market outcomes and decisions. Cultural embeddedness in the form of societal values and norms influences the views of market actors and their expectations (see for examples Lüde and Scheve 2012; Nessel 2012b). However, it should be noted that the interpretation of cultural norms and values differs between social groups and is frequently contested among them. Still, market actors and products need to find a minimum of cultural legitimacy (Deephouse and Suchman 2008; Zelizer 1983). Consumer organisations and social movement frequently call into question the "legitimate economic activity" of firms, and the "morality" of products (Nessel 2012b). Thus, the violation of cultural expectations by firms and attacks by consumer organisations on the "legitimacy" of firms' behavior may threaten individual firms and can increase the vulnerability of entire market segments (see more closely above).

In the previous section I demonstrated that the constitution and functioning of markets depends on consumers and firms building stable expectations towards anticipated market outcomes. These expectations are always precarious due to the difficulty to estimate their interaction with others (double contingency, trust) as well as the difficulty of setting own market strategies (uncertainty). Following central insights of the new economic sociology, structural, institutional and cultural conditions are social macrostructures that stabilize firms' and consumers' expectations, and help to reproduce markets over time. However, previous research in economic sociology rarely considered that a change in these social structures may lead to the destabilization of market expectations, and thus to the decline of markets.

How actors adjust to changing social structures is prerequisite to the social resilience of markets. To adapt to changes in markets and markets' environment consumers and firms have to develop mechanisms to deal with uncertainties that challenge their routine ways of actions. The structural, institutional, and cultural approaches presented above implicitly analyze some of these adaptation mechanisms. Harrison White points to the fact that firms can cope with uncertainties by observing their competitors. The concept of "cultural legitimacy" refers to organisations' requiring of a minimum of social acceptance, while needing to anticipate changing cultural norms and expectations. Firms not only have to take other firms into account, but they need to observe societal expectations to survive. Similarly, it could be argued that companies must take political decisions into account to determine future market strategies. The same is true for consumers. Consumers need to anticipate changes in the political and cultural environment of markets as well as markets' internal functioning to form stable expectations towards the actions of others. As Albert O. Hirschman (1970) argued, these skills diminish consumers' disappointments, reveal slack resources of firms, and, thus, stabilize markets. Observations of structural, institutional, and cultural conditions as well as the development of skills to adapt to their change are, accordingly, mechanisms to strengthen the social resilience of firms and consumers. As firms and consumers strengthen their social resilience they contribute to the existence of markets over time.

3 Consumer Organisations and Markets[2]

Though often neglected, the study of consumer organisations offers opportunities to develop new insights in the field of economic sociology in general and the social resilience of markets in particular (Nessel 2014). In this section, I present four case studies of consumer organisations in Germany. I focus on the specific strategies of consumer organisations to advocate for the interests of consumers vis-à-vis firms and political actors. As I show, these strategies can either contribute to stabilize or destabilize consumers' and firms' expectations. In the following analysis, an actor-centered stance is taken. I show that the strategies of consumer organisations affect, under some circumstances, the structural, institutional and cultural embeddedness of markets. I argue that consumer organisations' strategies can lead to new challenges for market actors, as they influence the environment of markets. At the same time, consumer organisations act as a prism of the market. They provide information for consumers and firms to interpret actual and future buying and investment strategies, and to cope with change in and outside markets.

Consumer organisations claim to represent consumer interests vis-à-vis government and business. Depending on the mode of organisation and the mode of institutionalization two types of consumer organisations in Germany can be distinguished.[3] First, are organisations set up by individual consumers. These organisations advocate on behalf of the interests of individual members, usually in specific market and policy fields (sectoral and member based consumer organisations). Examples include tenant associations (Mieterbund), consumer self help groups, as well as Utopia and Foodwatch. The latter two organisations are analyzed in more detail in the subsequent sections. Second, are organisations founded and financed

---

2   The following analysis is based on qualitative case studies that include intensive qualitative document analysis and expert interviews. Expert interviews have been conducted with representatives of consumer organisations (15), business associations (4), journalists (2), representatives of ministries (3), unions (1) and experts of consumer policy (6) (Nessel 2014).

3   In what follows I focus on strategies of consumer organisations and their impact on markets. Organisational structures can not be discussed in detail (see Nessel 2014; see Kleinschmidt 2010 on STW; see Trumbull 2006 on some aspects of Vz, vzbv and STW).

by the German federal state. These organisations include other organisations as members and claim to represent the interests of consumers in (almost) all market fields (all purpose and state funded consumer organisations). These second level organisations include sectoral consumer organisations but no individual consumers. In Germany, typical examples are organisations that run consumer centers in the 16 federal states of Germany (Verbraucherzentralen der Länder, Vz); and the Federation of German Consumer Organisations (Bundesverband der Verbraucherzentralen, vzbv), a nationwide representative of the 16 federal organisations that run consumer centers, as well as 25 other nationwide operating consumer associations in Germany (such as Mieterbund and other private consumer self help groups).[4] Another organisation, Stiftung Warentest (STW), also represents an all-purpose state financed consumer organisation, though there are some differences to the afore mentioned German consumer groups (see Kleinschmidt 2010 and below). Vz, vzbv and STW were founded by political decisions between 1953 and 1964 and are, until today, financed by federal or national mandate. In Germany, only these organisations have been granted political and legal rights to "legitimately" persue consumer interests within the institutional architecture of German consumer policy (Nessel 2014; Trumbull 2006).

Sectoral and all purpose consumer organisations differ in their modes of organisation and in type of institutionalization. I suggest another important difference between these two types of organisations: The stances they take against companies, consumers and government. As I will show in more detail, the strategies of consumer organisations can be distinguished in terms of their degree of conflict and cooperation with other market and non-market actors. In the next section, I analyze four consumer organisation in Germany: state funded and founded Vz/vzbv and STW, the first two deploying more conflictual, the latter more consensual strategies; and, the private organisations Foodwatch (conflictual) and Utopia (consensual). I will show that these organisations deploy different strategies that affect the expectations of consumers and businesses, and the social resilience of markets in different ways.

---

4 For a more detailed account of the organisation of consumer centers, federal and national organisations representing consumers in central Europe, and some insights in German consumer policy see Trumbull (2006).

3.1 Federal Associations of Consumer Centers and the Federation of German Consumer organisations

The 16 Federal Associations of Consumer Centers in Germany (Vz) and the Federation of German Consumer organisations (vzbv) were both established by national and federal governments between 1953 and 1963. In large parts they are state funded (about 90 percent). Both organisations have been officially declared to represent the interests of consumers in public and vis-à-vis politics, legislators, and firms. Because of political decisions, these organisations were structured as second level organisations. Vzbv comprises 25 nationwide operating consumer-orientated organisations (e.g. tenant organisations and consumer self help groups) as well as the 16 federal associations of consumer centers (Vz). Each of the 16 Vz represents consumer interests in one of the 16 federal German states. Vz is comprised of local consumer organisations such as local tenant associations or church based consumer help groups. Vz and vzbv both are second level organisations without individual consumers as members. Strictly speaking, vzbv and Vz represent the interests of their member organisations, and thus of specific social groups. However, both organisations claim that they advocate for the general interests of all consumers in Germany. This claim is supported and legitimized by national and federal law and politics. Only these two organisations are granted institutional rights to advocate for consumer interests in the legal and political arenas.

Vzbv and Vz deploy three main strategies to promote consumer interests: political representation at the national (vzbv) and federal level (Vz), legal strategies (class action lawsuits and warnings), and consumer information. Political representation is executed in political hearings, in political decision-making, and in building public opinion. Since the 1960s, Vz and vzbv are the legal and political representatives of consumer interest. They are part of the institutional architecture of consumer policy in Germany, and they represent the buyer's side against business associations in policy making (Trumbull 2006). In addition to their formal participation in the development of institutional market rules, both organisations have close social networks that include members of national parties and ministries (political lobbying).

Alongside their political representation, vzbv and Vz are guaranteed legal resources to enforce consumer interests. These legal resources include the right to file lawsuits and warnings against firms. To file lawsuits, Vz needs to act on behalf of the "general interest" of consumers in Germany. In contrast to U.S. law, class action lawsuits are not granted to a group of individual consumers in Germany (Strünck 2005). That is, individual consumers cannot collectively claim their legal rights. Class action lawsuits can only be filed by the Vz. Neither a group of consumers nor a consumer organisation other than Vz can pursue consumer rights in the legal arena. In Germany, class action lawsuits do not compensate consumers' individual losses (e.g. due to fraudulent market behavior or not adhered warranty rights). Instead, if class action lawsuits are successful, they result in modified legal market rules that prohibit certain behaviors of firms, strengthen warranty rights, or codes of conduct.[5] Besides class action lawsuits, Vz can warn companies to refrain from certain business practices. If a firm complies with warnings, it signs a declaration to stop the criticized practice. Non-compliance with this declaration is associated with a financial penalty by law. In many cases, warnings lead companies to refrain from certain business practices. In other cases, firms do not accept warnings.[6] If firms do not accept warnings, legal conflicts between Vz and businesses follow. If Vz is successful in legal conflicts, firms do have to change their criticized market practices. Legal resources granted to Vz by law form a powerful means to change market rules and the behavior of firms. However, it should be noted that class action lawsuits and warnings are restricted to two areas of German law: warranty law and competition law (e.g. Strünck 2005).

By means of political representation, legal advocacy and enforcement, Vz and vzbv seek to change the political and legal framework of markets, that is, their institutional embeddedness. Political and legal strategies can challenge companies significantly. If the formal embeddedness of markets changes in favor of consumers, as Vz and vzbv intend, consumers' bargaining power against firms and their market position are enhanced. Furthermore, the political and legal problematization of existing market practices increase firms' uncertainty about the suitability of their strategies. Companies must constantly expect that political and legal changes may put current strategies into question. Legal attacks on companies also threat firms' public reputation, as newspapers and expert journals frequently report on legal conflicts between Vz and firms, thus questioning firms' practices in public. Finally, class action lawsuits expose firms to financial risks as non-compliance with legal rules are penalized. Because penalties are almost always small in amount, this threat is, above all, significant only to smaller companies.

Consumer information is another strategy vzbv and Vz deploy. On the one hand, consumer information is addressed through public campaigns, publications on consumer issues, consumer conferences and consumer training. This kind of consumer information is meant to increase consumers' general knowledge about

---

5   "Whereas the U.S. rests on the 'private initiative model' of class actions, it is the 'consumer organisation claim model' as well as the 'administrative authority model' that prevail in Europe" (Strünck 2005: 209).

6   For an overview of firms' reactions to warnings see for example vzbv 2012.

the functioning of markets. In this sense, it aims to increase consumer literacy. Consumer literacy enables consumers to better evaluate the quality of goods and services, to know their rights against firms, gives them the skills to exercise these rights, and to cope with change in markets. On the other hand, Vz provide consumer information in consumer centers. In consumer centers, consumers can obtain information regarding all aspects of purchasing decisions (Benner and Weiser 2009). Consumer centers provide information on concrete market offers and legal aspects of contracts, thus helping consumers to evaluate the "quality" of vendors and products. In this respect, the information provided in consumer centers facilitates consumer choices. However, most of German consumers visit consumer centers to get support in legal conflicts with firms.[7] Legal advocacy is the main function of consumer centers in Germany. The same is true for European consumer centers, which have been established by the European Union to help consumers cope with legal problems in transnational trade. Legal advocacy in consumer centers does not include direct legal representation, but promotes consumer self-help. Consumer centers inform about warranty rights and offer means to solve fraud issues with firms. Taken together, consumer centers reduce consumers' uncertainty about the quality of goods and services, and they help them to solve legal conflicts with firms.

To be effective, consumers need to trust consumer center consultants. Relationships between consultants and consumers are based on trust. However, unlike the relationship between firms and customers, the relationship between consumer consultants and consumers are structured differently. In the latter case, the advisory institution pursues no direct financial gain and is formally obliged to provide "objective" information (Benner and Weiser 2009). In this regard, Vz function as a "judgment device" (Karpik 2010, p. 96).

Consumer centers take up and display consumer problems in market exchange. In doing so, "consumer complaints help monitor how markets work" (Benner and Weiser 2009). As do European consumer centers, German consumer centers "identify failing markets from a consumer perspective,"[8] while collecting consumer complaints. Consumer complaints are often taken up by political parties to take legal and political action against failing markets. Consumer complaints brought forward in consumer centers build an empirical foundation for European

---

7   These and other consultations have to be privately financed by consumers. The fees to get consumer help is, however, and compared to lawyers advice, relatively small in amount, dependent on the inquiry.

8   See European Commission (2012), http://ec.europa.eu/consumers/archive/complaints/index_en.htm.

and German authorities to change the political embeddedness of markets (Benner and Weiser 2009; European Commission 2012).

Consumer information and education reduce consumers' individual uncertainty in market transactions. Both strategies provide individual consumers with skills and information to cope with market uncertainties. They thus enhance individual consumers' resilience. In contrast, political and legal strategies deployed by vzbv and Vz seek to change existing market practices and legal regulations to improve consumers' collective bargaining power in markets vis-à-vis firms. As vzbv and Vz simultaneously seek to change the legal and political environment of markets and hence the collective position of consumers, they call into question the routine market strategies of firms. In doing so, they make firms more vulnerable to forecast market strategies.

3.2 Stiftung Warentest

Like vzbv and Vz, Stiftung Warentest (STW) was established by way of political decisions (Kleinschmidt 2010; Trumbull 2006). While Vz and vzbv were set up to represent the legal and political interests of consumers in Germany, STW is supposed to provide consumers with information about the quality of goods and services through comparative product testing. Vz, vzbv on the one hand, and STW on the other hand are the representative consumer organisations within German consumer policy. STW is organized as a foundation. The organisation was endowed with 500.000 Marks in 1963, and granted another 75 million Euro in 2012 to guarantee its financial sovereignty. However, unlike vzbv and Vz, STW receives only a small annual public subsidy (about 11 percent). It actually generates about 90 percent of its annual revenue from the sale of consumer magazines. The establishment of STW in 1964 institutionalized the idea of comparative product tests in Germany. In the late 1930s, the first permanent product testing organisations emerged in the United States. At the end of the 1950s many European countries had established test organisations (Kleinschmidt 2010). Since the 1950s, consumers have faced a massive increase in consumer goods and advertising. Both developments increased market complexity. The objective of test organisations is to reduce consumers' uncertainty about the quality of products and services through comparative product testing. They function as a counterpart to one-sided consumer information by companies. To provide consumers with a higher degree of information, German government established STW as a "neutral organisation" to perform "objective" product tests (Kleinschmidt 2010).

Comparative product testing goes through several stages. The first is the selection of the market objects and the characteristics to be tested. Second, is laboratory testing (for goods), and social research such as survey research, document analysis, and observation (for services). Third, the results of comparative product tests are evaluated and presented in test magazines. Test results are presented either as "quality judgments" or as "market overviews". Quality judgments evaluate certain properties of goods and services and display these properties in differentiated test tables. They refer to a whole product or to only some characteristics of a product (e.g. handling, safety, durability, technical performance). Quality characteristics are differentiated in grades ranging from "very good", "good", "satisfactory", "sufficient" to "poor". These different grades are defined by statistically weighting previously defined aspects of goods (e.g. handling, performance, etc.). In 2012, approximately 41.000 products were tested and rated by quality judgments.

In market overviews, services and service providers in a market segment are evaluated without assigning a final quality judgment. In market surveys, it is "less an in-depth test as an overview of the characteristic of a large number of service features" (STW 2012). In contrast to quality judgments, individual consumers have to closely compare test tables based on market overviews since STW does not present final rankings of products and services. Still, as market overviews compare and make quality aspects visible, they help consumers to evaluate products. Because all offers in a market are compared in market overviews, the structure of the competition in market segments is elucidated. A striking example of market overviews was the comparison between interest rates of consumer loans by German banks.

Test results are disseminated in test magazines, via media and by vendors. In Warentest's magazines *test* and *financial test*, and on its website, the organisation publishes detailed quality judgments and market overviews. *Financial test* publishes all test results in the market segments of financial services (including private retirement, investment, and health insurances). In addition, the magazine publishes a monthly overview of shares and funds. Results of tests in all other market segments are published in *test*. The results of both magazines are furthermore published in special issues and yearbooks. To address the media and consumers who do not buy the organisation's magazines, selected results of tests are communicated via press conferences, and (e-mail) newsletters to consumers and journalists. Furthermore, edited press releases for newspapers, television, and radio stations are offered. This latter kind of public communication widely disseminates the work and test results of the STW. STW test results are published in newspapers, magazines and through television and radio announcements. Printed media publishes 12 articles, television programs report on 5 articles of STW in average every day. This type of information strategy is primarily dedicated to consumers and journalists. However, this kind of communication is also intended to pressure politicians to take action against market failures (e.g. unsafe products). Through the media, the communication of comparative product tests also informs consumers who do not receive magazines about quality aspects of goods and services.

Warentest's results are finally published by firms. After signing a licensee contract, firms can advertise their products with quality judgments (usually "very good" and "good"). Companies use quality judgments by the independent STW to convince consumers of the quality of their products. Many German firms use STW's test results and logo on products, and in advertising. In this respect, the STW acts as an external institution to certify the quality of products. As empirical research shows, many consumers rely on the judgments of STW as a credible source of information in their buying decisions. Both, consumers and business attribute a high degree of confidence to test results published by STW (Kleinschmidt 2010, p. 124; Schrader 2008).

Quality judgments diminish uncertainty on the buyers' side, and help firms verify to consumers the quality of their products. Positive test results expand sales (Raffée and Silberer 1984; Schrader 2008). In contrast, poor test results have serious negative consequences on the resources of firms. Poor tested products and services are removed from the shelves, since consumer demand for these products decreases. Not surprisingly, firms react to poor test results by changing their products or removing them from the market completely (Raffée and Silberer 1984; Schrader 2008). Negative test results suggest that firms have slack resources. In many cases, poor test results lead to an improvement of products and services. Hence, test results by STW lead to innovations in markets and diminish the risk of "lemon markets". Comparative testing, therefore, has a direct impact on the expectations of consumers and firms, providing both with information on the quality of products, and thereby enhancing quality production in markets (Trumbull 2006; Kleinschmidt 2010).

3.3 Utopia

Utopia "[is] Consumer power – Our consumption is changing the world". This is how the organisation, found in 2007, presents itself to the public. Utopia understands "consumer power" as the capability of consumers to bring about change in markets through strategic purchasing. Utopia organizes strategic purchasing by motivating consumers to take ecological and political concerns into account when choosing between goods (buycott), and by channeling consumers' voice to firms. Utopia's central strategy is to provide a community platform and an online consumer magazine. The online consumer magazine publishes information about product features, and about the political and ecological "performance" of firms. In addition, its publications provide information about the ecological impact of production and consumption. In contrast to STW, members of Utopia themselves can contribute to articles, and evaluate products and firms by means of Web 2.0 applications (see below).

Utopia seeks to provide consumers with information so that they can exercise "political" or "ethical" consumption. Consumer information is displayed in multiple categories on the organisation's website (e.g. "magazine", "purchasing advice/ product guide", and "opinion"). For example, Utopia's "product guide" recommends "green" and "sustainable" products as well as "point of sales" to purchase them. Products and suppliers listed in the product guide are selected by Utopia. Utopia classifies products in "sustainable" and "less sustainable" products. However, unlike the judgments of STW, Utopia's quality judgments are not only formulated by experts, but also by members of the organisation.[9] Utopia members can quantitatively rank products on a scale from one to five. Members also can qualitatively evaluate products by written comments on the website (user generated content). In addition to the information presented by Utopia experts, members' evaluations of products help consumers assess the sustainability of products. Similar to test results of STW, these quality judgments reduce the uncertainty of consumers regarding the quality of products. By providing qualitative comments on products and their features, Utopia members also act as "feedback agents" to firms, as they provide them in-depth information about their offerings in the eyes of consumers.

The evaluation of products and services with the help of consumers is Utopia's first strategy to change markets. The provision of Web 2.0 applications to facilitate the dialogue between consumers and producers is its second organisational strategy. To put consumers and producers in dialogue about corporate strategies and products, Utopia offers "blogs", "live chats" and "company profiles". In company profiles on Utopia's website, companies can inform consumers about new products and strategies. Consumers can evaluate and comment on the information that

---

9   To become a "member" of Utopia, consumers can register on its website. The organisation counts 25.000 members. It should be noted, that Utopia's organisational structure comprises a foundation and a private enterprise that is structured as a "social entrepreneurship". Due to this, consumers can not formally become members of the organisation. Strictly speaking, Utopia members are "registered users" of its website. However, Utopia takes into account some of its users demands, integrates them in its strategy and provides applications for community building within the group of "users" as well as between the "users" and the organisation (Nessel 2014).

firms give regarding their products. Firms can then reply to consumers, and so on. Through Utopia's Web 2.0 applications, "firm-consumer dialogues" are initiated. Utopia, thus, channels the voice of consumers directly to firms. Firms receive information about given or future consumer preferences, as well as relevant social values that guide consumer choices (sustainability). As Albert O. Hirschman argued (1970), the voice of consumers constitutes an important resource for companies to optimize their business strategies. Similar to the quality evaluation of products mentioned above, direct communication between consumers' voice and firms provides the latter with detailed information about current market strategies from the point of view of the consumer. Firms may, then, better identify consumer demands, and set their strategies accordingly. Furthermore, as firms expose their strategy to a public dialogue with consumers on the Utopia website, firms can enhance their social legitimacy.

That firms try to enhance their social legitimacy in cooperation with consumer organisations can be seen in another project of Utopia, the "Change Maker Project". The core of Utopia's Change Maker Project is to motivate firms to implement and maintain sustainable corporate practices (including the integration of "sustainable principles" in management processes and value chains, the reduction of emissions and greenhouse gases, surpassing social standards of an industry etc.). If firms cooperate with Utopia, fill a letter of declaration, and fulfill the above mentioned criteria, they are awarded with the title "Change Maker". Utopia thus certifies firms and enhances the credibility of their sustainability strategies. As the Change Maker title is presented on a public conference, and as firms tout with the title on their websites, firms can enhance their social legitimacy by showing that they comply with social and ecological consumer concerns. The Change Maker Project is intended to motivate firms to fulfill sustainable business strategies. To do so, Utopia eschews blaming firms in favor of a strategy that underlines firms' "positive" improvements in sustainable production and management decisions.

Consumer information provided by Utopia and STW, as well as the corporate dialogue deployed by Utopia are characteristic examples of cooperative strategies of consumer organisations. On the one hand, these cooperative strategies provide firms with information about existent and future preferences of consumers, thus reducing uncertainty about the suitability of their strategies. On the other hand, consumers can stabilize their expectations regarding the quality of products through expert and members evaluations on product features.

In the next section I present an organisation that, similar to Vz and vzbv, utilizes more conflicting strategies against firms to pursue consumer interests.

3.4 Foodwatch

Foodwatch (FW) was founded in 2002 by former Greenpeace International director Thilo Bode. FW presents itself as a non-profit membership organisation, and as an alternative to state financed Vz and vzbv. FW actually comprises 25.000 individual members. In terms of individual members, Foodwatch is the largest consumer organisation in Germany.[10] It aims to "promote consumer protection through consumer advice and information". To achieve these goals, two strategies are deployed: the dissemination of consumer information by means of media campaigns, and the public and political representation of consumers. Media campaigns and strategies are at the core of FW tactics, and these campaigns and strategies characterize FW in the field of consumer organisations in Germany. Similar to the protest of social movements, three aspects are specific to FW's media campaigns: First, perceived consumer grievances are identified and blame is attributed to a source, usually to firms and politics (diagnostic frame). Second, solutions for the abolition of perceived problems of consumers are formulated (prognostic frame). And third, consumers are mobilized to support political demands (motivational frame).

In order to create media attention, FW annually awards a "negative" prize to firms ("Golden Cream Puff"). The Golden Cream Puff "rewards" the "most misleading advertising" of firms. The campaign strategy of FW exerts pressure on firms and politics by influencing public opinion. To do so, FW scandalizes existing market practices and market rules, taking individual firm's behavior as a proxy for wrong doing. Campaigns seek to change market behavior of firms and political actors to take legal action against perceived market failures. As social movement

---

10 However, taking the sheer financial resources as a basis, FW as well as other private consumer organisations in Germany are rather "small". FW obtains 1,5 million Euros from donations and member fees, Utopia 1 million Euro. In contrast, vzbv obtains 16 million Euros form the German federal state, the biggest local Vz (Vz NRW) 35 millions mostly by the EU and the German state of North Rhine Westphalia and its communities. STW operates with 46 million Euros mostly from sales of consumer magazines. However, state funding and political establishment of Vz and STW cause, until today, some restrictions on their strategies (see in more detail Nessel 2014). For example,Vz and vzbv can, in contrast to FW, not deploy conflictual media campaigns as a strategy as both organisations are formally restricted to the political and legal representation of (some) German *consumer associations*. And STW, in contrast to Utopia, is obliged to "neutral" product tests without the help of consumers and without the opportunity to taking a political stance (e.g on sustainability). That is, the institutional architecture of German consumer policy affect both, private and state funded consumer organisations in their strategies.

theory in general, and framing theory in particular, shows, the impact of media campaigns is determined by internal organisational resources and external environmental factors. Beneficial internal resources to assert campaign goals include the professionalization of the organisation and its close social ties to journalists who, in many cases, extensively report on FW campaigns, and thus broaden public perception of the organisation and its claims. Moreover, its 25.000 members and the additional support of subscribers to campaigns form a symbolic capital to emphasize its claims. External factors that determine the success of FW campaigns include the societal resonance of the deployed campaign frame as well as cultural and political opportunities (e.g. consumer awareness for issues of food security). Finally, external shocks (e.g. food scandals) affect campaign success, as external shocks indicate market failures and favors political and consumer support for claims.

For companies, the potential threat of FW campaigns is less material – in contrast to some social movements and environmental organisations, FW eschews calls to boycott firms. The potential threat to firms is more symbolic, as FW campaigns primarily address the targets' reputation. Public media campaigns, directly or indirectly, influence the normative expectations of consumers, competitors of targets, and investors. FW takes market practices of individual firms as a proxy to question the practices of the food industry as a whole. Or, as the organisation did recently, the banking industry. To attract media and consumer attention, the organisation accuses firms of systemically misleading consumers in "labeling" and advertising, and of intentionally discriminating against consumers.

Some firms and business associations react to FW attacks by counter campaigns to influence public opinion. Thus, campaigns subsequently lead to public debates about the credibility of firms. Campaigns thus put into question the expectations of companies about their own strategies as well as consumers' expectations regarding firms. Following neo-institutional arguments, it can be concluded that firms try to affirm their legitimacy by public expression for and/or direct implementation of claims. This is true, when firms perceive FW as a representative body of all, or at least, great parts of consumer interests. In what follows I present some empirical findings that show that some, but not all, firms do indeed react to FW claims and integrate FW demands into their business strategies.

In some cases, the claims of FW campaigns led to changes in corporate strategies and market offerings. Since the beginning of FW's biggest campaign in 2007, "270.000 Consumer complaints to manufacturers have been sent" (Foodwatch 2012). 37 product advertisements were criticized during the "golden puff" campaign, and subsequent protest actions were started against these advertisements. Out of 37 companies, 15 have withdrawn their product from the market, changed their recipe or modified product advertising (ibid). How firms react to the "golden puff" nomination, the 2012 "winner's" reaction reveals an underlying logic. The company responded to the attack by withdrawing its product. In a newspaper interview, the management justified its reaction as follows:

> "Question: How did you react to the criticism in the campaign [a high amount of sugar in a tea for children]?
> Answer: We have adjusted the product and in November there is a new sugarless tea.
> Question: Although you find your tea useful?
> Answer: We did not want to confuse the consumer and we didn't want to fight out against FW in public. The slander always is stronger than the argument."
> (Tagesspiegel 11.11.2012).

These examples illustrate that companies indeed do react to potential risks resulting from media campaigns by consumer organisations. More than immediate material losses, the potential reputational risks seem to be a strong incentive for firms to fulfill or, at least, to respond to claims. That firms do interpret media campaigns as a serious threat to their reputation and market position is also shown in empirical studies of social movement research. For example, King and Soule (2007) present ample evidence that some companies react to reputational risks with the integration of stakeholder claims into their strategies. However, it is not clear so far, which factors lead to full, or partial integration of claims by some firms, whereas other firms simply reject them. Though many firms react to FW claims, many others neither take direct action nor publicly state to take them into account. The divergent reaction of firms to stakeholder claims yet remains unaccounted for in economic sociology and social movement theory. In the next section, I provide some thoughts on the puzzling reactions of firms to consumer organisations' diverse strategies. For the argument pursued here it should be noted, that FW campaigns sometimes result in changing individual production strategies, and in the withdrawal of products from the market. Moreover, public struggles between consumer organisations and firms can deepen crises in market segments. Crises in market segments are likely when other stakeholder organisations support social protests and when their claims find broad cultural resonance (frame resonance). Especially after external shocks, such as the financial or the BSE crisis, social protests can strengthen the political will to change existing market rules, and to prohibit certain market strategies. External shocks can also hinder or diminish investments in market segments. Both factors can lead to crises in market segments and to diminished markets. A recent example of the impact of external shocks is the politically initiated "energy revolution" in Germany. The nuclear disaster that took place in Fukushima, Japan and the scandalizing campaigns by social movements following it, lead to political decisions to end nuclear energy in Germany by the Year 2020. Though the long-term impact of consumer organisations' media campaigns has yet to be studied, it seems obvious that media campaigns can increase the vulnerability of individual companies, and the vulnerability of entire market segments (King and Soule 2007; Nessel 2014).

Campaigns and public consumer information about risks in market exchange are FW's main strategy to change existing market practices. Alongside this strategy, FW deploys political lobbying and seeks legal representation in hearings to push forward its claims. To endow political claims with "legitimacy," FW mobilizes consumers to sign online petitions. The number of individual supporters of online petitions frequently exceeds the member base of the organisations. That is, FW claims find the support of consumers who are not member of the organisation. The number of organisational members and non-organisational supporters builds FW's symbolic capital. Building on this symbolic capital, FW claims to represent consumers in the political arena, and against the state financed vzbv and Vz. The individual membership base and the frequent support of nonmembers in campaigns has guaranteed FW its status in the political arena. The organisation is frequently invited to political hearings and participates in some fields of consumer policy in Germany, especially in policy fields related to food issues.

However, in contrast to vzbv and Vz, the organisation, does not possess formally granted political rights. Instead, it is FW's public dissemination of "counter-expertise" to government and industry-related consumer information and its individual member base that justifies its participation in particular issues of consumer policy. The inclusion of private consumer organisations alongside state financed consumer organisation in German consumer policy can be seen as the integration of "civil society" in political processes (Leggewie 2006, p. 155f.). FW proliferation of "counter-expertise" through campaigns and political statements addresses the cultural and political embeddedness of markets. On the one hand, this strategy challenges the expectations of consumers and firms as well as the expectations of a broader market environment (investors and journalists). On the other hand, FW indirectly (via public opinion building) and directly (via political representation) influences the political embeddedness of markets. FW publicly blames companies and politics for market failures and for discrimination against consumers. FW strategies, the scandalizing campaigns and harsh political demands, are examples of conflicting strategies deployed by consumer organisations. Unlike Utopia, FW does not seek to change markets in cooperation with firms, but against them. Confrontational strategies aim to change the expectations of companies, politicians and investors through public mobilization. Public mobilization through campaigns and political protest seeks to change firms behavior and to change the cultural and political embeddedness of markets.

4 Consumer Organisations and the Social Resilience of Markets

In line with new economic sociology it has been argued so far that the permanent reproduction of markets depends on consumers and firms building stable expectations regarding market outcomes. With the concept of social embeddedness, new economic sociology has identified some structural, institutional, and cultural conditions that build the basis for the reproduction of markets. How market actors react to a change in these social structures yet remains understudied. In this article I argue that actors' skills to adapt to the changing structural, institutional, and cultural environment of markets are at the core of the social resilience of markets. Only if market participants adjust their expectations to changing market conditions in an "appropriate" way, will markets reproduce over time. In contrast, challenges to routine ways of doing things in markets and to anticipate future market developments make them more likely to fail. Markets are at risk to fail over time, if consumers and firms do not "appropriately" adjust their expectations and strategies to environmental change of markets, and markets' internal developments.

In the previous analysis of consumer organisations in Germany, six strategies have been analyzed in relation to the expectations of firms and consumers and, accordingly, to the social resilience of markets. These strategies include consumer information, consumer literacy, corporate dialogue (cooperation between consumer organisations and firms), legal strategies (warnings and class lawsuits), political strategies (political participation and lobbying), and scandalizing campaigns. An overview of strategies deployed by consumer organisations in Germany is summarized in the following table (Table 1).

Table 1 Strategies of consumer organisations in Germany (Nessel 2014)

Strategies	Utopia	Stiftung Warentest	Vz/Vzbv	Foodwatch
Consumer information	Yes	Yes	Yes	
Consumer literacy	Partly	Partly	Yes	
Corporate dialogue	Yes	Partly		
Legal strategies			Yes	
Political strategies			Yes (formal)	Yes (informal)
Scandalizing Campaigns				Yes
Stance towards politics and firms	Cooperative	Neutral/ Cooperative	Conflicting	Conflicting

Consumer information, corporate dialogue and consumer education represent cooperative strategies of consumer organisations. These strategies stabilize the expectations of consumers and firms. Thus, cooperative strategies increase the social resilience of markets. In contrast, legal and political strategies, and media campaigns are confrontational strategies. These confrontational strategies seek to change the legal, cultural and political environment of markets in favor of consumers. They are intended to directly enhance consumers' bargaining power against firms. In addition, they indirectly influence investors perception of firms' market position and provide politicians with information of market "failures". Conflicting strategies thus increase the vulnerability of firms and, thus, of markets. In conclusion, I compare differences within and between cooperative and conflicting strategies and analyze their impact on the expectations of firms and consumers, and on the resilience and vulnerability of markets.

Mainly, consumer information has a stabilizing effect on the expectations of consumers. The STW evaluates the quality of products and services through comparative testing. Having been established by German authorities, STW is formally obliged to provide "objective" information to consumers. STW does so by expert opinions ("external laboratories" or experts of the organisation). Similarly, consumer advice of Vz in consumer centers is based on opinion of the organisation's experts. Unlike comparative product tests conducted by STW, consumer centers take the individual social and financial situation of consumers as a basis to help them choose suitable goods and services. STW and Vz both offer consumer information on almost all aspects of goods and services. To evaluate the quality of products, Utopia, instead, focuses on the assessment of sustainability. And in contrast to STW and Vz, Utopia evaluates the (sustainable) quality of goods and services with the help of its members. Though it differs in practice, the information strategy of all three organisations reduces the uncertainty of consumers regarding the quality of goods and services and help consumers to reduce market complexity.

Furthermore, publications of the three organisations address consumer literacy.[11] Consumer literacy refers to consumer skills to better cope with the changing conditions of markets. As Hirschman (1970) has argued, disappointed expectations of consumers about the quality of products and services destabilize markets.

---

11 In this article, I have focused only superficially on consumer literacy in the section on Vz and vzbv. Vz and vzbv are the two German consumer organisation that deploy this strategy most intensively. However, Utopia and STW *touch* consumer information in almost all of their publications. I have neglected this fact to make clear the main differences between the strategies of the presented consumer organisations (see in more detail Nessel 2014). Though STW and Utopia seek to enhance consumer literacy, it is not *characteristic* for their strategy as it is for Vz and vzbv.

Following Hirschman, it can be concluded that consumer information and literacy help consumers to evaluate new and existent products, as well as to adapt to legal and cultural change in market's environment. Consumer information and consumer literacy both stabilize markets as they increase the resilience of consumers at the actor level. However, it should be noted that not all consumers take consumer information and consumer literacy into account (Nessel 2014). Generally, consumers with high economic and cultural capital are more likely to use comparative product tests when purchasing. And the target group of Utopia is first and foremost a "vanguard from the green consumer movement", neglecting other groups. However, as some studies on comparative product testing have shown, test results indirectly encourage quality competition in markets, and via public media also reach consumers who do not buy test magazines (Raffée and Silberer 1984; Schrader 2008). This effects of consumer information can thus improve the social resilience of markets at the system level, but with the above mentioned restrictions, that is, the unequal distribution of market opportunities between different social groups.[12]

In this article, I have analyzed corporate dialogues as another strategy deployed by consumer organisations. Corporate dialogues designate cooperation between firms and consumer organisations in joint projects (e.g. Utopia's Changemaker project). Corporate dialogues point to the provision of communication channels that put consumers and firms in constructive dialogue. Corporate dialogues are meant to help firms to adjust strategies and products to consumer demands. Within corporate dialogues, consumers can express their voice to firms. Firms can use consumers voice to reduce uncertainty regarding given and future consumer preferences. Firms can use the feedback from STW and Utopia as a prism of the market. By observing expert evaluations (STW, Vz) and consumer judgments (Utopia) about their products, firms may obtain important information to cope with uncertainties regarding consumer preferences. The voice of consumers can reflect a firm's slack resources and help firms to optimize business strategies (Hirschman 1970; Nessel 2014). Cooperative consumer organisations channel the voice of consumers to firms, and thus increase the impact of the voice option. In conclusion, consumer information, consumer literacy, and corporate dialogue, have a stabilizing effect on the expectations of those consumers and firms that take these cooperative strategies into account when setting buying or production decisions.

In contrast to cooperative strategies, conflictual strategies increase the vulnerability of markets. Conflictual strategies challenge firms' routines and enhance their uncertainty about future strategies. Legal and political strategies have a di-

---

12   A closer analysis of consumer organisations and social inequality is presented in Nessel 2014.

rect impact on firms' flow of resources and the strategies of individual market participants. In particular, collective action suits can have sever negative financial impacts on smaller companies. Legal and political strategies can also result in changing legal market rules, thus calling into question the practices of firms. When existing market rules are prohibited or changed, or more generally speaking: consumer protection is increased, the political embeddedness of markets changes (see also Trumbull 2006). As studies in economic sociology show, the political embeddedness of markets affects the strategies of firms and the forms of market competition (Bourdieu 2005; Fligstein 2001). If uncertainty about the development of market regulation increases, the uncertainty of companies in the definition of future strategies does as well. Furthermore, potential investors will be more reluctant to invest in firms and market segments, if they feel uncertain about legal and political developments.

Even more than political and legal strategies, campaigns increase the vulnerability of firms (see also Strünck 2005). Campaigns of confrontational consumer organisations aim to scandalize market practices of companies publicly. The public questioning of firms exposes them to reputational risks. Attacks on the reputation of firms can challenge established expectations of consumers and investors and subsequently lead to the reduction of sales or investments (King and Soule 2007). Companies have to take into account that campaigns will negatively affect their reputation in the eyes of consumers and investors. A decline of reputation can lead to material losses. As King and Soule (2007) show empirically, stock prices for "attacked" firms decline as the press follows negative campaigns of social movements. Not surprisingly, some firms are extremely sensitive to consumer organisations' campaigns and take their demands into account. Due to reputational risks, some firms take products from the market, change product's recipes or advertising, or respond to media campaigns with counter-attacks. That consumer organisations' attacks on a firm's reputation significantly challenge the existence of that firm has also been shown in sociological neo-institutionalism. Empirical and theoretical findings in neo-institutionalism illustrates that firms' "survival rates" are closely intertwined with "social legitimacy" (Deephouse and Suchman 2008). If the social legitimacy of firms is challenged by consumer organisations, they are exposed to increased vulnerability. Scandalizing campaigns challenge firms' social legitimacy and thus their "survival rate".

However, cooperation between consumer organisations and firms can increase the social legitimacy of the latter. Firms can observe consumer organisations to anticipate actual and anticipated demands of consumers and adjust their strategies as well as their expectations to them. In this sense, consumer organisations can also help firms to identify and forecast potential crises. The criticisms of consumer organisations can be interpreted by firms as a loss of confidence in the eyes of consumers and investors. The problematization of market practices by consumer organisations cannot only challenge firms, but can strengthen their resilience as well. If firms perceive consumer organisations as a vanguard of relevant consumer interests, attacks on individual companies are a signal for them and their competitors to screen strategies about possible problems of consumer acceptance. Attacks also point to problems in the implementation of technical and social strategy decisions. That companies watch consumer organisation and adjust their strategies to their claims has been shown in studies on the impact of comparative product testing by STW (Raffée and Silberer 1984; Schrader 2008). Firms frequently take into account tests results to adjust their new market products accordingly. Firms also anticipate test methods to align their products in advance of it. This impact of consumer tests is due to the fact that negative test results diminish sales of products and services (Raffée and Silberer 1984). Negative Test results increase the (financial) vulnerability of companies in the short run, but can help individual firms, *and their competitors*, to better evaluate consumer preferences in the long run.

The certification of corporate strategies by external actors such as NGOs or consumer organisations can also be a resource for firms to increase social legitimacy and to increase sales (Münch 2008; Nessel 2014). External certification of firms reduces the uncertainty of consumers about the quality of products (Karpik 2010). At the same time, external certification allows companies to reduce uncertainty about the future acceptance of new products or management standards. Observing consumer organisations provides firms with information about consumer preferences, future changes of markets, or markets' environment. Harrison White has identified this mechanism of mutual observation as a stabilizing factor of markets. I have shown in this article, that the mutual observation between firms and consumer organisations has a similar effect on the resilience of individual firms, and on the stability of markets more general.

Firms' observations of and their cooperation with consumer organisations helps them to cope with uncertainties, and to plan future strategies. Moreover, consumer organisations stimulate the social skills of consumers and increase their knowledge in evaluating products by means of consumer information and consumer literacy. The mutual observation of market actors as well as their ability to adapt to changes in the structural, institutional, cultural, but also the technical environment of markets are mechanisms that increase the social resilience of markets. In contrast, the problematization of market practices as well as political-legal strategies deployed by consumer organisations to change market rules increases the vulnerability of firms and consumers. Scandalizing campaigns, legal and regulatory measures can furthermore deepen the decline of entire market segments. The decline of markets is likely, when exogenous crises coincide with political wills to take action against market practices. Confrontational strategies of consumer organisations can motivate political interventions in markets and impede investment by consumers and investors. Confrontational strategies of consumer organisations can also negatively affect the expectations of firms' competitors, consumers and investors, and hence deepen market crises. The extent to which cooperative and confrontational strategies of consumer organisations influence the resilience of entire markets demands more study. The results of this paper suggest that the vulnerability of markets is increased when consumers, firms, and investors are *massively* confused by confrontational strategies of consumer organisations. In contrast, cooperative strategies of consumer organisations seem to contribute to the resilience of markets, if firms and consumers take consumer information, consumer literacy, and consumer voice into account to anticipate changes in the social and technical embeddedness of markets and stabilize their expectations accordingly.

References

Beckert, J. (1996). What is Sociological about Economic Sociology? Uncertainty and the Embeddedness of Economic Action. Theory and Society, 25, 803-840.
Beckert, J. (2010). How Do Fields Change? The Interrelations of Institutions, Networks, and Cognition in the Dynamics of Markets. Organization Studies, 31(5), 605-627.
Benner, E., & Weiser, B. (2009). Verbraucherberatung als Instrument einer Verbraucherpolitik in der Sozialen Marktwirtschaft. DIW Vierteljahresheft zur Wirtschaftsforschung, 78(3), 144-159.
Bourdieu, P. (2005). The Social Structures of the Economy. Cambridge: Polity Press.
Deephouse, D. L., & Suchman M. (2008). Legitimacy in organizational institutionalism. In R. Greenwood, C. Oliver, R. Suddaby & K. Sahlin-Andersson (eds), The Sage Handbook of Organizational Institutionalism (49-77). London: SAGE.
DiMaggio, P., & Powell, W. (1983). The Iron Cage Revisited: Institutional Isomorphism and Collective Rationality in Organizational Fields. American Sociological Review 48 (4), 147-160.
Engels, A. (2011). Wirtschaft und Rationalität im Neo-Institutionalismus. In A. Maurer & U. Schimank (eds), Die Rationalitäten des Sozialen (113-133). Wiesbaden: VS Verlag für Sozialwissenschaften.
European Commission (2012). Consumer Complaints. http://ec.europa.eu/consumers/archive/complaints/index_en.htm, (18.9.2014).
Fligstein, N. (2001). The Architecture of Markets. An Economic Sociology for the Twenty-first Century Capitalist Societies. Princeton: Princeton University Press.
Foodwatch (2012). Bilanz: 5 Jahre abgespeist.de – die foodwatch-Kampagne gegen legale Verbrauchertäuschung. http://www.foodwatch.org/uploads/media/Pressematerial_abgespeist-Bilanz_Zusammenfassung_2012-11-22.pdf [28.3.2014].
Fuhse, J. (2009). The Meaning Structure of Social Networks, Sociological Theory, 27(1), 51-73.
Granovetter, M. (1974). Getting a Job: A Study of Contacts and Careers. Chicago: University of Chicago Press.
Granovetter, M. (1985). Economic Action and Social Structure: The Problem of Embeddedness. The American Journal of Sociology, 91(3), 481-510.
Hirschman, A. O. (1970). Exit, Voice, and Loyalty. Responses to Decline in Firms, Organizations, and States. Harvard: Harvard University Press.
Karpik, L. (2010). Valuing the Unique: The Economics of Singularities. Princeton: Princeton University Press.
King, B., & Soule, S. (2007). Social Movements as Extra-Institutional Entrepreneurs: The Effect of Protest on Stock Price Returns. Administrative Science Quarterly, 52, 413-442.
Kleinschmidt, C. (2010). Comparative Consumer Product Testing in Germany. Business History Review, 84, 105-124.
Leggewie, C. (2006). Deliberative Demokratie – Von der Politik-zur Gesellschaftsberatung (und zurück). In S. Falk, D. Rehfeld, A. Römmele & M. Thunert (eds), Handbuch Politikberatung (152-160). Wiesbaden: VS Verlag für Sozialwissenschaften.
Lüde von, R., & Scheve von, C. (2012). Rationalitätsfiktionen des Anlageverhaltens auf Finanzmärkten. In K. Kraemer & S. Nessel (eds), Entfesselte Finanzmärkte. Soziologische Analysen des modernen Kapitalismus (309-326). Frankfurt/.: Campus.

Münch, R. (2008). Jenseits der Sozialpartnerschaft. Die Konstruktion der sozialen Verantwortung von Unternehmen in der Weltgesellschaft. In A. Maurer & U. Schimank (eds), Die Gesellschaft der Unternehmen – Die Unternehmen der Gesellschaft (163-190). Wiesbaden: VS Verlag.
Mützel, S. (2010). Koordinierung von Märkten durch narrativen Wettbewerb. In J. Beckert & C. Deutschmann (eds), Wirtschaftssoziologie. SH 49 KZfSS (87-106). Wiesbaden: VS Verlag.
Nee, V. (2005). The New Institutionalism in Economics and Sociology. In: N. Smelser & R. Swedberg (eds), The Handbook of Economic Sociology (p. 49-74). Princeton: University Press.
Nessel, S. (2012a). Der Lebensmittelmarkt als soziales Feld. Theoretische Erweiterungen der Feldanalyse zur Untersuchung von Märkten, In S. Bernhard & C. Schmidt-Wellenburg (eds), Feldanalyse als Forschungsprogramm. (59-81). Wiesbaden: VS Verlag.
Nessel, S. (2012b). Ethisches Investment, Islamic Finance und politische Fonds. Eine Analyse multipler Entscheidungsrationalitäten auf Finanzmärkten. In K. Kraemer & S. Nessel (eds), Entfesselte Finanzmärkte. Soziologische Analysen des modernen Kapitalismus (281-308). Frankfurt a.M.: Campus.
Nessel, S. (2014). Verbraucherorganisationen und Märkte. Eine wirtschaftssoziologische Untersuchung. Dissertation Thesis Universität Graz.
Podolny, J. (2001). Networks as the Pipes and Prisms of the Market. American Journal of Sociology, 107(1), 33-60.
Raffée, H., & Silberer, G. (eds) (1984). Warentest und Unternehmen. Frankfurt a.M.: Campus.
Schrader, U. (2008). Transparenz über Corporate Social Responsibility (CSR) als Voraussetzung für einen Wandel zu nachhaltigerem Konsum. In H. Lange (ed), Nachhaltigkeit als radikaler Wandel. Die Quadratur des Kreises? (149-166). Wiesbaden: VS Verlag.
Stiftung Warentest (STW) (ed) (2012). Jahresbericht 2012. Berlin: Stiftung Warentest.
Strünck, C. (2005). Mix-Up: Models of Governance and Framing Opportunities in U.S. and EU Consumer Policy. Journal of Consumer Policy, 28(2), 203-230.
Swedberg, R. (1994). Markets in Society. In N. J. Smelser & R. Swedberg (eds), The Handbook of Economic Sociology (233-253). Princeton: Princeton University Press.
Tagesspiegel (2012). „Auch der Ruder-Achter isst Babybrei". Interview von Heike Jahberg mit Claus Hipp. http://www.tagesspiegel.de/wirtschaft/claus-hipp-im-interview-auch-der-ruder-achter-isst-babybrei/7375406.html [03/28/2014].
Trumbull, G. (2006a). Consumer Capitalism: Politics, Product Markets, and Firm Strategy in France and Germany. Ithaca: Cornell University Press.
Verbraucherzentrale Bundesverband (vzbv) 2012. Übersicht der Verfahren Fluggastrechte. http://www.vzbv.de/cps/rde/xbcr/vzbv/fluggastrechte_verfahren_vzbv.pdf [03/28/2014].
Verbraucherzentrale Bundesverband (vzbv) 2013. Verfahren des vzbv zu Kostenfallen im Internet. http://www.vzbv.de/cps/rde/xbcr/vzbv/Kostenfallen_im_Internet.pdf [03/28/2014].
White, H. (1981). Where Do Markets Come From? American Journal of Sociology, 87(3), 517-547.
White, H. (2000). Modeling Discourse in and around Markets. Poetics, 27(2), 117-135.
Zelizer, V. (1983). Morals and Markets: The Development of Life Insurance in the United States. New Brunswick.
Zukin, S., & DiMaggio, P. (1990). Introduction. In S. Zukin & P. DiMaggio (eds), Structures of Capital: The Social Organization of the Economy (pp. 1-35). Cambridge: Cambridge University Press.

Part III
RESILIENCE IN THE SOCIAL SPHERE: THEORETICAL AND EMPIRICAL EVIDENCE

Responses to Discrimination and Social Resilience Under Neoliberalism

The United States Compared[1]

Michèle Lamont, Jessica S. Welburn, and Crystal M. Fleming

Members of stigmatized groups often live with the expectation that they will be overscrutinized, overlooked, underappreciated, misunderstood, and disrespected in the course of their daily lives. How do they interpret and respond to this lived reality? What resources do they have at their disposal to do so? How are their responses shaped by neoliberalism? How can responses to stigmatization foster social resilience?

This chapter enriches our understanding of social resilience by considering whether and how stigmatized groups may be empowered by potentially contradictory contextual forces – more specifically, by cultural repertoires that enable their social inclusion.

---

[1] This research developed in the context of an international research project. Conversations with our collaborators Joshua Guetzkow, Hanna Herzog, Nissim Mizrachi, Elisa Reis, and Graziella Silva de Moraes fed our thinking in multiple ways. Our chapter also benefited from the input of the members of the Successful Societies Program and the support of the Canadian Institute for Advanced Research, as well as from comments from Kathleen Blee, Robert Castel, Anthony Jack, Carol Greenhouse, and Andreas Wimmer.

"We consider repertoires to be social scripts, myths, and cultural structures and that the content of these repertoires varies to some extent across national contexts" (Lamont & Thévenot 2000).[2] We also consider that certain repertoires can foster resilience by feeding the capacity of individuals to maintain positive self-concepts; dignity; and a sense of inclusion, belonging, and recognition.[3] We argue that societies provide individuals with different means for bolstering their identity and building resilience. This is accomplished by making available repertoires that are fed by national ideologies, neoliberalism, and narratives concerning the collective identity of their groups.[4]

The research was presented in a number of settings where the reactions of the audience broadened our thinking: the Institut Marcel Mauss; Ecole des Hautes études en sciences sociales; the Centre Maurice Halbwachs; Ecole normale supérieure; the Obervatoire sociologique du changement, Sciences Po; the seminar "Cities are Back in Town," Sciences Po; the Humanities Center, University of Pittsburg; the Departments of Sociology at Yale University, Boston University, Brandeis University, and Brown University; the Faculty of Social Sciences and History of the Diego Portales University, Santiago de Chile; the POLINE conference on Perceptions of Inequality, Sciences Po (Paris, May 2011); the Nordic Sociological Association meetings (Oslo, August 2011); the Adlerbert Research Foundation Jubilee Conference on "Creating Successful and Sustainable Societies" (Gothenburg, November 2011); and the meetings of the Association for the Study of Ethnicity and Nationalism (London, March 2012). Funding for the comparative study of responses to stigmatization and for data gathering in Brazil was provided by a faculty grant and a Weatherhead Initiative grant from the Weatherhead Center for International Affairs, Harvard University. Research on African American responses to stigmatization was funded by a grant from the National Science Foundation (# 701542). Research on Israeli responses to stigmatization was funded by a grant from the US-Israeli Binational Science Foundation. Michèle Lamont acknowledges the generous support of the Canadian Institute for Advanced Research. We thank Travis Clough for his technical assistance.

2   On repertoires, see Swidler (1986), and Tilly (2006). Although collective imaginaries provide to a group a sense of shared past and future, as well as shared identity (see the introduction to Hall & Lamont 2013, pp. 1-31), the term "repertoire" can be apply to such collective imaginaries, as well as to other relatively stable schemas or cultural structure.

3   On recognition, see Taylor (1991), Honneth (1996), and Fraser and Honneth (2003). Walton and Cohen (2011) have shown that social belonging increases self-reported well-being among African American college students. In future research, we will consider how various types of responses to stigmatization influences subjective well-being. On collective imaginaries and health, see Bouchard (2009).

4   Other repertoires may be more relevant in other societies and historical periods. We take Jenkins (1996) theory concerning social identity as a point of departure: we understand it as resulting from both self-identification (e.g., what it means for African Americans

Considering repertoires is an essential macro complement to the generally more micro approaches to resilience and responses to stigma. It shifts the focus on social resilience conceived as a feature of groups as opposed to a feature of individuals. It also brings to light neglected conditions for recognition and social inclusion, which are essential dimensions of successful societies (Hall & Lamont 2009). For instance, Wright & Bloemraad (2012) show that societies that adopt multicultural narratives about collective identity and multicultural policies (i.e., that score high on the multiculturalism index) signal to immigrants that they value their contributions to the host society. These societies not only provide recognition to immigrants but also foster their emotional and cognitive engagement in this host society as manifested for instance in their greater political participation. This means that repertoires matter. Also, while stigmatization and discrimination toward particular groups is a universal feature of societies, national histories of group boundaries, conflict, and reconciliation vary. Societal trajectories of group relations shape the opportunities and resources individuals have at their disposal for understanding and dealing with stigmatization and thus affect their resilience.

Although this chapter concerns primary the United States, we adopt a comparative approach and also describe responses to stigmatization in Brazil and Israel, countries where the boundaries separating the main stigmatized group from other groups differ in their degree of permeability and porousness (Lamont & Bail 2005). In the three national settings under consideration, we focus on responses to stigmatization among members of groups that are marked on different bases and with different intensities, that is: (a) African Americans in the New York metropolitan area; (b) Afro-Brazilians in Rio de Janeiro; and (b) Ethiopian Jews, Mizrahis (Oriental Jews), and Arab citizens of Israel in the greater Tel Aviv. "Whereas the first three groups have historically been stigmatized based on phenotype, Mizrahis are discriminated against based on ethnicity – although they are a majority group in Israel. For their part, Arab Israelis are primarily stigmatized because of their ethno-religious identity – that is, as Arabs and non-Jews".[5]

The comparison is informed by interviews conducted with large samples of "ordinary" middle class and working class men and women in each of these three national contexts (with 150 interviews in the United States, 160 in Brazil, and 125 in

---

to belong to this group) and group categorization (the meaning given to this group by outgroup members; see also Cornell & Hartman 1997 and Brubaker & Cooper 2000).

5   Bases of stigmatization are historically contingent, with (for instance) biological racism being replaced by cultural racism in the so-called "post-racialism" era in the United States (Bobo 2011).

Israel).[6] These individuals are ordinary in the sense that they are not characterized by, nor selected on the basis of, their involvement in social movements related to identity politics (unlike Moon 2012). They were selected as research participants generally randomly based on criteria such as place of residence, occupations, and level of education (see Appendix for details). This approach is most appropriate for documenting the whole range of responses to stigmatization found in a population without privileging social actors who are most politicized. This is necessary because we are concerned with how the consolidation of collective identity may affect everyday responses to racism.[7]

The empirical focus of interviews is accounts of rhetorical and strategic tools deployed by individual members of stigmatized groups to respond to perceived stigmatization (a broad term that includes or accompanies perceived assaults on dignity, blatant racism, and discrimination). Responses to stigmatization can be individual or collective, and they take a variety of forms such as confronting, evading or deflating conflict, claiming inclusion, educating or reforming the ignorant, attempting to conform to majority culture or affirming distinctiveness, wanting to "pass" or denouncing stereotyping, and engaging in boundary work toward undesirable "others" when responding to stigmatization. They also include "exit" strategies, such as "limiting contacts," "absorbing it," "ignoring the racists," and "managing the self" (Fleming et al. 2011). These responses (including decisions to not respond) occur both in private (when individuals ruminate about past experi-

---

6   This research was conducted by three groups of social scientists who have engaged in a collaborative study since 2005. We adopted a comparative approach with parallel research designs and data collection procedures. Core collaborators in Israel are Joshua Guetzlcow (Department of Anthropology and Sociology, Hebrew University), Hanna Herzog, and Nissim Mizrachi (Department of Anthropology and Sociology, Tel Aviv University). For Brazil, collaborators are Elisa Reis and Graziella Silva (Interdisciplinary Center for the Study of Inequality, Federal University of Rio). For the United States, the core team consists of Crystal Fleming (Department of Sociology, State University of New York at Stony Brook), Michèle Lamont (Department of Sociology and Department of African and African American Studies, Harvard University), and Jessica Welburn (Department of Sociology and Department of African-American Studies, University of Michigan). The U.S. team benefitted from the assistance of Monica Bell, Mellisa Bellin, Steven Brown, Moa Bursell, Nathan Fosse, Nicole Hirsch, Véronique Irwin, Anthony Jack, Michael Jeffries, and Cassi Pittman.

7   The notion of "everyday response to stigmatization" is inspired by Essed (1991)'s notion of everyday racism as "... integration of racism into everyday situations through practices that activate underlying power relations" (50). It also expands on Aptheker (1992)'s definition of anti-racism as rhetoric aimed at disproving racial inferiority. For a discussion of everyday antiracism, see Pollock (2008). On stigma, see Goffman (1963).

ences and try to make sense of them) and in public (when they interact with others while reacting to specific events or incidents) (see Bickerstaff 2012 on public and private responses).

As we explored responses to stigmatization, we paid special attention to interviewees' references to national histories and scripts and to collective myths, as well as to their views concerning what grounds cultural membership and belonging – criteria ranging from economic success to morality and cultural similarities (Lamont 2000). In doing so, we aimed to capture what repertoires respondents drew on in describing situations of stigmatization and how they dealt with them. We also gathered information on their beliefs about, and explanations for, equality and differences between human groups.[8] Although comparative studies of race relations are generally focused on political ideology and state structures (e.g., Marx 1998; Lieberman 2009) or elite discourse (e.g., Van Dijk, 1993; Eyerman, 2002),[9] we connect such ideologies to individual narratives about daily experiences, intergroup relationships, and group boundaries.[10]

Our topic is particularly significant at the present juncture and this, for two reasons: First, to the extent that neoliberalism is often associated with individualization, depoliticization, and a flight away from social justice movements (Lazzarato 2009; Greenhouse 2011), we need to better distinguish between responses to stigma aim to correct the situation of the individual or that of the group (see also Ancelovici (Chapter 12) on French responses to class domination). Second, in the current period of growing economic inequality, members of stigmatized groups are often more vulnerable (Pierson and Hacker 2010; also Welburn 2012 on the downwardly mobile African American middle class).[11] In this period of increased

---

8   This approach is developed in Lamont (2000). Drawing on the sociology of science, it focuses specifically on how ordinary people construct facts on the nature of human groups based on various types of evidence. See also Morning (2009) on racial conceptualizations and Roth (2012) on racial schemas.

9   Space limitation precludes a comparison of our approach with the influential critical discourse analysis approach to racism (e.g., Wodak 2001) or to more political studies of white and black anti-racism (Feagin & Sikes 1994; Picca & Feagin 2007; for a review, see O'Brien 2007.)

10 On groupness and ethno-racial boundaries, see Zolberg & Woon (1999); Lamont (2000); Lamont & Molnar (2002); Todd (2004); Wimmer (2006); Pachucki, Pendergrass & Lamont (2006); Bail (2008); Brubaker (2009); Alba (2009); and Massey & Sanchez (2010).

11 In May 2012, the Bureau of Labor Statistics reported that 7.4 percent of whites were currently unemployed compared with 13.6 percent of African Americans. Research has also consistently shown that African Americans have considerably less wealth than whites, which includes lower homeownership rates, less saving, and few invest-

insecurity, it is particularly urgent to better understand which resources (cultural and others) enable the development of their social resilience and the lessening of vulnerabilities.

Our concern is subjectivities in the neoliberal age. The growing literature on the neoliberal subjectivities has focused primarily on the transformation of middle and upper-middle class selves under late capitalism (e.g., Hearn 2008), described alternatively (under the influence of Giddens 1991, Boltanski and Chiapello 1999, and others) as having self-actualizing, networked, branded, and cosmopolitan selves. Social scientists have generally neglected the national scripts or myths made available to "ordinary" working class people, who make up half of our respondents and more than the majority of the American population. This group is also neglected in studies of everyday responses to racism – despite a huge literature on African Americans' responses to racism, particularly through social movements (but for a few exceptions, e.g., Frederick (2010) on African Americans' aspirations to be millionaires).

The paper opens with two examples of experiences and responses to stigmatization by African American men. It discusses what most African Americans interviewees believe is the best way to respond to racists: confrontation. It also explores how this response is shaped by American national histories and myths. Second, drawing on the collective work of our collaborators in Brazil and Israel (as presented in a special issue of Ethnic and Racial Studies by Lamont and Mizrachi 2012), we sketch how responses to stigmatization in these countries are also shaped by national collective myths, including those that concern the history, place, and salience of ethno-racial minorities in the polity. Third, we take a closer look at the American case to examine how responses to stigmatization are shaped by (a) repertoires about matrices of human worth that are connected to neoliberalism and that emphasize competition, consumption, individualization, and personal achievement and (b) repertoires tied to African American collective identity, its tradition of resilience, and its distinctive criteria of worth. Information on research design, selection, interviews, and data collection and analysis are available in the Appendix.

Drawing only on questions we asked interviewees concerning their ideal or "best approaches" to responding to stigmatization, the chapter highlights the responses to stigmatization in Brazil, Israel, and the United States. We found that

---

ments (e.g., Conley 1999; Oliver & Shapiro 2006; Pew Charitable Trust Foundation 2011). For example, Shapiro & Oliver (2005) find that African Americans control only ten cents for every dollar whites control. A 2011 report by the Pew Charitable Trust Foundation shows that the wealth gap has only grown since the 2008 global recession.

the most popular response among African Americans we talked to is confronting racism (Fleming et al. 2011), which is motivated by a national history of de jure racial exclusion and fed by the lasting legacy of the civil rights movement. In contrast, most Afro-Brazilian interviewees assert the centrality of racial mixture (variously defined) in their society, including the notion that "we are all a little black." In this context, they promote accommodation over confrontation (Silva & Reis 2011) as more compatible with national identity and culture (with reference to the notion of racial democracy). For their part, interviewees from stigmatized Jewish groups in Israel emphasize shared religion over ethno-racial identity and respond to stigmatization by asserting the Jewish identity they share with the majority group (Mizrachi and Herzog 2011). Finally, in the face of strong ethnic and religious discrimination, Arab Israelis respond by evoking the universal respect of human dignity. They also avoid making claim based on group rights (Mizrachi and Zawdu 2012). We suggest that in each case, these responses are facilitated by widely available cultural myths about national belonging – more specifically, by the American dream, the myth of Brazilian racial democracy, and Israeli Zionism.

A closer look at the American case reveals that African Americans draw on two additional repertoires in responding to stigmatization. First, they use a repertoire made more readily available by neoliberalism, which focuses on scripts that value competition, consumption, individualization (Bourdieu 1998), and personal achievements (in line with market fundamentalism (Somers 2008). These scripts of response go hand in hand with individualist explanations of low achievement, poverty, and unemployment, which are often associated with poor moral character (laziness, lack of self-reliance), as opposed to market and structural forces.[12] Second, they use a repertoire that is connected to group identity and that celebrates shared culture and experiences. These narratives are sources of pleasure and comfort that can act as a counterweight to feelings of isolation and powerlessness, and as such, enable social resilience. These repertoires also emphasize moral strength and a history of survival that mitigate self-blaming and may also act as a resource for social resilience. Finally as Lamont (2000) argued based on interviews conducted in 1993, we also find an alternative moral matrix of evaluation that allows African Americans to not measure themselves by the dominant standard of socio-

---

12 Similarly, Greenhouse (2011) argues that the moral construction of African Americans and poverty has been profoundly transformed under neoliberalism – with a stronger stigmatization of welfare dependency and celebration of a neoliberal self. This means that the tools with which African Americans respond to racism are themselves the product of neoliberalism.

economic success.[13] These alternative repertoires can potentially act as sources of social resilience by broadening the criteria of social inclusion.

National narratives that stress the American history of racism and fight against racial domination (of the type associated with the American civil right movement and with African American social movements, such as the Black Panthers) and representations of shared African American collective identity characterized by resilience can enable collective responses oriented toward confrontation. But scripts central to neoliberalism may favor also primarily individualist responses to stigma, particularly the pursuit of individual mobility.

Addressing whether individual or collective responses have positive or negative association with social resilience is beyond the scope of this chapter. However, we point out ways in which the various repertoires respondents draw on may affect social resilience. For instance, although a focus on personal achievement may encourage African Americans to escape stigma through an agentic, autonomous and universalist logic (as one respondent puts it, "get the skills to get the job – may the best man win"), it may also limit the appeal of alternative matrixes of evaluation (e.g., the notion that blacks have a caring self and solidarity) (Lamont 2000) that emphasizes morality, downplays socioeconomic success, and thus sustains positive self-images despite low social status.

This chapter builds directly on Successful Societies: How Institutions and Culture Affect Health, which focused on the capability of individuals and groups to respond to the challenges they encounter and on how institutions and shared cultural repertoires serve as resources and buffers against the "wear and tear of inequality" that epidemiologists address (Clark et al. 1999; Hertzman & Boyce 2010). National identity, scripts provided by neoliberalism, and scripts about collective identity, are some of the main repertoires or toolkits on which individuals draw to gain recognition and respond to the challenges they face (Lamont 2009). Thus, resilience is maintained not only by inner moral strength and resourcefulness or by social support (often emphasized in popular and scholarly writings) but also through the repertoires that sustain recognition or the institutionalization and circulation of positive conceptions of individual or collective selves. From this perspective, members of stigmatized groups vary with regard to their ability to reshape group relations in ways that allow for the widespread adoption of representations and narratives asserting the dignity and worth of their group.

---

13   This is one of the three elements of definition of social resilience at the center of Hall and Lamont (2013). The two other dimensions are ability to imagine better futures that are within one's reach and the ability to resist discrimination, exploitation, and exclusion.

This argument complements social psychological approaches to resilience. Social psychologists typically focus on the psychological orientations that foster individual resilience, such as privileging the in-group as a reference group (Crocker, Major & Steele, 1998)[14] and having a strong racial identification or biculturalism (Oyserman & Swim 2001). They also consider the impact of cognitive ability, positive self-perception, and emotional regulation on resilience, as well as the broader environment, generally network and community support (see Son Hing2012, chapter 5).[15] In contrast, again, our analysis centers on the cultural supply side of the equation, that is, on cultural repertoires and the relative availability of alternative ways of understanding social reality (also Harding et al. 2010).

It is important to note that institutional and structural forces also play a crucial role in shaping responses and diffusing repertoires. Indeed, a large literature addresses the role of public policies in defining the conditions of reception for minority groups, including how they understand their place in the polity (e.g., Kastoryano 2002, Ireland 2004, Koopmans et al. (2005, Wimmer & Min 2006). These topics are beyond the scope of this chapter, so we leave them aside. For the most part, we also leave aside the important questions of how repertoires diffuse, why individuals or groups are more likely to draw on one script rather than another (see, e.g., Lamont 1992; Schudson 1988), and variations in the salience of ethno-racial identities across groups.[16]

---

14 See also Pinel (1999) on "stigma consciousness" and Clark et al. (1999) on how minority groups cope psychologically with the "perceived stressor" of racism and prejudice. Also Son Hing 2012. See Link & Phelan (2000) for a broader review of the literature on stigma, which is most often concerns with the stigma of "stressors" such as mental illness and physical disabilities and their impact on health.

15 Son Hing (2012, Chapter 5) considers that "protective factors (i.e., strengths or capabilities) may reside within the individual (e.g., emotional regulation, self-enhancement), the family (e.g., secure attachments, authoritative parenting), or the community or environment (e.g., community resources, programming)." Cultural repertoires are not part of the protective factors they have paid attention to.

16 Of the three groups of African descent, African Americans are most likely to self-define through their racial identity, and they are more likely to label an interaction or a person as "racist." Afro- Brazilians and Ethiopian Jews have racial identities that are less salient or that are expressed primarily through class (in Brazil) or religious (in Israel) frames. Thus, national contexts make various kinds of historical scripts, myths, or repertoires more or less readily available to social actors to make sense of their reality (Lamont & Thévenot 2000; see also Swidler 1986; Mizrachi, Drori & Anspach 2007.) Along with Wimmer (2008) and Brubaker (2009) we analyze not only social identity but also identification processes and the development groupness. However, unlike these scholars, we are centrally concerned not only with cognition but also with the role of emotion (particularly anger, pain, pride, and other feelings directly associ-

African Americans Experiencing and Responding to Stigmatization

How does it feel to be outside of a boundary? Most of the African American men and women we interviewed perceive themselves as being underestimated, distrusted, overscrutinized, misunderstood, feared, overlooked, avoided, or plainly discriminated against due to their ethnical belonging at some point in their lives. This perception can be persistent for some respondents and situational for others. Two examples provide suitable illustrations. They both concern two strikingly similar narratives in which an African American man finds himself inside an elevator with outgroup members.[17]

In the first case, Marcus, a black court employee, enters an elevator in which there is a middle-aged Indian woman who also works at the court.[18] He describes the situation thus: "She clutches her purse. I almost fainted. I almost fainted .... It devastated me. But it's happened to brothers before. Welcome to the Black race, brother. You've got it. I've got it." Her reactions prompt Marcus's anger and humiliation because, as he explains, he often feels that people think he does not belong in the court building. For instance, he is routinely questioned about whether he truly works at the court and knows others who work there. Marcus has to carefully consider how he should respond to the situation. Should he ignore the slight and let it go? Should he confront the woman, and if so, how? And what will be the costs of confrontation (emotional, interactional, potentially legal)? Marcus wants to maintain his image of professionalism and stand up for himself. How can he do both? He explains that these are the questions that often emerge when he experiences stigmatization. The repeated experience of such an internal dialogue can take a toll and contribute to the "wear and tear of everyday life" that results in huge disparities in the health and well-being of ethno-racial groups in the United States and elsewhere.

In a second example, Joe, a recreation specialist, faces a more blatant racist situation. His account viscerally expresses perceptions of the health impact of anger

---

ated with identity management; see Archer 2003; Summers-Effler 2002). And we also connect the drawing of group boundaries to everyday morality (e.g., Lamont (2000) and Sayer (2005) in the case of class).

17 For a discussion of the place of our argument in the literature on African American anti-racism (e.g., in relation to the work of Karyn Lacy, Joe Feagin, and others), see Fleming et al. (2011).

18 We use "African American" and "black" interchangeably to reflect the use of these terms by our respondents.

in the experience of stigmatization (see Mabry & Kiecolt 2005). He finds himself alone with several white men in an elevator. He recalls the scene thus:

> One made a joke about Blacks and monkeys. I said, "Man, listen, I ain't into jokes." ... His demeanor changed, my demeanor changed. All of the positive energy that was in there was being sucked out because the racial part. And the other guys, you could actually see them shrinking up in the corner because they didn't want no parts of it.... [I told myself] get out of it because if I stay in it, I'm going to be in that circle and [won't be able to] get out.... The stress level rose. My tolerance was getting thin, my blood pressure peaking and my temper rising. By the grace of God, thank you Jesus, as I stepped off the elevator, there was a Black minister walking past. I said, "Can I speak to you for a minute because I just encountered something that I got to talk about because I'm this far [to exploding]?" I had been at the job for a week. This is all I need to get me fired. He said, "You're a better man than me." [Now] I'm trying to get through the affair [to decide] if I was to go to the city [to complain].

Joe knows that anger and impulse control are imperative if he wants to keep his job. He has to manage his emotions and finds an outlet when a chance encounter with an African American pastor offers relief – or a buffer – from a fellow group member who can relate to. Similar to the majority of our interviewees, Joe factors in pragmatic considerations when weighing various courses of action (Fleming et al. 2012). But his normative response is that one needs to confront racism. This gap between ideal responses and situational constraints may have consequences for the emotional well-being of our respondents.

When probed about the "best approach" for dealing with racism (using an open-ended question format), three quarters of the 112 African American interviewees who addressed this question focused on how to respond (what we call "modalities" of responses): half of them (47 percent) favored confronting or challenging racism and discrimination. They prefer to "name the problem," "openly discuss the situation," and "make others aware that their action makes me uncomfortable." This compares to a third (32 percent) who prefer conflict- deflecting strategies – believing that it is best to ignore, accept, forgive, manage anger, or walk away (Fleming et al. 2012). The rest favor a mixed strategy, choosing to "pick their battles" or to "tolerate." Two thirds (65 percent) focused not on "modalities" but on what they consider to be the specific "tools" for responding to discrimination. For one third of them (37 percent), the best approach is educating stigmatizers and (in some cases) fellow blacks about tolerance, diversity, and the lives and culture of African Americans. For one fifth of them (17 percent), the best tool is to increase formal education for African Americans to improve mobility outcomes for members of the group.[19]

An illustration of the desire to confront is provided by a prison instructor. When asked how we should deal with racism, he responds:

> Confront it. 'Cuz people will try to tell you that it doesn't exist and it does exist... confront it. Not in a negative way, but just bring it up, discuss it. White folks will try to act like it doesn't exist and then they'll try to reverse it on you,

This is typical of the responses voiced by many interviewees. Their shared belief in the legitimacy of confrontation as a response is bolstered by the widespread availability of national scripts about the racist history of the United States, to which they often make reference in the context of the interviews (whether they talk about the history of chattel slavery, Jim Crow, or the experiences of their parents growing up in the South). Equally important is their awareness of the civil rights movements (including the struggles around school desegregation, the Newark Riots, the marches on Washington) and their current experiences with discrimination at work or elsewhere. More specifically, among 302 mentions of landmark historical events made during the course of the interviews, 30 percent concerned slavery, 16 percent concerned the 2008 elections, 15 mentioned the civil rights movement, and 11 mentioned the race riots. For instance, one interviewee explains that "my wife's father had a black garage in South Carolina. The Ku Klux Klan burned it down. That's why they moved up here, to get away from it. A lot of older people, they don't even like to talk about it ... We just had to deal with it."

As suggested by the examples of Marcus and Joe (and as observed by social psychologists), the ideal of confronting racism is tempered by pragmatic consideration concerning costs (material, symbolic, or emotional). Individual strategies are constrained by what respondents believe is possible and doable given their needs and dependency on resources. In the presence of obstacles to confronting, a majority of middle class African American respondents focus on hard work and achievement as the key to challenging racial inequality (also Welburn & Pittman 2012)[20] essential to the pursuit of the American dream. Many embrace this crucial

---

19 A number of other tools (e.g., gaining information) were mentioned by only a few respondents and thus are not reported here. Some respondents mentioned more than one "best approach" for dealing with racism.

20 The forty five African-American middle class respondents interviewed by Welburn & Pittman (2012) more frequently explain racial inequality by motivational than by structural problems. These authors find 79 mentions of the former in interviews (e.g., decline in values and morality, lack of efforts, making excuses)compared with 65 men-

national collective myth (Hochschild 1995), through educational and economic achievement, and through the consumption it enables (as one respondent, a network technician, puts it: "You need to do something positive with your life. The American dream is out there; all you got to do is grab it and run with it." We will see that this individualist response coexist with a more collectivist strategy grounded in a shared African American identity.

The continued commemoration of the African American history of discrimination and courage (e.g., through the institutionalization of Black History Month, the existence of African American studies as an academic discipline, as well as important aspects of black popular culture) enables interviewees to believe that it is legitimate to denounce and confront racism and discrimination. This orientation is less frequent among respondents in Brazil and Israel (Silva & Reis 2012; Mizrachi & Herzog 2012).

National Responses Compared

Israel

Similar to the African Americans we spoke with, Israelis anchor their responses to stigmatization in national history and myths. Indeed, Mizrachi and Zawdu (2012) show that ordinary Ethiopian Jews use the Zionist national narrative to neutralize the stigma associated with blackness – unlike political activists who have attracted the attention of the Israeli media in 2011. They downplay their phenotypical markings (e.g., skin tone) and define their identity as "just another group of immigrants," similar to other Jewish immigrant groups who eventually assimilate and prosper in Israel (often referring to the Russian Jews who preceded them en masse in the 1990s). This identification as "Jewish immigrants" grounded in the Zionist narrative serves as an equalizer: it legitimates their participation in the larger society. Similarly, the Mizrahis mobilize an assimilationist state ideology as a cultural tool for gaining recognition – an ideology that defines all Jews, regardless of regional, phenotypical, or other characteristic, as members of the polity. Both groups find in this ideology empowering repertoires of religious citizenship that makes their responses to stigmatization possible (Dieckhoff 2003). These accounts contrast with the responses to stigmatization by Arab Israelis, which appeal to universal human dignity, as opposed to shared religion (Mizrahi & Herzog 2012). Members of this

---

tions of the latter ("fewer opportunities for African American males," "racism and discriminations," and so on).

group attempt to depoliticize social difference by avoiding the use of a language of human rights and mobilize Jews in their social network in their defense (ibid.). Their ethno-religious identity, however, remained explicit and firmly differentiated from that of the Jews.

Brazil

When interviewing middle class and working class Afro-Brazilians about their views on the best approach for responding to stigmatization, Silva and Reis (2012) find that they most frequently embrace a dialogical and fuzzy "racial mixture" script as a response. This term is used to describe the multiracial character of the Brazilian population ("we are all a little black") and its hybrid culture and identity, as much as the notion that everyone, independently of phenotype, can be fully committed a multiracial society. Racial mixture is a crucial collective myth for the Brazilian nation (along with the myth of racial democracy), and it acts as a more inclusive and less politically loaded cultural basis for cultural membership than does shared religion in the Israeli case.[21] Silva and Reis remark that few interviewees consistently used one single concept of racial mixing throughout the interview, switching between meanings according to contest (Silva & Reis 2012, p. 396). In a recent review of the literature on racial mixture, Telles and Sue (2009) suggest that in Latin America especially, the centrality of mixed racial categories does not translate into a decline in racial inequality. Marx (1998) also analyzes the role of the state in creating racial boundaries and hierarchies. Governments feed collective imaginaries by defining rules of membership across a number of policy areas that have a direct impact on those who experience exclusion as well as on shared conceptions of cultural membership (alternatively, ethnic boundaries also shape state action – see also Lieberman (2009) for a cross-national illustration concerning state responses to aids in Brazil, India, and South Africa).

This analysis suggests that some strategies are more likely to be found in some contexts than others (e.g., promoting racial mixture in Brazil and confronting

---

21 Silva and Reis (2012) identify four uses of the term "racial mixture:" (a) to describe whitening among blacks, (b) to celebrate Brazilian négritude (which is defined as mixed); (c) to describe Brazilian national identity; and (d) to describe a personal experience or non-racist strategy for responding to racism, that is, "non-essentialist racialism" which can mobilize by whites as well). Although the last two frames are used by more than 50 percent of the respondents, the last one is the most popular (being used by 66 percent of the 160 respondents), and the first one is the least popular (being used by 17 percent only).

in the United States). However, the use of repertoires is linked not only to their availability but also to proximate and remote determinants that make that some individuals are more or less likely to use certain repertoires than others (Lamont 1992). A more detailed look at the interaction between repertoires, social resources, situational cost, and opportunity structure will be the object of future analysis. For now, suffice to restate that national ideologies do not push individuals toward a single strategy – they simply make strategies more or less likely across contexts, enabling and constraining them.

The United States: Other Repertoires

Neoliberalism

We now provide a closer look at African American responses enabled by neoliberalism, that is, responses that emphasize (a) self-reliance and autonomy (connected to individualization and the privatization of risk (Sharone 2013)), (b) competitiveness and educational and economic achievement, and (c) the signaling of social status through consumption. These individualist responses may be alternative to, and often threaten, collective responses, such as social movement and political mobilization (Bourdieu 1998; see below).

It may be objected that these responses exist independently of neoliberalism because they are central to the tenets of the American creed (as described by Hochschild 1995; also see Fischer 2010). However, their centrality and availability are likely to be accentuated in the neoliberal era because the two types of repertoires (the American dream and neoliberalism) become intertwined under the influence of market fundamentalism (see Greenhouse 2011; also Richland 2009). In the neoliberal era, the American dream is less about individual freedom and equality and more about individual success, performance, competition, and economic achievement.

Although there is great variation in how African Americans interpret "the American dream," some defining it as nightmare, many of our interviewees believe that the best response of racism is for blacks to work to get ahead through education and that they should persevere regardless of persistent discrimination (also Welburn & Pittman 2012 based on data on African Americans living in New Jersey). Moreover, the desire to "make it big" is very salient in interviews, and a large number of the individuals we talked to dream of starting their own business; they mention the distance from racists that being self-employed can provide together with the advantage of financial security (also Frederick 2010). They also value hard work and its most important outcome, financial independence. It is worth quoting one working class man who is a particularly vocal advocate of economic achievement. He describes the people he likes as "hustlers" who, like him, hold several jobs and are willing to do anything to make money. He talks about his friend Thomas, who he says "does landscaping in the morning for a company. Then he has his own contracts in the middle of the day, sleeps and goes to work for Fed Ex at night....I like to see hustlers because that's something that I do: just hustling. No laws are being broke, no one is being hurt."

Respondents also put a great emphasis on self-reliance for themselves and others. In so doing, they may want to mark distance toward the stereotype of low-income African Americans who depend on others for their subsistence and "don't want to pull their own weight." For instance, a woman who works for a dry-cleaning business and a grocery store and who admits to struggling financially says:

> I don't like beggars. I don't like anybody's looking for a handout, I like people that want to get out and do something for themselves and help themselves. ... I just can't deal with beggars.

This script, which is found in many interviews, is embraced by white and black American working class men alike (Lamont 2000; also Pattillo-McCoy 1999). It is reinforced by the script of privatization of risk central to neoliberalism (Hacker 2006) and is embodied in the Personal Responsibility and Work Opportunity Act of 1996, which implicitly defined the poor as lazy and immoral (Guetzkow 2010).

Similar responses are found among middle class respondents, with a focus on professional achievement and improving their social and economic status. The majority of the respondents in this class category describe themselves as strongly committed to such goals. They also often define themselves by their ability to "do the job" as well or better than whites, and they conceive of competence as an important anti-racist strategy (Lamont & Fleming 2005). Others celebrate the virtue of competition and define African American culture as embracing it (as a transit technician puts it, "We love to compete. Anything you put us in that's athletic, we just excel. [We] love to compete.") These respondents say they want to hire other African Americans when possible but that incompetence defines the limits of racial solidarity (as one respondent says: "You fuck up and I am done with you.") The conditions for cultural memberships that are imposed on middle class African Americans may put limitations on their racial solidarity toward low-income blacks if achievement and economic success are sine qua non for cultural membership (Lamont & Fleming 2005).

Formal education and individual educational attainment are viewed by many as essential in a highly competitive neoliberal climate, especially for African Americans who have experienced greater job market instability than members of other racial groups in recent years. Accordingly, when asked about the best way to respond to racism, the pursuit of education is frequently mentioned. As one of them puts it, speaking of young African Americans:

> You can't take a diploma from them ... It's recorded ... They are African-Americans so... there are some strikes. Get all the education so when you're sitting down with the competition, at least you know [what it's like]. He has it, your competition has it. You're going to get it. I'll go in debt to get my sons the education money ... You can take sports away, but you can't take a diploma away.

Echoing this interviewee, a writer also celebrates education as a tool for gaining inclusion while noting its limitation. She also stresses the importance of financial independence and points the importance of "being on top":

> My mother said, "Girl, go to school. Get your education. They can't take it out of your head ... you'll get the job. You'll get fair treatment." So that's what I expected from a job. But that's not what it's all about ... Go get your education, but don't make that everything. Have you some side something going on ... When the cards fall, as they will, you have to decide you want to be on top. And the only way you can be on top is if you get something for yourself.

Along similar lines, a teacher explains the importance of education for autonomy, the utility of separatism, and the self-reliance of African Americans in a context of pervasive racism:

> Even though we will never be integrated fully, we will never be accepted, as long as we can educate a number of our people, we can challenge these different cultures that we face each and every day. Or we can have our own hospitals, our banks, our own, be our and have our own so we don't have to be subjected with negativity each and every day.

While getting a formal education is not exclusive of collective solutions (as getting education may contribute to "lifting the race") and of collective empowerment ("to put our people in place ... to create a future for us"), the prime beneficiary of a college degree is its holder. One interviewee, a property manager, emphasizes that collective empowerment in more important than individual success when he says (after stating "you need the monetary flow ... if you want to make your own rules"):

> I don't believe in pursuing in the American dream by just having physical things. It's more important that we establish the institutions that would give our people longevity and empowerment in the future. The American dream tells us to be successful as individuals, where[as] everybody else comes here and is successful as a group. Our American dream is an illusion because most of our dreams are through credit [...] which makes us sharecroppers.

He asserts the importance of collective empowerment over the simple accumulation of goods and individual achievement for fighting racism. Nevertheless, of the respondents who discussed formal education when we questioned them about the best tool for responding to stigmatization, a third spoke of its importance for the improvement of the group, and two thirds referred to its importance for the individual. This is in line with the neoliberal emphasis on the privatization of risk and with the related question of how African Americans explain their fate (as resulting from individual effort or linked fate). Recent research demonstrates that African Americans have become more individualist in their explanation of inequality over the past few decades (Bobo et al. 2012; Welburn & Pittman 2012).

As a correlate of the emphasis put on economic and educational achievement, some African American respondents also emphasize consumption as a means to providing proofs of cultural citizenship. Some respondents define their success in term of what they are able to afford to buy – whether a house, a car, or an education for their children. Being able to use money as an equalizer (e.g., by shopping at brand stores, sporting professional attire, or driving a nice car) is often seen as a fool-proof means of demonstrating that one belongs and that one has achieved a middle class status that lessens, to some extent, the stigma of being black in contemporary American (Lamont and Molnar 2002; Pittman 2012).[22] Although the literature emphasizes conspicuous consumption of luxury goods among African Americans (ibid.), we find that our respondents are most concerned with consuming items that are associated with a "decent" or "normal" middle or working class lifestyle. For instance, the dry-cleaner and grocery store employee expresses regrets: "I wish I had my own condo, a decent car to drive I take a vacation and sit at home." Also, many interviewees value having the means to support themselves, to

---

22 These behaviors had already been noted for the black middle class in Franklin Frazier's 1957 *Black Bourgeoisie*, and in reaction to Wilson's (1978) writing on the spatial and cultural isolation of the black middle class.

buy health insurance, and to have "a little cushion." But as is the case for elite African Americans (Lamont & Fleming 2005), using access to economic resources as a criterion for cultural membership excludes all low-income African Americans.

It would be important to ascertain whether and how neoliberalism has transformed African American understandings of the conditions for gaining cultural membership and whether economic achievement looms larger in these scripts today than it did a few decades ago, reinforcing themes central to the national scripts centered on achievement and individualism (Sears et al 2000). This is not an easy task because the spread of neoliberalism occurred concurrently with economic, educational, political, and legal gains for African Americans, which led some to believe in the advent of a "post-racial America," especially in the wake of Barack Obama's presidential election in 2008. Although racial discrimination persists, it is equally difficult to ascertain the relative impact of neoliberalism on stigmatized groups in other countries. However, given the relative significance of governmental efforts to promote neoliberal policies and to protect workers from its impact across advanced industrial societies, one can presume that this impact has been particularly important in the United States.[23] More than ever, many African Americans may have become convinced that self-reliance, economic success, individual achievement, and consumption are the best response to stigmatization. However, many of our respondents are nostalgic about a time when black collective movements were dynamic, and they have vivid memories of the systematic dismantling of radical collective movements, such as the Black Power movement, by the state. Thus, it is not surprising that there is a clash between individualist responses inspired by neoliberalism and other responses enabled by repertoires celebrating collective identity, as we suggest in the next section.

African American Collective Identity

The collective identity and vision of a common past serves as a buffer against stigmatization for a number of African Americans. This is accomplished through (a) a shared narrative of "we-ness" that can act as a source of comfort and pleasure; (b) an awareness of a shared tradition of resilience in the context of continued discrimination, which helps individuals make sense of their experience; and (c)

---

23 This is confirmed by Greenhouse's (2011) ethnographic analysis of the entanglements of politics and identity in the major American legislation of the 1990s. See also Chauvel (2010) on the impact of the welfare state on the economic instability of youth across advanced industrial societies.

an identity defined in opposition to that of whites that reinforces non-economic matrixes of worth. We gathered evidence on these questions by probing interviewees on what it means for them to be African Americans, what makes their group distinctive, and related questions.

In the context of interviews, a large number of individuals explained that African Americans have a common culture and social experience or a shared "background" that provides them a sense of pleasure. This sense of "cultural intimacy" (Herzfeld 1996) is described by one middle-aged African man thus:

> That's what I like about our people. Good or bad, we're coming together.... We all got an uncle somewhere that chases young girls, and a grandmother somewhere who has certain sayings.... Or an aunt who can cook a sweet potato pie.... You put us together in a restaurant and we'll walk out of there laughin' because it's going to be something that we have in common. And that's just our people; it's just the way it is. I haven't met anybody that didn't have a grandmother like my grandmother. Or an aunt. Somebody.

Similarly, one interviewee describes African Americans as "having a bond," as being "on the same frequency," and another explains that African Americans generally knowing where other blacks "are coming from." It is noteworthy that this sense of cultural intimacy is also salient in discussions of interracial relationships, where the absence of shared experiences of discrimination is described as a major challenge. This is illustrated by one middle class interviewee who discards white romantic partners after one negative experience. Referring to his former girlfriend, he explains that "she can't get the joy out of watching Mandela walk out of jail.... She can't understand when three white police officers shoot two black males for nothing. She could say 'they shouldn't have been out there.' See, I'd have to choke her...."

When probing interviewees about what are the distinctive characteristics of African Americans, we find that the notion of "a shared culture" is frequently mentioned spontaneously, ex aequo with similar responses that all point to other aspects of "cultural sameness:" morality, the importance of religion, the importance of caring, the richness of black culture, and black aesthetics and popular culture (each received 11 percent of the 307 responses given to this probe). These figures support the relatively high salience of shared culture in "folk" or "racial" conceptualization of blackness among African Americans (Morning 2009; Silva 2012).

Psychologists have shown that shared identity provides a feeling of comfort and of being understood that can act as buffers or provide solace when one feels being underestimated, distrusted, overscrutinized, misunderstood, feared, overlooked, avoided, or discriminated against (e.g., Neblett et al. 2004). As such, widely available repertoires presenting and making salient African American shared identity and culture can act as resources that sustain social resilience. Such repertoires are crucial sources for recognition that have been neglected by social psychologists who tend to focus on networks, family, and community as environmental sources of resilience (as summarized by Son Hing 2012, chapter 5). If they are absent, individuals are more likely to find themselves vulnerable, isolated, and less able to respond to assaults on their sense of dignity – as was the case for Joe before he ran into a black minister when exiting an elevator in the incident related earlier. Such repertoires are likely to be more widely available in societies that support multiculturalism (see Kymlicka 2007; Wright & Bloemraad 2012) and adopt institutional structures that mitigate a clear ingroup-outgroup demarcations (Emmenegger et al. 2011).

In describing what African Americans have in common, a number of respondents often mention resilience and a tradition of overcoming barriers. Indeed, when probing interviewees about the distinctive characteristics of African Americans, we find that, respectively, 15 percent and 12 percent of the responses concern "resilience" and a shared history of overcoming racial barriers. Accordingly, respondents refer with respect and admiration to the stories their parents have told them about their past experiences with combating or dealing with racism. These stories make salient shared identity and past struggles. They also provide individuals standardized tools for making sense of their individual experience and for avoiding internalizing negative messages. As such, they do contribute to the social resilience of their group. However, a number of respondents also mentioned what they perceive to be the more negative features of African Americans: self-destructiveness, lack of solidarity, lack of self-respect, the use of Ebonics, hip hop fashion, and the prevalence of youth violence – for a total 12 percent of the characteristics mentioned. Thus, collective identity can be a source of collective shame as well as a source of pleasure and pride.

African American social resilience is also likely to be strengthened by a widely available repertoire that defines blacks in opposition to whites and puts their "caring self" above the "disciplined self" of whites. Based on interviews conducted in 1993, Lamont (2000) argued that the African American working class men she talked with perceived themselves as more caring and accepting, as "having the spirit" or "soul" or as more in contact "with the human thing" than whites. Some contrasted this portrayal with a view of whites as materialist, power obsessed ("he who has the gold makes the rules'), arrogant, and self-serving – as manifested in the "illusion of white superiority." Lamont (2000) argued that by defining themselves as more moral than whites, African Americans promoted a matrix of evaluation that counterbalanced the emphasis on economic achievement promoted by neoliberalism. This matrix functions as an alternative measuring stick and enables low to middle income earners to cultivate a sense of dignity and self-pride despite their lower socioeconomic status. These observations appear to hold for the respondents we interviewed in 2012 (a topic to be explored in future publications.)[24]

Awareness of the need to cultivate alternative matrixes of evaluation is strong among some respondents. A few emphasize the importance of celebrating a range of achievements by African Americans and of cultivating knowledge of black culture and tradition (knowing "their roots") among young people. They also lament the weak sense of black pride in their community. For instance, a property manager explains:

> Most of our problems as Black people stem from the fact that we do not have our connection to our roots ... We don't look back to our story for any type of strength or encouragement ... We don't have a village where there are elders who direct the youth.

This man stresses the importance of giving black children a sense of purpose and pride by reconnecting them with their group identity (also Bouchard 2009). He wants to broadcast an alternative collective narrative about the group's past and future that may bolster social resilience – in lieu of scripts of consumerism and individual achievement that are enabled and made more salient by neoliberalism. Strengthening the connection with the past could provide a way for low-income blacks to gain a sense of cultural membership despite their being low on the totem pole of individual achievement – a way not to be "loser" in an increasingly dominant neoliberal competition.

Conclusion: What Confers Social Resilience?

In examining the question "How can responses to stigmatization confer social resilience?" this chapter has focused on social resources that may sustain recognition by focusing on the cultural repertoires on which African Americans draw to consider what are the ideal responses to racism. We have suggested that these repertoires act as resources that sustain social resilience, conceived as features of groups. Such repertoires are part of an environment that feeds the sense of empowerment and worth of group members. They may be unevenly available across social contexts, depending on the success of mobilization efforts enacted by the stigmatized as well as their allies and the extent to which societies support multiculturalism or other means of creating more porous boundaries between various types of ingroups and outgroups.

---

24 For a complementary perspective, see Stephens et al. (2012).

In the preceding section, we have argued that exposure to cultural repertoires that make salient and celebrate a shared culture has positive effects on social resilience. This complements findings from social psychology described by Son Hing (2012, see Chapter 5) that strong ingroup (racial) identification fosters resilience for those who experience lower levels of discrimination. Indeed, among ethnic minority youth in Scotland, the more girls experienced collective self-esteem, the lower their depression and their anxiety (Cassidy, Howe, and Warden 2004). Similarly, Asian American children experiencing discrimination from their peers have higher self-esteem if they feel more positively toward their ethnic group (Rivas-Drake, Hughes, and Way 2008). This work suggests that the mere fact of partaking in a similar experience and of sharing a similar narrative may provide a buffer in the form of social support. Although psychologists are generally not concerned with the cultural sources of such strong group identities, our chapter illuminates this part of the puzzle.

Future research should explore which of the three types of repertoires considered here – national myths, neoliberalism, and collective identity and history – have the most positive impact on social resilience. However, this cannot be an easy task for several reasons: (a) although social actors generally privilege a repertoire, they often alternate between them across situations and over time, making it difficult to establish a direct causal relationship between types of repertoires, social resilience, and well-being; (b) the three types of repertoires may be becoming increasingly braided, especially under the growing influence of neoliberalism; and (c) Neoliberal themes may have simultaneously beneficial and pernicious effects on social resilience. Indeed, they may promote self-blaming for failure (see Chapter 5), encourage African Americans to escape stigma through a universalist logic (e.g., compete to "get the skills to get the job" according to the principle of "the best man for the job"), and limit the appeal of alternative moral matrixes of evaluation that may allow low-status individuals to fare better. To complicate matters further, neoliberalism may also encourage stigmatized group to make claims based on human rights (also see Chapters 2 and 3) while undercutting in practice collective claims by promoting individualization. Finally, neoliberalism may promote competition with members of other stigmatized groups and thus affect negatively the potential for collective mobilization.[25]

---

25 Future research should draw on ethnographic observation to assess how accounts of responses to stigmatization compare with actually responses. This is essential to better understand the relationship between interaction and available grammars of action – two deeply intertwined aspects of social life, which each gives us only a partial view of human action.

There is also the possibility that individuals are using repertoires differently under neoliberalism: they may be increasingly skeptical of collective projects and collective myths and find refuge in their private lives. For example, this is suggested in the paradoxical fact that in early 2011, the French were found to be more pessimistic about the future than most other national groups being compared yet were producing more children.[26] Privatization may be more likely in a context where individuals have few resources to realize their dream and yet are asked to deploy entrepreneurialism and other neoliberal virtues.

It is too early to determine whether patterns in responses to stigmatization are converging across the national cases we are considering and whether, overall, African Americans are better off (e.g., in terms of subjective well-being) than their Brazilian or Israeli counterparts. Also, more comparative analysis is needed before we can draw conclusion on the relative impact of neoliberalism on social resilience for African Americans compared with Afro-Brazilians and stigmatized groups in Israel. Nevertheless, we venture to predict that the former are less culturally buffered from the pernicious effects of neoliberalism than their counterparts in Brazil and Israel, given the centrality of individualism and economic achievement in the collective myth of the American dream. Moreover, the fact that in the United States, the "losers" of market fundamentalism (as measured by unemployment rate and other indicators) are disproportionately symbolic "outsiders" (immigrants and African Americans) can also increase the legitimacy of neoliberal themes in this national context. Although the American dream empowers many, it often leaves those who cannot achieve it without hopes. This is both the grandeur and the tragedy of the American collective imaginary.

Methodological Appendix

Case Selection

Our countries of comparison were selected to maximize differences in frequency in perceived discrimination across cases, the latter being an indicator of the strength or permeability of boundaries across national contexts. The selection was based on a comparison by Lamont and Bail (2005) of the relative strength of social

---

26 The annual BVA-Gallup international survey revealed the French to be the "world champions of pessimism." It found that 61 percent of French thought that 2011 would bring economic difficulties compared with an average of 28 percent in the 53 countries surveyed (http://www. bva.fr/fr/sondages/les-perspectives_economiques.2011 .html).

boundaries in various realms (labor market, spatial segregation, and so on), as well as that of symbolic boundaries (pertaining to collective identity) across half a dozen countries. We had hypothesized that overall, perceived discrimination, and by extension, the range and salience of anti-racist strategies, would be greater for Muslim Palestinian citizens of Israel than for Negros in Brazil, for whom interracial sociability and interracial sexual relationships are relatively frequent. We originally viewed the American case as an intermediary one, one in which racism would be very salient, but also one in which intergroup boundaries would be weaker than in Israel, with different patterns of response. Of course, as data collection proceeded, we became increasingly aware of the complexity of the comparison, which would be far less linear and more multidimensional than we had anticipated.

Research Design

The research designs for the three national cases were largely parallel in each site. We conducted interviews with a relatively large number of respondents (by the standards of qualitative methods), with the goals of reaching saturation and of systematically comparing anti-racist strategies across populations. The data collection consisted of open-ended two-hour interviews with working and middle class men and women. In the United States, we conducted interviews in the New York metropolitan area, which presents a full spectrum of social classes for both majority and minority groups. In Brazil and Israel, we chose as major metropolitan centers Rio de Janeiro and Tel Aviv because, similar to New York, they are mixed cities where relationship between members of various ethno-racial groups are frequent and highly routinized without the clear predominance of one particular group (on mixed cities, see Monterescu & Rabinowitz 2007). These metropolises should not be viewed as representative of the national population because there are large regional variations in the spatial distribution of ethno-racial groups in each of the three countries under consideration.

Selection of Respondents

Respondents were limited to native-born interviewees (with the exception of Ethiopian immigrants to Israel). The samples comprise males and females in roughly comparable numbers for each site. Middle class respondents have a two- or four-year college degree and are typically professionals or managers. The working class respondents have a high school degree (or equivalent) but no college degree. The age range is between 20 and 70 years, with small variations across the three countries.

Sampling

Methods for sampling respondents varied slightly cross-nationally in response to the specific challenges associated with locating respondents from various class and racial groups across sites given the local patterns of social and spatial segregation and concentration and cultural factors.

In the United States, middle and working class respondents were recruited using two primary techniques. First, we used a survey research company to recruit participants. The company used census track and marketing data to identify potential participants who met a number of criteria. Then the company mailed letters announcing the study to these randomly sampled African Americans living in northern New Jersey and called potential participants to encourage participation and confirm their eligibility for the study. Second, to increase our sample size, we used snowball sampling techniques, with no more than three referrals per participants. This method was particularly fruitful for recruiting working class respondents and men, who were less likely to respond to requests from our survey research company. Respondents were paid $20 for their participation.

In the case of Brazil, sampling procedures were as follows. Because the number of black middle class individuals remains limited, we identified respondents through firms (e.g., in the sectors of oil and telecommunication), networks (i.e., Facebook for black professionals), and professional associations in addition to some snowball sampling from a wide networks of contacts (with up to three referees per respondents). Working class respondents were identified by a survey firm and paid for their participation (this was not the case for the middle class because we anticipated that this would not create a good context of exchange for the interview).

Finally, in Israel, the sample was constructed through multi-entry snowballing. Interviewers reached out to individuals meeting our various sampling criteria in a large range of settings. They aimed to diversify the composition of the sample in terms by occupation.

Interviews and Data Analysis

In the three sites, most respondents were interviewed by an ethno-racial (but not a class) ingroup member (for all but a few exceptions). The interviews were confidential, conducted in a location of the respondent's choosing, and were recorded with the interviewee's consent. Respondents were questioned on a range of issues concerning what it means to be an "X" (e.g., African American), similarities and differences between them and other ethno-racial groups, their views on social mobility and inequality, past experiences with racism, what they have learned in their family and at school about how to deal with exclusion, and so on. Discourse was elicited by asking respondents to describe past, most recent, and general experiences with racism and discrimination; relationships with coworkers, neighbors, family members, and community members involving discrimination; and the strategies they used for handling these situations.

The interview schedule, first developed for the American case, was carefully adapted to the Brazilian and Israeli cultural contexts. Most importantly in the Brazil case, instead of explicitly asking questions about racial identity, we waited for it to emerge spontaneously in the context of the interview. If it did not, we asked questions on this topic at the end of the interview – the salience of racial identity being one of the key foci of the project.[27] In Israel, we were particularly interested in the articulation between various types of stigmatized identities (blackness, Arab identity, and the backwardness that are often likened in views about the Mizrahis).

The interviews were fully transcribed and systematically coded by a team of research assistants with the help of the qualitative data analysis software Atlas.ti. The coding scheme was developed iteratively by the three national teams of coders, with the American coders taking the lead. This coding scheme includes more than 1,500 entries. A substantial portion of the interviews were coded by more than one person. Codes and a list of interviewees are available upon request.

Studying Responses to Stigmatization

In the three countries, we documented responses to stigmatization by asking interviewees about ideal or "best approach" for dealing with racism, independently of context, their responses to specific racist incidents, the lessons they teach their

---

27 We initially postponed mentioning the centrality of race in our project in our interviews with African Americans, but this created awkward situations because most respondents expected the study to be concerned with this topic.

children about how to deal with racism, their views on the best tools their group has at its disposal to improve their situation, and their reactions to a list of specific strategies. We also considered how these responses vary with a number of social and cultural indicators (including gender, class, age; whether individuals live in integrated or segregated environments; whether racist incidents occurred in public or private spaces and entailed violence, assaults against one's dignity, or institutional discrimination).

References

Alba, R. (2009). Blurring the Color Line: The New Chance for a More Integrated America. Cambridge, MA: Harvard University Press.

Aptheker, H. (1991). Anti-Racism in U.S. History: The First Two Hundred Years. Westport, CT: Greenwood Press

Archer, M. (2003). Structure, Agency and the Internal Conversation. New York: Cambridge University Press.

Bail, C. (2008). The Configuration of Symbolic Boundaries against Immigrants in Europe. American Sociological Review, 73 (1), 37-59.

Bickerstaff, J. (2012). Ethnic Versus Racial Identification: Variation in the Antiracist Responses of First Generation French Blacks. Du Bois Review: Social Science Research on Race, 9(1), 107-31.

Bobo, Lawrence D. 2011. Somewhere between Jim Crow and Post-Racialism: Reflections on the Racial Divide in America Today. Daedalus, 140(2), 11- 31.

Bobo, L. D., Charles, C. Z., Krysan, M. & Simmons, Alicia D. (2012).The Real Record on Racial Attitudes." In Social Trends in the United States 1972-2008: Evidence from the General Social Survey, edited by Peter V. Marsden (pp. 38-83). Princeton, NJ: Princeton University Press.

Boltanski, L. & Chiapello, E. (1999). Le nouvel esprit du capitalisme. Paris: Gallimard.

Bouchard, G. (2009). Collective Imaginaries and Population Health. In Successful Societies: How Institutions and Culture Affect Health, ed. by Peter A. Hall and Michèle Lamont (pp. 169-200). New York: Harvard University Press.

Bourdieu, P. (1998). The Essence of Neo-liberalism. Le Monde Diplomatique. http://mondediplo.com/x99 8/12/o8bourdieu.

Brubaker, R. (2009). Ethnicity, Race, and Nationalism. Annual Review of Sociology, 35, 21-42.

Brubaker, R. & Cooper, F. (2000). Beyond Identity. Theory and Society, 29, 1-47.

Cassidy, O'Connor, Howe, C. & Warden, D. (2004). Perceived Discrimination and Psychological Distress: The Role of Personal and Ethnic Self-Esteem. Journal of Counseling Psychology, 51(3), 329-39.

Chauvel, L. (2010). Le destin des générations structure sociale et cohortes en France du XXè siècle aux années 2000. Paris: Presses Universitaires de France.

Clark, R., Anderson, N. B., Clark, V. R. & Williams, D. R. (1999). Racism as a Stressor for African Americans: A Biopsychosocial Model. American Psychologist, 54(10), 805-16.

Cornell, S. & Hartman, D. (1997). Ethnicity and Race. Making Identity in a Changing World. Thousand Oaks, CA: Pine Forge Press.

Crocker, J., Major, B. & Steele, C. (1998). Social Stigma. In Handbook of Social Psychology, ed by D. T. Gilbert, S. T. Fiske & G. Lindzey (eds). Boston: McGraw-Hill.

Dieckhoff, A. (2003). The Invention of a Nation: Zionist Thought and the Making of Modern Israel. New York: Columbia University Press.

Emmenegger, P., Häusermann, S., Palier, B. & Seeleib-Kaiser, M. (2011). The Age of Dualization: The Changing Face of Inequality in De-industrializing Societies. New York: Oxford University Press.

Essed, P. (1991). Understanding Everyday Racism: An Interdisciplinary Theory. London: Sage Publications.

Eyerman, R. (2002). Cultural Trauma: Slavery and the Formation of African American Identity. Cambridge, UK: Cambridge University Press.

Feagin, J. R. & Sikes, M.P. (1994). Living with Racism: The Black Middle Class Experience. Boston: Beacon.

Fischer, C. (2010). Made in America. A Social History of American Character and Culture. Berkeley: California University Press.

Fleming, C., Lamont, M., & Welburn, J. (2012). Responding to Stigmatization and Gaining Recognition: Evidence from Middle Class and Working Class African-Americans." Ethnic and Racial Studies, 35(3): 400-17.

Fraser, N. & Honneth, A. (2003). Redistribution or Recognition? A Political-Philosophical Exchange. London: Verso.

Frazier, F. (1957). The Black Bourgeoisie: The Book That Brought the Shock of Self-Revelation to Middle-Class Blacks in America. New York: Free Press Paperbacks.

Frederick, M. (2010). Rags to Riches. Religion, the Media and the Performance of Wealth in a Neoliberal Age. In C. Greenhouse (ed.), Ethnographies of Neoliberalism (pp. 221-37). Philadelphia: University of Pennsylvania Press.

Giddens, A. (1991). Modernity and Self-Identity: Self and Society in the Late Modern Age. Cambridge, UK: Polity Press.

Goffman, E. (1963). Stigma. New York: Simon and Schuster.

Greenhouse, C. (2009). Ethnographies of Neo-liberalism. Philadelphia: University of Pennsylvania Press.

Greenhouse, C. (2011). The Paradox of Relevance: Citizenship and Ethnography in the United States. Philadelphia: University of Pennsylvania Press.

Guetzkow, J. (2010). Beyond Deservingness: Congressional Discourse on Poverty, 1964-1996. Annals of the American Academy of Political and Social Sciences, 629, 173-99.

Hacker, J. (2006). The Great Risk Shift. New York: Oxford University Press.

Hall, P. A., & Lamont, M. (eds) (2009). Successful Societies: How Institutions and Culture Matter for Health. New York: Cambridge University Press.

Harding, D., Lamont, M., & Small, M. (2010). Reconsidering Culture and Poverty. Special Issue of Annals of the American Academy of Political and Social Sciences, 629, 6-27.

Hearn, A. (2008). Meat, Mask, and Burden: Probing the Contours of the Branded 'Self." Journal of Consumer Culture, 8(2), 197-217.

Hertzman, C., & Boyce, T. (2010). How Experience Gets Under the Skin to Create Gradients In Developmental Health. Annual Review of Public Health, 31, 329-47.

Herzfeld, M. (1996). Cultural Intimacy: Social Poetics in the Nation State. London: Routledge.

Hochschild, J. (1995). Facing Up to the American Dream: Race, Class, and the Soul of the Nation. Princeton, NJ: Princeton University Press.

Honneth, A. (1996). The Struggle for Recognition: The Moral Grammar of Social Conflicts. London: Polity Press.

Ireland, P. R. (2004). Becoming Europe: Immigration, Integration, and the Welfare State. Pittsburgh: University of Pittsburgh Press.

Jenkins, R. (1996). Social Identity. London: Routledge.

Kastoryano, R. (2002). Negotiating Identities: States and Immigrants in France and Germany. Princeton, NJ: Princeton University Press.

Koopmans, R. Statham, P., Giugni, M., & Passy, F. (2005). Contested Citizenship: Immigration and Cultural Diversity in Europe. Minneapolis: University of Minnesota Press.

Krysan, M. (2012). From Color Caste to Color Blind? Contemporary Era Racial Attitudes, 1976-2004. In H.L.Gates et al. (eds), The Oxford Handbook of African American Citizenship (235-278). New York: Oxford University Press.

Kymlicka, W. (2007). Multicultural Odysseys: Navigating the New Global Politics of Diversity. New York: Oxford University Press.

Lamont, M. (1992). Money, Morals, and Manners. the Culture of the French and the American Upper-Middle Class. Chicago: University of Chicago Press.

Lamont, M. (2000). The Dignity of Working Men: Morality and the Boundaries of Race, Class, and Immigration. Cambridge, MA: Harvard University Press.

Lamont, M. (2009). Responses to Racism, Health, and Social Inclusion as a Dimension of Successful Societies. In P. Hall & M. Lamont (eds), Successful Societies: How Institutions and Culture Matter for Health (pp. 151-168). New York: Cambridge University Press.

Lamont, M., & Bail, C. (2005). Sur les Frontières de la Reconnaissance. Les Catégories Internes et Externes de l'Identité Collective. Revue Européenne De Migrations Internationales, 21(2), 61-90.

Lamont, M., & Fleming, C. (2005). Everyday Anti-Racism: Competence and Religion in the Cultural Repertoire of African-American Elite and Working Class. Du Bois Review, 2(1), 29-43.

Lamont, M., & Mizrachi, N. (2012). Ordinary People Doing Extraordinary Things, One Step at the Time: Responses to Stigmatization in Comparative Perspective. Ethnic and Racial Studies, 35(3), 365-81.

Lamont, M, & Molnar, V. (2002). The Study of Boundaries in the Social Sciences. Annual Review of Sociology, 28, 167-95.

Lamont, M., & Thévenot, L. (2000). Rethinking Comparative Cultural Sociology: Repertoires of Evaluation in France and the United States. London and Paris: Cambridge University Press and Presses de la Maison des Sciences de l'Homme.

Lazzarato, M. (2009). Neoliberalism in Action: Inequality, Insecurity, and the Reconstitution of the Social. Theory, Culture and Society, 26(6), 109-33.

Lieberman, E. (2009). Boundaries of Contagion: How Ethnic Politics Have Shaped Governmental Responses to Aids. Princeton, NJ: Princeton University Press.

Link, B. G., & Phelan, J. (2000). Evaluating the Fundamental Cause Explanation for Social Disparities in Health. In C. Bird, P. Conrad P. & A. M. Fremont (eds), Handbook of Medical Sociology (pp. 33-46). Nashville: Vanderbilt University Press.

Mabry, B., & Kiecolt, J. K. (2005). Anger in Black and White: Race, Alienation, and Anger. Journal of Health and Social Behavior, 46(85), 1-101.

Marx, A. (1998). Making Race and Nation: A Comparison of South Africa, the United States and Brazil. Cambridge, UK: Cambridge University Press.

Massey, D. S., & Sánchez, M. R. (2010). Brokered Boundaries: Creating Immigrant Identity in Anti-Immigrant Times. New York: Russell Sage Foundation.

Mizrachi, N., Drori, I., & Anspach, R. (2007). Repertoires of Trust: The Practice of Trust in a Multinational Organization Amid Political Conflict. American Sociological Review, 72, 143-65.

Mizrachi, N., & Herzog, H. (2012). Participatory Destigmatization Strategies among Palestinian Citizens of Israel, Ethiopian Jews and Mizrahi Jews. Ethnic and Racial Studies, 35(3), 418-35.

Mizrachi, N., & Zawdu, A. (2012). Between Global Racial and Bounded Identity: Choice of Destigmatization Strategies among Ethiopian Jews in Israel. Ethnic and Racial Studies, 35(3), 436-452.

Moon, D. (2012). Who am I and Who are We? Conflicting Narratives of Collective Selfhood in Stigmatized Groups. American Journal of Sociology, 117 (5), 1336-70.

Monterescu, D., & Rabinowitz, D. (2007). Mixed Towns/Trapped Communities: Historical Narratives, Spatial Dynamics and Gender Relations in Jewish-Arab Mixed Towns in Israel/Palestine. London: Ashgate Publishing.

Morning, A. (2009). Toward a Sociology of Racial Conceptualization for the 21st Century. Social Forces, 87(3), 1167-92.

Neblett, E. W., Shelton, J. N., & Sellers, R. M. (2004). The Role of Racial Identity in Managing Daily Racial Hassles. In G. Philogene (ed.), Racial Identity in Context: The Legacy of Kenneth Clark. Washington, DC (pp. 77-90). American Psychological Association Press.

O'Brien, E. (2007). Antiracism. In H. Vera & J. Feagin (eds), Handbook of the Sociology of Racial and Ethnic Relation. New York: Springer.

Oliver, M. L. & Shapiro, T.H. (2006). Black Wealth/White Wealth: A New Perspective on Racial Inequality. New York: Routledge.

Oyserman, D., & Swim, J. K. (2001). Social Stigma: An Insider's View." Journal of Social Issues, 57(1), 1-14.

Pachucki, M., Lamont, M., & Pendergrass, S. (2006). Boundary Processes: Recent Theoretical Developments and New Contributions. Poetics, 35(6), 331-51.

Pattillo-McCoy, M. (1999). Black Picket Fences. Privileges and Perils Among the Black Middle Class. Chicago: University of Chicago Press.

Pew Charitable Trust Foundation (2011). Wealth Gaps Rise to Record Highs Between Whites, Blacks and Hispanics." Retrieved from http://www.pewsocialtrends.org/2011/07/26/wealth-gaps-rise-to-record-highs-between-whites-blacks-hispanics/.

Picca, L. H., & Feagin, J. R.(2007). Two-Faced Racism. White in the Backstage and Frontstage. New York: Routledge.

Pierson, P., & Hacker, J. (2010). Winner-Take-All Politics. New York: Simon and Schuster.

Pinel, E. C. (1999). Stigma Consciousness: The Psychological Legacy of Social Stereotypes." Journal of Personality and Social Psychology, 76(1), 114-28.

Pittman, C. (2012). Race, Class, and Social Context: an Examination of the Impact of Race on the Consumption Preferences and Practices of Middle and Working Class African American. Unpublished dissertation, Department of Sociology, Harvard University.

Pollock, M. (2008). Everyday Antiracism: Getting Real About Race. New York: The New Press.

Richland, J. B. (2009). On Neoliberalism and Other Social Diseases: The 2008 Sociocultural Anthropology Year in Review. American Anthropologist, 2, 170-76.

Rivas-Drake, D., Hughes, D., & Way, N. (2008). A Closer Look at Peer Discrimination, Ethnic Identity, and Psychological Well-Being Among Urban Chinese Sixth Graders. Journal of Youth and Adolescence, 37(1), 12-21.

Roth, W. (2012). Race Migrations: Latinos and the Cultural Transformation of Race. Stanford, CA: Stanford University Press.

Sayer, A. (2005). The Moral Significance of Class. New York: Cambridge University Press.
Schudson, M. (1988). How Culture Works. Theory and Society, 18, 153-180.
Sears, D. O., Sidanius, J., & Bobo, L. (eds) (2000). Racialized Politics: The Debate about Racism in America. Chicago: University of Chicago Press.
Shapiro, T. M., & Oliver, M.L. (2006). Black Wealth, White Wealth, A New Perspective on Racial Inequality. London: Routledge.
Sharone, O. (2013). Unemployment Experiences: Job Searching, Interpersonal Chemistry, and Self-Blame. Chicago: University of Chicago Press.
Silva, G. M. D. (2012). Folk Conceptualizations of Racism and Antiracism in Brazil and South Africa. Ethnic and Racial Studies, 35(3), 506-22.
Silva, G. M. D., & Reis, E. (2012). The Multiple Dimensions of Racial Mixture: From Whitening to Brazilian Négritude. Ethnic and Racial Studies, 35(3), 382-99.
Somers, M. (2008). Genealogies of Citizenship. New York: Cambridge University Press.
Son Fling, L. (2012). Responses to Stigmatization: The Moderating Roles of Primary and Secondary Appraisals. Du Bois Review, 9(1), 149-68.
Stephens, N. M., Fryberg, S. A., & Markus, H. R. (2012). It's Your Choice: How the Middle Class Model of Independence Disadvantages Working Class Americans. In Facing Social Class, edited by S. T. Fiske & H. R. Markus (pp. 87-106). New York: Russell Sage Foundation.
Summers-Effler, E. 2002. The Micro Potential for Social Change: Emotion, Consciousness and Social Movement Formation. Sociological Theory, 20, 21-60.
Swidler, A. (1986). Culture in Action: Symbols and Strategies. American Sociological Review, 51, 273-286.
Taylor, C., with commentary by K. A. Appiah, J. Habermas, S. C. Rockefeller, M. Walzer, S. Wolf. (1994). Multiculturalism: Examining the Politics of Recognition. Edited and introduced by Amy Gutman et al. Princeton, NJ: Princeton University Press.
Telles, E E., & Sue, C. A. (2009). Racial Mixture: Boundary Crossing in Comparative Perspectives. Annual Review of Sociology, 35, 129-46.
Tilly, C. (2006). Regimes and Repertoires. Chicago: University of Chicago Press.
Todd, J. (2004). Social Transformation, Collective Categories and Identity Change. Theory and Society, 34(4), 429-63.
Van Dijk, T. A. (1993). Elite Discourse and Racism. Newbury Park, CA: Sage.
Walton, G. M., & Cohen, G. L. (2011). A Brief Social-Belonging Intervention Improves Academic and Health Outcomes for Minority Students. Science 331(6023), 1447-51.
Welburn, J. (2011). Managing Instability: Conceptions of Opportunity and Success among African Americans from Middle-Income Households. PhD dissertation, Harvard University.
Welburn, J. & Pittman, C. (2012). Stop Blaming 'The Man': Perceptions of Inequality and Opportunities for Success in the Obama Era Among Middle Class African-Americans. Ethnic and Racial Studies, 35(3), 523-40.
Wilson, W. J. (1978). The Declining Significance of Race. Chicago: University of Chicago Press.
Wimmer, A. (2008). The Making and Unmaking of Ethnic Boundaries: A Multi-Level Process Theory. American Journal of Sociology, 113(4), 970-1022.
Wimmer, A. & Min, B. (2006). From Empire to Nation-States. Explaining Wars in the Modern World. American Sociological Review, 71(6), 267-97.

Wodak, R. (2001). The Discourse-Historical Approach. In Methods of Critical Discourse Analysis, edited by R. Wodak & M. Meyer. London: Sage.

Wright, M. & Bloemraad, I. (2012). Is There a Trade-Off between Multi- culturalism and Socio-Political Integration? Policy Regimes and Immigrant Incorporation in Comparative Perspective. Perspectives on Politics, 10, 77-95.

Zolberg, A. & Woon, L. L. (1999). Why Islam is Like Spanish: Cultural Incorporation in Europe and the United States. Politics and Society, 27(1), 5-38.

The Resilience of Punctuated Cooperation

Hendrik Vollmer

1 Introduction: resilience as resource and topic

Resilience has become a widely publicized and almost universally accepted end of social and institutional practice and, for social scientists struggling for recognition among competing forms of expertise about vulnerability, risk, and crisis management, concepts of resilience have continued to gain appeal (e.g., Boin & van Eeten 2013, p. 430). Researchers and theorists have set out to identify processes and structures that might strengthen the ability of groups, firms, states, businesses or armies to withstand adversity. The search for resilience has been as much a search for knowledge as it has been a search for virtue – and for results ideally marketable in the form of advice to an enlightened government of resilience (Chandler 2014). In this way, deliberations of what it means to be or to become resilient have been mixed up with arguments about why certain forms of resilience are desirable. As a result, anything ambiguous, risky or bad with respect to the virtue of the concept or its empirical manifestation cannot for long remain an example of 'true' resilience.

To untangle the resulting imbroglio of conceptual and normative, empirical and moral narratives, it is helpful to differentiate between using some understanding of 'resilience' as a resource, on the one hand, and addressing resilience as a topic of inquiry on the other (Zimmerman & Pollner 1971). In the former case, social and institutional practice as much as fellow social scientists tend to be held accountable for discrepancies with respect to an initial concept or benchmark of resilience. That allows marketing expertise, offering consultancy, and cracking down on competing concepts that allegedly cannot live up to 'true' resilience. In the case of considering resilience as a topic, any discrepancy between an initial understanding of resilience and its empirical or conceptual qualification will instead charge the analyst with an obligation to rethink her or his understanding and to mobilize some form of additional knowledge, theory or data in order to account for variations. This offers an opportunity for advancing the social science of resilience academically. Whereas in the former case, the concept of resilience serves as a resource in producing evaluations, advice and blame, in the latter it opens up a space for contributions by different types of social research and theory.

The present contribution will stick with the accountability of the analyst to be on topic rather than with the liability of being in line with some understanding of being 'truly' resilient. The initial understanding of resilience that informs such an effort can be sparse. Initial engagement with the topic requires little more than a suitable set of examples as a slice of subject matter, a bit of common ground to be explored. The minimal understanding to guide such an exploration here will be that resilience is an attribute of individuals or collectives that struggle with but do not succumb to disruptions (e.g. Janssen & Anderies 2007, pp. 45 f.; Weick & Sutcliffe 2007, p. 71; Djalante et al. 2011, p. 3). The slice of subject matter to be explored is offered by a set of phenomena that speak to the topic of resilience by demonstrating actual, although not in any sense ideal, achievements of particular forms of resilience. They indicate resilience as something that members of a collective accomplish through their "practical sense" (Bourdieu 1977, pp. 113 f.; Garfinkel & Sacks 1986, pp. 162-164) rather than by following a guideline or concept of resilience.[1]

This strategy of making observations about resilience with reference to a particular set of examples – and a condition of social life that may be characterized as punctuated cooperation (Vollmer 2013) – is not unlike how contributions to the theory of high reliability have approached their topic: as an empirical fact to be studied in the field by investigating a limited but significant set of examples. Reliability has been investigated as an achievement of organizations that prevail against great odds like, for example, the odds of building a nuclear reactor on a naval vessel that is simultaneously used as an airport for heavily armed jet fighters (Roberts

---

[1] It should be noted that this emphasis on practical sense among participants of social situations is very different from the emphasis on 'resilient populations' that is occasionally found in political and academic discourse (Zebrowski 2014). Resilience as a result of practical sense, it will turn out, associates resilience with differences in strategies across participants, positions and fields, and thus with heterogeneity across members of the collective, which cannot sit well with any 'biopolitical' construction of 'a' population.

1990; Weick & Sutcliffe 2007, pp. 35-41). This orientation has arguably resulted in an understanding of operational reliability that in many respects still outperforms recent conceptualizations of resilience (Aguirre & Best 2015) but, speaking to resilience as a topic rather than using it as a conceptual resource, that is not the issue here. The present contribution will emulate the analytical strategy of high reliability research by looking at how participants of social situations respond to disruptions, at situations of violence, at military organizations, and at nation-states as empirical achievements of resilience against the odds.[2]

The argument to be made about the regular character of such accomplishments of resilience does not to presume these accomplishments to be perfect and can happily acknowledge its limited character with respect to its selection of empirical cases, its use of particular concepts from social theory, and the resulting understanding of resilience. The observations of accomplishments in resilience that are subsequently offered are tenuous and limited – but they are also highly suggestive. The paper proceeds by exploring resilience among participants of disruptive social situations (2.) and then develops an understanding of resilience in participants' strategies that is reiterated with respect to larger social contexts like organizations and nation-states (3.).

If these examples still indicate just one particular type of resilience among, perhaps, many others (e.g., Gunderson 2000, pp. 426 f.; Jaeger 2010, pp. 14 f.; Boin & van Eeten 2013, pp. 431 f.) this will not appear to constitute a particularly rare specimen. The fact that such resilience in strategies emerges in different situations, contexts, aggregations, and on different scales encourages some generalization from the slice of examples toward understanding resilience more generically in terms of distinct distributions of strategies in social fields (4.). In conclusion, this provides further opportunity to consider the position of sociology with respect to resilience as a topic of inquiry and its continued use as a resource in offering consultancy, benchmarks, and evaluations (5.). The switch from investigating a topic in academic research to marketing it as a resource to outsiders and stakeholders will certainly remain an appealing move for any social science competing for expert jurisdiction and research funds in a competitive academic and professional environment. Social scientists, however, would be wiser for *not* pulling it at this point with respect to resilience.

---

2   For a similar approach see Boin and van Eeten (2013).

2 Responding resiliently to disruptiveness

In investigating the bend-but-not-break signature of resilience, social situations among co-present participants offer a paradigmatic focus for understanding how people cope with disruptions without falling prey to them. Closer examination of disruptive situations turns the quest for resilience into a quest for participants' strategies that can subsequently be tracked down in broader social contexts. These strategies refer to sets of moves that are correlated in a regular manner with actual occasions (Vollmer 2013, pp. 65 f.), for example with certain events or with other moves (as in game theoretical matrices), and, more generally, are associated with participants' sense of how to act given their circumstances (Bourdieu 1977, pp. 4-9; Martin 2011, pp. 163-169).

The problem of identifying resilience in strategies that are adopted by participants in responding to disruptions is the apparent variety of disruptive events and activities that participants respond to. The variety of possible circumstances of disruptiveness makes it difficult to immediately derive a general understanding of resilience in strategies from a common measure of success in coping with specific disruptions. For example, if participants face the disruptiveness of, say, an annoying guest at a dinner party, they may respond by taking the person to the side for a talking-to, by calling on those who have brought him or her along to do likewise, or by quietly hoping that a lack of attention will ultimately discourage the trouble-maker from further action. Respective strategies may work more or less well depending, for example, on the age, background, or level of intoxication of the disruptive guest, responses by bystanders (and their age, background, intoxication, etc.), the prior relationship among everybody involved, etc. It is hard to see how any optimism about resiliently dealing with dinner party troublemakers that may or may not result from respective assessments were to translate into expectations of any sort with respect to other settings like, for example, dealings with stone-throwing protesters, club-swinging riot police, or volatility in financial markets. Yet despite the wide variety of social situations in which participants face different sorts of disruptions, despite the different opportunities of response associated with ongoing events and activities, and despite the in any case uneven odds of dealing with disruptions successfully, there is remarkable order in how participants respond to disruptions across situations. It appears reasonable to focus on these regularities first and then come back to the question in which sense these regularities of response, i.e. of strategies of responding to disruptions, allow for some success in dealing with disruptiveness.

Perhaps the sociologically most iconic disruptive situations are the breaching experiments performed by Harold Garfinkel and his students, some of which are in fact quite similar to the annoying dinner guest example (Garfinkel 1967, pp. 35-75). More recently, after the pioneering work of Randall Collins (2008), violent situations have likewise been receiving a lot of attention by social scientists. In social theory, the investigation of critical situations by Giddens (1979, pp. 123-128) has been a common reference point for illustrating the fundamental importance of ontological security in social interaction (Giddens 1984, pp. 60-64). Giddens' investigation in turn has referred extensively to the study of Bruno Bettelheim (1943) about being imprisoned in a concentration camp. Less drastic but still congenial examples of disruptive situations are 'scenes' (Goffman 1963, pp. 185-187) in which embarrassment as a particular species of disruptiveness is employed strategically by certain participants. A first common denominator of these in many respect quite different situations is the tendency among participants to feel a strong sense of boundary between what and who is within the situation and everything and everybody else outside of it. The notorious bystander effect is a manifestation of this sense as it shows that people can be quite close to a situation and still not be 'in.' Those who are in, feel the sense of being in very strongly, something which Goffman (1974, pp. 378 f.) has described as 'engrossment' (Vollmer 2013, pp. 78 f.).

This *strong sense of enclosure* that is common to a wide variety of disruptive situations sometimes results from a physically enforced entrapment, for example, in the case of imprisonment in a concentration camp. Sometimes the sense of being trapped is maintained by the social and psychological forces of being occupied with and absorbed by ongoing action or, on the other side of the boundary, by the caution exercised in not becoming involved. Sometimes, the boundary thus maintained is challenged as when making a 'scene' involves drawing in outsiders that would rather not take part (Goffman 1963, pp. 186 f.). Irrespective of its ultimate source or motivation, the sense of being either 'in' or 'out' is more pronounced in situations of disruptiveness than it is in other walks of everyday life. The experience of disruptions is strongly associated with a sense of being in a situation clearly demarcated from the rest of the world, one in which "situational closure" (Goffman 1963, pp. 151-153) is strong. One may hesitate to call this sense of exposure strategic since it is often associated with a reduced level of opportunity among participants, most notably with respect to exit. But whilst enclosure itself is often not strategic, the sense of enclosure clearly is: it commits participants' attention to a division of the world, orienting them to the significance of where they stand with respect to a disruptive situation, to the significance of exiting and entering this situation, to (possibly) drawing others in, and themselves out – all of which is highly strategic in the sense of finding appropriate moves given present predicaments.

The second common characteristic of participants' responses in different situations of disruptiveness is a convergence of moves within an *endogenous order* that is emerging. While the sense of enclosure appears to impress itself onto participants almost involuntarily and immediately, this process of ordering indicates the contingency of responding to disruptions in gradually establishing a sense of what is going on. Since order within the situation is emergent and not immediate, it makes apparent the selectivity of participants' strategies of response. Participants could, for example, try to reaffirm some normative idea of appropriateness in 'cleaning up' a situation gone wrong, whether by appealing to a standard of behavior or to an external authority. They could also seek to establish order by collecting more information, possibly turning the quest for order into an epistemic, more emphatically cognitive, and, in the aftermath of a disruption, perhaps somewhat forensic endeavor. Or they could call on social relationships with other participants in order to establish order by rallying for some form of collective action. While there is always some overlap of these aspects within the endogenous order of disruptive situations, what is apparent across many disruptive situations is that participants strongly orient to one another. Normative and cognitive aspects of response do play a role, but mostly just to the extent that they can be identified with participants' social relations and respective positions, e.g., as fellow passengers, soldiers, or friends. "We never talk this way, do we?" is a typical response by the subjects of Garfinkel's breaching experiments (Garfinkel 1967, p. 44). Rather than appealing to general values, norms or bodies of knowledge, participants tend to appeal to one another, their respective positions, memberships, and social ties.

In achieving some sense of order within disruptive situations, participants thus focus on the relational rather than the normative or cognitive aspects of what is going on (Vollmer 2013, pp. 91-94, 151-155, 217-224). The clearest example of this is, perhaps, the unique endogenous order within situations of violence. Such situations are always disruptive, regardless of the motivation, the commitment, or the training of participants (Collins 2008, pp. 19 f., 39-82). There is, as Collins discusses at length, always an element of "confrontational tension" in violent situations as participant fail to find a basis of mutual entrainment. Situations of violence are typically brief encounters among nervous participants. The rare instances in which participants do appear to come to grips with violence are characterized by grave one-sidedness (strong perpetrators against helpless victims), by a highly asymmetric rush of events (experienced as a 'tunnel of violence'), or by both in what Collins (2008, pp. 83-133) calls "forward panic." If participants successfully establish order in a situation of violence, they almost always do so by segregating into groups and by taking stratified positions with respect to the action. It is not a particular motivation to be violent but participants' attentiveness to unique positions of strength, weakness, membership or status that infuses violent situations with some degree of order and stability (Collins 2008, pp. 371-462). Positions, rather than norms or some shared understanding of what violence would be about appear as viable orientations. As with the sense of enclosure, neither violence nor the endogenous order within disruptive situations per se are strategic in the sense of calculated choices. The sense of endogenous order, however, is strategic in both the technical sense – of correlating moves to actual occasions and with respect to positions, membership in groups, or differences in strength – and the common sense of 'strategically' doing yourself a favor – in effectively orienting participants to one another as friend, foe, leader, or fellow sufferer.

Furthermore, as Collins (2008, pp. 10-19) shows in contrasting violent situations with the persistent collective myths that exist about them (in which violence tends to be depicted as a well-motivated and prolonged struggle among competent fighters), the endogenous order within disruptive situations tends to be very much at odds with the understanding of the situation from without. Almost all situations of disruptiveness, at least if they are of any interest to outsiders, are subject to a process of *exogenous normalization* in which they are being reframed time and again. This turns them into episodes within a longer history of events in which their significance (whether as the 'battle of somewhere' or 'that evening when my wife made me suffer for her sociology class') is redrawn.

Conspicuously, the inherent selectivity of such retrospective re-ordering is very different from the one that is apparent in the endogenous order within disruptive situations. It is in exogenous normalization that cognitive, intellectual, and forensic aspects are brought to the fore in understanding the situation as a distinct episode in a larger chain of 'events.' The emphasis is on making sense in terms of hard-won, ideally somewhat proven, facts and 'lessons learned.' Some sense of position and membership, for example when blame is directed at certain groups and individuals, will often be involved in the resulting narratives but, contrary to what goes on within disruptive situations, it is always blame begging for evidence of guilt, as in the courts of post-disaster or post-war tribunals. In the normalization of disruptions, the cognitive, informational and factual aspect about who did what when to which effect is dominant (Vollmer 2013, pp. 95-102, 143 f., 182).

Considering this lack of correspondence between endogenous and exogenous order with respect to situations of disruptiveness, it is not surprising that there is little affinity between how insiders and outsiders orient to these situations and that, even much later, there is often little reconciliation of respective recollections. Bruno Bettelheim characterizes survivors' memory of being imprisoned in a Nazi concentration camp as "unforgettable but unreal" (Bettelheim 1943: 433). "Unforgettable" means: still virtually present as a recollection; "but unreal" means:

without connection to the actually present situation and the broader social context in which it is taking place. In the bigger picture of how the larger collective of participants within and beyond disruptive situations deals with the fallout of disruptiveness, this indicates a *dissociation* between situations of disruptiveness and the wider social world. This dissociation takes place in terms of enclosing participants within a disruptive situation and, in this manner, as an externality of participants' association within the situation. It prevails because productions of social order and context within and beyond the disruptive situations tend to be very different. Association within and dissociation without reinforce one another: the enclosure of situations of disruptiveness allows for strong differences between endogenous and exogenous production of order, the endogenous focus on the relational aspects of position, membership, or status emphasizes the specificity of the local order among the co-present while the exogenous production of context generalizes toward some broader (e.g., historical, biographical, or moral) significance of the disruption. The resulting incompatibility perpetuates the dissociation between disruptive situations and the rest of the world.

This picture of enclosure, endogenous order and association, exogenous normalization and dissociation is remarkably coherent across different situations of disruptiveness, and it is the outcome of a particular distribution of strategies among participants within and beyond these situations. These strategies are associated with different types of exposure to and concerns with particular disruptions. In understanding their association with resilience, the question of success now finally requires some consideration. Looking at two different (endogenous and exogenous) sets of strategies that are part of a broader, and apparently somewhat regular, distribution, the discussion of how these strategies allow individual participants to prevail needs to be complemented by a discussion of how they affect the larger collective.

In terms of individual coping and endurance, it clearly makes a lot of sense that there should be a marked difference of strategies between insiders and outsiders: the cognitive style of outsiders fits well with their role as bystanders that try to make out the significance of what is happening without getting more precariously involved; the relational style of insiders appears well suited to cope with events that challenge their routines, their knowledge and understanding of what to expect: if you have no idea what is going on, you may be well advised to look at what other people are doing and to find and hold your ground (position, status, tie) with respect to them and to ongoing events. There also appear to be collective benefits to this distribution of strategies: disruptiveness is truncated and set apart from those not directly exposed to it as the situation is closed off and its impact on further activity is made subject to reflective control by outsiders. If you consider the ultimate test of resilience to reside in the individual and collective ability to endure, then the roots of an evolutionary argument are apparent: individual exposure is minimized, a dynamic of association focusses those exposed on finding allies, otherwise the fallout on social order is contained and normalized through a dynamic of dissociation as life goes back to normal – or so it appears.

3 Extensions of punctuated cooperation

For the same reasons that association and dissociation result in containment, this distribution of strategies may encourage an underestimation of fallout if too much weight is given to collective normalizations of disruptions (Vollmer 2013, pp. 206-213). While the endogenous social order of punctuated cooperation quickly fades into the realm of the "unforgettable but unreal," life goes on for those exposed to it, and it goes on for them within the larger collective. Participants who were exposed to disruptions and to the endogenous order of disruptive situations may not nearly as quickly and smoothly be normalized as the retrospective understanding of the episode by others. Therefore, as life goes on, the strategies associated with the endogenous order of punctuated cooperation will not remain completely confined to the original situation of disruptiveness as the participants of this situation will not be either. As participants are reabsorbed by the collective, they confront a cost of the dissociation of disruptiveness within the collective in finding little correspondence of what for them is unforgettable with the reality that surrounds them. And they will continue to interact and decide, informing and irritating others. As life does not get fully back to normal for them, so it may not for whom they meet.

The sociological significance of the homecoming soldier unable to relay his experience but still very much impressed by it (Schutz 1964, p. 114), however, is not merely the diffusion of some residual disruptiveness among family, friends, and colleagues. Of greater sociological significance is perhaps the fact that the distribution of strategies that contains and dissociates disruptiveness is apparently not a temporary fix wrapped around single situations but a pattern that transcends the collective as a whole, from the battlefield to the kitchen, office and living room. As far as violence is concerned, there is a distribution of strategies associated with the endogenous order of making violence happen and with normalizing it exogenously that is neither confined to a single instance nor to a single set of participants or to a single collective into which participants are reabsorbed; not just one soldier, and not just one army, not just one family and one 'general public' that reiterates dissociation; the pattern of distributed strategies for the social containment of violence has, for all intents and purposes, become global. It is backed by the best known, most appreciated and most lamented mega-formations within contemporary social order – ruling bureaucracies incorporated into a global system of nation-states.

The endogenous production of order among participants of violent situations can be summarized in the rationale 'associate and stratify,' which means that the attentiveness to the relational that generally characterizes the endogenous order of punctuation cooperation is manifest, in situations of violence, as a concern with membership in coalitions and the comparative strength of positions. Again, taken as a strategy with some benefit for individuals coping with ongoing events, this seems perfectly reasonable: find out who your allies are and watch out who is likely to prevail! The endogenous outcome of this is that participants are joined in coalitions in which the actively violent are backed by a supporting cast that is audience to the action; the ability to bring about and sustain violence thus becomes an expression of situational stratification (Collins 2008, pp. 448-462). Ruling bureaucracies express this outcome of associating and stratifying on a more permanent basis across situations, episodes and settings. The modern nation-state itself can be regarded as the evolutionary outcome of organizing a support network for specialists in collective violence respectively associated and stratified, reared in competition with other organized and stratified support networks (Martin 2009, pp. 322-327; Tilly 1992). In the process of state formation, the means of violence are monopolized by a select few; hierarchies of positions are set up that regulate access to these means; a public is created as an audience of state action (which in times of peace proceeds to find other problems to concern itself with); a generalized form of membership and identity is established that segregates people into competing pockets of state citizens, and again into those well-equipped and institutionally supported and those unprepared, legitimately unfit and inadmissible to violent action. As participants of violent situations associate and stratify, so do citizens within nation-states, and nations-states within the system of competing nation-states (Tilly 1992, pp. 161-191). The rationale of association and stratification appears to inform people just as much as groups, armies, and states (Vollmer 2013, pp. 195-202).

That this is actually a reasonable orientation not only for those directly exposed to violent situations but for those orchestrating battles among aggregate units, not at least considering the debilitating dynamics of 'hot' and 'cold' military conflict, is altogether not clear at all. That the organization of collective violence contains of subset of insiders in stratified hierarchies in which everybody else remains an outsider to violent engagements appears like a scaling-up of strategies from violent situations to military bureaucracies and nation-states. The collective fitness of this strategy appears to be less the result of a particularly enlightened understanding of what collective violence is, what it should be about or what should be done about it, and more a reiteration of the 'enclose, dissociate, and make subject to normalization by outsiders' principle of punctuated cooperation discussed so far. Given the dissociation between endogenous and exogenous strategies of response, it may hardly be surprising that the collective understanding of violence and warfare has remained archetypal, if not altogether moronic in its concern with strength, size and belonging. While it would be tough to argue that strategies would translate from overcoming violent situations to preparing for or fighting wars by virtue of being sound at just about any scale, it is hard to question the resilience of these strategies against the background of the global triumph of the nation-state pandemic of which both the endogenous strategies and exogenous normalizations of collective violence are strikingly uniform correlates. If anything, the apparent dullness of the arrangement makes its historical resilience even more impressive.

In terms of sheer scale and uniformity, the extended and in many respects scale-invariant distribution pattern of strategies for coping with situations of violence is clearly a unique extension of punctuated cooperation. Yet a perhaps more convincing indication of the particular resilience offered by perpetuating the distribution of strategies sketched in the preceding sections can be attained if the general pattern of association and dissociation is identified in more unambiguously 'positive' examples that are already associated with the topic. The celebrated examples of high-reliability organizations with their members collaborating in small pockets of interlocked "heedful interrelating" (Weick and Roberts 1993, pp. 368-383) and "mindfulness" (Weick and Sutcliffe 2007, pp. 39-41) offer a convenient connection. Again there is an endogenous production of context among co-present participants that mobilizes their ability to associate and relate to one another. In this instance, however, the claim is not that this is a good strategy of coping with disruptions (or, for that matter, for inflicting them on others) but a good strategy for averting them (Roberts 1990, p. 168; Weick and Roberts 1993, pp. 366-368). With respect to resilience, this connection cannot be but good news: it indicates a possible convergence of strategies of response and strategies of prevention. The weak spot of such an argument is, regrettably, the exogenous normalization of high reliability. Just like the civilian control of nation-state armies can hardly be guaranteed by a thorough-going normalization of violence through the narrative of war stories or high-brow historical narrative, to maintain that certain organizations can be run with impressive reliability by insiders will provide little intelligence about what is actually going on inside these organizations.[3] As failure is surprisingly rare in the case of high-reliability organizations that follow the pattern of association

---

3   It is interesting to re-read Weick and Sutcliffe (2007, pp. 53-58) in this respect.

and dissociation, so is effective external control. One may interpret this as a sign of resilience, or merely as a delayed reckoning (Clarke 1993).

For a final example, the signature of punctuated cooperation and its particular distribution of strategies can also be identified and associated with resilience in the much discussed phenomenon of groupthink under conditions of stress and threat. Stress and threat are good examples of the changing and endogenous character of disruptiveness: both concern disruptions that feel very real to participants of certain situation but may actually never take place, like almost missed assignments that, as far as outsiders are concerned, just look like having been accomplished perfectly on time. Again, most examples of groupthink are instances of participants attending more to positions, membership and status than to other informational cues in facing disruptiveness (Janis 1982, pp. 174-197; Staw et al. 1981, pp. 507-511). In the case of groupthink, the literature has largely focused on the biased nature of groupthink as an interesting shortcoming of participants' strategies. But these strategies are also the basis of responses that may well be considered resilient as participants focus on well-trained performances in bringing about collective action (Janis 1982, pp. 256-259). This capability of being able to act is surely critical, not at least since research on stress has found tipping points toward breakdown to draw nearer if stress responses are failing to resolve sources of disruptiveness, even if they are low-level ones like future assignments or unmade decisions (Rudolph and Repenning 2002).

Assessing groupthink in terms of a pathological bias within responding to disruptiveness requires bracketing the fact that the groups under study are often under severe outside pressure to produce, often in situations in which taking the time to carefully reflect and evaluate all the information potentially 'at disposal' is not an option. In experimental settings, for example, subjects are often asked to muster their resolve and challenged to produce outcomes while experimenters proceed to make these tasks more difficult by interrupting, side-tracking or luring subjects into blind alleys. If a group is charged by a larger collective or a single experimenter to come up with decisions under pressure, groupthink allows insiders to accomplish just that, and leaves outsiders free to review or denounce it. In this way the groupthink phenomenon exemplifies the recurrent pattern of endogenous association, exogenous normalization, and dissociation.

These observations do not suggest any kind of evaluative assessment with respect to the particular form of resilience thus explored but they indicate that its signature distribution of strategies is quite common across different situations, recurrent across different contexts, and apparently somewhat successful in brute evolutionary terms. The organization of collective violence in nation-states is perhaps the best example of a specific pattern of resilience repeated on different scales across larger collectives. Similarities in the resulting distribution of strategies are also obvious with respect to subtler disruptions like those associated with stress and groupthink. Furthermore, the still very prominent, if not paradigmatic, understanding of high reliability organizations fits the general pattern of endogenous association and dissociation. The example of collective violence provides an idea about the specific capability thus afforded – a specialized capacity to engage with a particular type of disruption – and so do the claims of high-reliability theory. Just like groupthink, both also suggest specific externalities of such resilience, not at least with respect to the fact that the rest of the collective is left with very little control of this capability. While this has been criticized in discussions of high-reliability theory (Clarke 1993) and continues to be the bread and butter of much research in social psychology, it nowadays appears somewhat underappreciated with respect to collective violence. That, for example, the remarkable capacity of 'cohesive' military units to keep on fighting even when there is little overall sense to it (Shils and Janowitz 1948) may correspond to a certain lack of control and receptiveness to external information only tends to be perceived as problematic once soldiers do something 'truly' nasty, like 'fragging' their officers (Savage and Gabriel 1976, pp. 346-350).

If dissociation implies a certain lack of control, this certainly has to be as disconcerting with respect to risky technology as it is with respect to the use of physical force. If we continue to treat resilience as a topic rather than a resource, however, it can hardly mean that in this case we are not looking at resilience its proper form. It means that we need to probe further in order to understand the relationship between resilience in strategies and resilience in broader social formations – and that we should be prepared to expect certain costs to be associated with this.

4 Resilience in social fields

The prior discussion has suggested that the pattern of association and dissociation brings about effects that are structural in the sense of establishing boundaries between insiders and outsiders, which are sensed as constraints on experience and action. As a result, what somebody will understand about a distinct source of disruptiveness will in an important respect be a correlate of position on either side of the boundary that separates association within from dissociation without. The difference between insiders and outsiders places distinct limitations on participants: one group of participants is too close to the source of disruptiveness to adequately contextualize it in the broader setting (e.g., the war that is already lost or the experimental design of a social scientist); the other group of participants is some distance removed and often has some time to invest in normalizing events and activities exogenously. Understanding the gains and limitations of resilience against the background of this rift across positions with respect to particular disruptions would be ill-advised to take one position or segment of positions within the collective as a point of reference for producing generalized statements. One has to look at both the endogenous association of participants, on the one hand, and at the exogenous normalization and dissociation on the other, in order to understand the collective containment of disruptiveness; in the same manner, an assessment of resilience in terms of distributed strategies requires to investigate not only the regularity within strategies but also the regularity of how they are distributed.

A suitable understanding of resilience therefore needs to take into account the association of strategies with distinct positions. If the arrangement of these positions is somewhat regular, as the previous discussion of distributed strategies has been suggesting, resilience may most appropriately be analyzed in terms of strategies distributed across positions in *social fields*. The notion of field has recently been getting a lot of attention and a lot of social and organizational research is now using it in some form. One of the reasons for this is that use of the concept bridges the gulf between scholarship about social differentiation and scholarship on social inequality (Emirbayer and Johnson 2008; Fligstein and MacAdam 2012, pp. 28 f.). Another is that it can refer to the works one of the most eminent social theorists, Pierre Bourdieu (1977, pp. 184 ff., 1984, pp. 226 ff.; Lizardo 2012, pp. 240-242). There is no space here for an extended discussion of the concept or its lineage (instead see Martin 2003, 2011, pp. 244 ff., 268 ff.), but two aspects of social fields need to be singled out since they are of particular importance with respect to the topic of resilience: firstly, that the existence of fields is associated with some regularity in strategies distributed across positions; secondly, that the 'fieldness' of any field is gradual.

A field exists to the extent that occupants of a set of positions are, in their perceptions and actions, subject to a certain field-specific gravity, whether this gravity is defined by a distribution of capital across positions (Bourdieu 1985, p. 724), the particular imperatives of action associated with social objects (Martin 2011, pp. 270 f.), or by some collectively shared understanding of the field, its set of positions, purpose or rules (Fligstein and MacAdam 2012, p. 9). Irrespective of considerable variance with respect to such issues of definition, "one of the central claims of field theory, *on which all else rests*" is that "persons feel the imperatives of action associated with any situation" (Martin 2011, p. 307, emphasis is mine). The existence of a field thus rests on the fact that there exists a 'feel for the game' across occupants of positions and various situations. Seen from within any situation, the 'fieldness' of the field derives from the extent to which "patterns of local alignment (…) become globally organized" (Martin 2011, p. 307). Such fieldness is therefore in an important sense a result of regularity across strategies and could be seen to emerge from such regularity (cf. Vollmer 2013, p. 65 f.), for example, when people regularly recognize opportunities for making trades, when they acquire a sense of taste in 'properly' appreciating a work of art – or the heedfulness required by working on a flight deck.

Against this background, it is as if punctuated cooperation induces a localized field effect by drawing together specific positions and by segregating them from the rest of the collective, both within disruptive situations and exogenously. The former field effect may be short-lived and confined to the run of a single disruptive situation[4] but it can also be perpetuated, as among battle-seasoned troops and in high-reliability organization. The distinctness of the field effect, i.e. the fieldness of the field, is clearly felt by participants in both cases, whether in terms of the gravity of 'engrossment' within and the repulsion or distant attraction of gazing from without in facing disasters, or in terms of "collective mind" on flight decks (Weick and Robert 1993, pp. 364-368). The field effect associated with exogenous normalization is a direct result of the collective attention given to what first becomes a historical episode or distinct 'event' (Sewell 2005, pp. 100-103). As the example of collective violence demonstrates impressively, this exogenous field effect may at times impress itself on a very large scale of positions. The twin character of field effects – one larger field impressed by exogenous normalization and a smaller one produced by the more contained endogenous order of coping with disruptions – appears to be associated with the pattern of association and dissociation more generally. This distribution of strategies associated with punctuated cooperation tends to bring about not one, but two distinct field effects through which disruptiveness is contained within the gravity of a smaller field while actitivites in a larger field relate to this in a normalizing manner, for example through historical, bureaucratic, legal or political discourse.

If the particular resilience of punctuated cooperation is thus embedded in and reinforced by the shape of social fields and can as such be properly addressed as 'structural' in sealing disruptions off, making them the concern of the limited number of inadvertently exposed or deliberately seasoned participants in positions

---

4   Note that even Harold Garfinkel (1967, p. 58), clearly not somebody to postulate lightly a sense of structure in social situations, associates the situational closure involved in successfully performing breaching experiments with the temporary existence of a field: "I designed a procedure to breach these expectancies while satisfying the three conditions under which their breach would presumably produce confusion, i.e., that the person could not turn the situation into a play, a joke, an experiment, ad deception, and the like, or, in Lewinian terminology, that he could not 'leave the field'."

that are temporarily or enduringly bracketed, this kind of resilience comes at an evident price: The fact that disruptiveness does not affect the collective as a whole but members with different degrees of exposure and participation establishes incompatibilities of access, experience, action, and divergence of understanding. Different positions in different fields practice different strategies of response with different opportunities of perception, learning, and control. The larger collective essentially makes dealing with a specific type of disruption the special task assigned to a distinct set of positions. It may equip occupants with special means of coping (weapons, swimming nuclear-reactor powered airports, etc.) but neither will it share the experience associated with coping nor have an altogether appropriate understanding of it. The limits of control with respect to a bureaucratically entrenched system of military violence (Lasswell 1941; Melman 1997) and the governance of disaster-prone technology by insiders (Sagan 1993; Clarke 1993) thus correspond to systematic limits of collective cognition in segmented social fields.

The gravest problem with governing the effects of this kind of resilience in social fields is not that people would be generally inclined to exploit their positions unilaterally but that "it makes little sense to put people in a distorted world and ask them to see straight" (Martin 2011, p. 230). The field offers a *cognitive economy* that allows occupants of position to focus attention on what is relevant in holding their ground (Martin 2011, pp. 315-317). Stress responses are a good illustration of how the endogenous order of punctuated cooperation makes use of such cognitive economy in focusing participants on well-trained responses (Vollmer 2013, pp. 120-129), and such coping can be supported by their positions within a field and the resources these positions give them access to (e.g., in terms of social or symbolic capital). Making use of this cognitive economy backs up the ability to cope and thus contributes to resilience. Increasing resilience therefore cannot mean streamlining strategies of response in order to liberate them from the 'bias' of specific positions; it needs to work with the cognitive economy of social fields in improving on a given containment of disruptions. The challenge is to make use of distributed cognition in a manner that preserves the heterogeneity of strategies that correlates with resilience in distributed strategies and social fields.

If some degree of "structural secrecy" (Vaughan 1996, pp. 238-277) is therefore on the price tag for resilience in social fields, it will be crucial to manage and, if possible, reduce this cost without destabilizing the boundaries which allow one set of participants to cope and the others to contain, normalize, reflect or ignore. Rather than destabilizing these boundaries and questioning the heterogeneity of coping with disruptiveness, enlightened governance would need to make sure that collective resources of coping and intelligence which is hidden from decision-makers are effectively mobilized. This is evidently a tricky business of both accommodating some degree of structural secrecy and overcoming it during times when mutual orientation and exchange of information are needed. The vulnerability of respective communication across different segments of social fields to issues of timing and misunderstanding among heterogeneous parties is evident (Vaughan 1996, pp. 278-333). However, the risks of intervening across boundaries, fields and sub-fields into complex ecologies of response and learning in the name of improving on prior resilience are hardly less complex (Kette and Vollmer 2015).

5 Conclusion

Such considerations refer back to concepts of resilience as a resource in assessments of abilities to cope with disruptiveness. The particular type of resilience explored here suggests caution with respect to such assessments since it indicates an ability to cope that is entrenched in distributed strategies and structures, is tied up with managing some the most fatal means of destruction available today and continues to pose a challenge to sociological investigation. The resilience of punctuated cooperation points to strategies and structures that bring about and make use of heterogeneity in containing disruptiveness. This resilience places limitations on the access to and knowledge of disruptions subject to strategies and positions, which affects the external control of and collective learning from disruption and disaster, much of which remains limited to subsets of participants, particular positions, fields and subfields. These limitations need to be understood in terms of distributions across positions which to a certain extent appear complementary with respect to what occupants know and cannot know, control and cannot control. Collectively, this distribution and correlated heterogeneity are associated with the ability to cope and prevail.

It is one thing to criticize the difficulties of exerting influence on the military-industrial complex or the lack of control over the handling of nuclear weapons or nuclear reactors but it is another to stop practitioners in their tracks with external directives. The pattern of association, containment, and dissociation in coping with disruptions pulls apart strategies as well as positions, and the question is not merely whether these currents can be rerouted to converge on standards of resilience deemed generally desirable: it needs to be about the extent to which they should (cf. Janssen and Anderies 2007). If there is a general lesson to be drawn from the resilience of punctuated cooperation toward a general understanding of resilience in strategies and structures, it will have to include an argument in favour of heterogeneity. Not one truly resilient, but different strategies of coping make for containment; not one field, but a number of fields to support both the engrossment by and normalization of disruptions, to allow for both deep involvement and detached forensics. Such heterogeneity is evident at the elementary level of social situations in which some confront disruptiveness while others gaze idly and it is recurrent in the heterogeneity across fields and positions in cases in which coping with certain disruptions is extended and perpetuated. The evident complexity and ambiguity that results from this heterogeneity is a good reason for keeping open the topic of resilience for various kinds of conceptual and empirical engagement (Boin and van Eeten 2013, p. 443) and it cautions against narrowing the discussion down prematurely in the name of all-embracing concepts or benchmarks of resilience. Against the idea that resilience cannot be bad, use of the concept might well "apply to forces that are constructive as well as detrimental for human survival" (Kaufmann 2013, p. 67) once the concept is thoroughly integrated into social theory. Parts of the requisite theory, not at least with respect to understanding field effects on participants' experience and action have yet to be fully developed, and it is evident that producing the requisite data necessitates a re-assessment of both the ontology and methodology of social research (Martin 2011; Vollmer 2013, pp. 227-233).

One could argue that in the meantime there will still be much to gain and little to lose in offering at least some expertise on resilience on the market for academic advice. Benefiting from the still fluid collective understanding of resilience, there are ample opportunities of 'disowning' a calamity (Downer 2014) in the event of having placed the wrong bets. The stifling effects of using narrower notions of resilience as a resource in placing these bets, however, may ultimately be more severe on academics themselves than on their reputation in the market for 'true' resilience. Rather than trying to cut down the heterogeneity of empirical and theoretical intelligence about resilience, its heterogeneous strategies and structures, it may be the best bet for both the social practice and the social science of resilience to keep the topic open for the broad engagement it will continue to require.

References

Aguirre, B. A. & Best, E. (2015). How Not to Learn. Resilience in the Study of Disaster. In: H. Egner, M. Schorch & M. Voss (eds) Learning and Calamities: Practices, Interpretations, Patterns (pp. 216-232). New York and London: Routledge.

Bettelheim, B. (1943). Individual and Mass Behavior in Extreme Situations. Journal of Abnormal and Social Psychology 38, 417-452.

Boin, A. & van Eeten, M. J. G. (2013). The Resilient Organization. A Critical Appraisal. Public Management Review 15, 429-445.

Bourdieu, P. (1977). Outline of a Theory of Practice. Cambridge: Cambridge University Press.

Bourdieu, P. (1984). Distinction. A Social Critique of the Judgement of Taste. London: Routledge & Kegan Paul.

Bourdieu, P. (1985). The Social Space and the Genesis of Groups. Theory and Society 14, 723-744.

Chandler, D. (2014). Beyond Neoliberalism: Resilience, the New Art of Governing Complexity. Resilience 2, 47-63.

Clarke, L. (1993). Drs. Pangloss and Strangelove Meet Organizational Theory: High Reliability Organizations and Nuclear Weapons Accidents. Sociological Forum 8, 675-689.

Collins, R. (2008). Violence. A Micro-sociological Theory. Princeton, Oxford: Princeton University Press.

Djalante, R., Holley, C. & Thomalla, F. (2011). Adaptive Governance and Managing Resilience to Natural Hazards. International Journal of Disaster Risk Science 2 (4), 1-14.

Downer, J. (2014). Disowning Fukushima: Managing the Credibility of Nuclear Reliability Assessment in the Wake of Disaster. Regulation & Governance 8, 287-309.

Emirbayer, M. & Johnson, V. (2008). Bourdieu and Organizational Analysis. Theory and Society 37, 1-44.

Fligstein, N. & MacAdam, D. (2012). A Theory of Fields. Oxford: Oxford University Press.

Garfinkel, H. (1967). Studies in Ethnomethodology. Englewood Cliffs, NJ: Prentice-Hall.

Garfinkel, H. & Sacks, H. (1986). On Formal Structures of Practical Actions. In: H. Garfinkel (ed.), Ethnomethodological Studies of Work (pp. 160-193). London and New York: Routledge & Kegan Paul.

Giddens, A. (1979). Central Problems in Social Theory. Action, Structure and Contradiction in Social Analysis. Berkeley and Los Angeles: University of California Press.

Giddens, A. (1984). The Constitution of Society: Outline of the Theory of Structuration. Oxford: Polity Press.

Goffman, E. (1963). Behavior in Public Places. Notes on the Social Organization of Gatherings. New York: Free Press.

Goffman, E. (1974). Frame Analysis. An Essay on the Organization of Experience. New York: Harper & Row.

Gunderson, L. H. (2000). Ecological Resilience – in Theory and Application. Annual Review of Ecology and Systematics 31, 425-439.

Jaeger, C. (2010). Risk, Rationality, and Resilience. International Journal of Disaster Risk Science 1 (1), 10-16.

Janis, I. L. (1982). Groupthink. Psychological Studies of Policy Decisions and Fiascoes. Boston: Houghton Mifflin.

Janssen, M. A. & Anderies, J. M. (2007). Robustness Trade-offs in Social-Ecological Systems. International Journal of the Commons 1, 43-65.
Kaufmann, M. (2013). Emergent Self-Organisation in Emergencies: Resilience Rationales in Interconnected Societies. Resilience 1, 53-68.
Kette, S. & Vollmer, H. (2015). Normalization and Its Discontents. Organizational Learning from Disaster. In: H. Egner, M. Schorch & M. Voss (eds.) Learning and Calamities: Practices, Interpretations, Patterns (pp. 181-198). New York and London: Routledge.
Lasswell, H. D. (1941). The Garrison State. American Journal of Sociology 46, 455-468.
Lizardo, O. (2012). The Three Phases of Bourdieu's U.S. Reception: Comment on Lamont. Sociological Forum 27, 238-244.
Martin, J. L. (2003). What Is Field Theory? American Journal of Sociology 109, 1-49.
Martin, J. L. (2009). Social Structures. Princeton, NJ: Princeton University Press.
Martin, J. L. (2011). The Explanation of Social Action. Oxford: Oxford University Press.
Melman, S. (1997). From Private to State Capitalism: How the Permanent War Economy Transformed the Institutions of American Capitalism. Journal of Economic Issues 31, 311-330.
Roberts, K. H. (1990). Some Characteristics of One Type of High Reliability Organization. Organization Studies 1, 160-176.
Rudolph, J. W. & Repenning, N. P. (2002). Disaster Dynamics: Understanding the Role of Quantity in Organizational Collapse. Administrative Science Quarterly 47, 1-30.
Sagan, S. D. (1993). The Limits of Safety: Organizations, Accidents, and Nuclear Weapons. Princeton, NJ: Princeton University Press.
Savage, P. L. & Gabriel, R. A. (1976). Cohesion and Disintegration in the American Army: An Alternative Perspective. Armed Forces and Society 2, 340-376.
Sewell, W. H. (2005). Logics of History: Social Theory and Social Transformation. Chicago and London: University of Chicago Press.
Schutz, A. (1964). Collected Papers, Vol. II: Studies in Social Theory. The Hague: Martinus Nijhoff.
Shils, E. A. & Janowitz, M. (1948). Cohesion and Disintegration in the Wehrmacht in World War II. Public Opinion Quarterly 12, 280-315.
Staw, B. M., Sandelands, L. E. & Dutton, J. E. (1981). Threat-Rigidity Effects in Organizational Behavior: A Multilevel Analysis. Administrative Science Quarterly 26, 501-524.
Tilly, C. (1992). Coercion, Capital, and European States, AD 990-1992. Revised paperback edition. Oxford: Blackwell.
Vaughan, D. (1996). The Challenger Launch Decision: Risky Technology, Culture, and Deviance at NASA. Chicago and London: University of Chicago Press.
Vollmer, H. (2013). The Sociology of Disruption, Disaster and Social Change: Punctuated Cooperation. Cambridge: Cambridge University Press.
Weick, K. E. & Roberts, K. H. (1993). Collective Mind in Organizations: Heedful Interrelating on Flight Decks. Administrative Science Quarterly 38, 357-381.
Weick, K. E. & Sutcliffe, K. M. (2007). Managing the Unexpected. Resilient Performance in an Age of Uncertainty. Second edition. San Franciso, CA: Wiley.
Zebrowski, C. (2014). The Nature of Resilience. Resilience 1, 159-173.
Zimmerman, D. H. & Pollner, M. (1971). The Everyday World as a Phenomenon. In J. D. Douglas (ed.), Understanding Everyday Life: Towards a Reconstruction of Sociological Knowledge (pp. 80-103). London: Routledge & Kegan Paul.

Contributors

Wolfgang Bonß is Professor of Sociology and speaker of the research center "RISK" at the University of the armed forces in Munich (Germany). From 1986 to 1995 he was senior researcher at the Institute of Social Research in Hamburg. He serves for the Scientific Advisory Board of the Research Forum Public Security and is Co-editor of the "European Journal for Security Research". His research interests are sociological theory, reflexive modernity, and sociology of risk. Recent publication: Risk. Dealing with Uncertainty in Modern Times, in: Social Change Review 2013, 11: 7-36.

Cordula Dittmer is Senior researcher at the Disaster Research Unit (DRU) FU Berlin (Germany). Her main interests are disaster research, transdisciplinarity, resilience, gender- and postcolonial theory, peace- and conflict studies. Recent publications: Martin Voss and Cordula Dittmer: Resilienz aus katastrophensoziologischer Perspektive, in: Rüdiger Wink (ed.): Multidisziplinäre Perspektiven der Resilienzforschung. Wiesbaden (forthcoming). Cordula Dittmer and Claudia Simons (ed.): Post-/Dekoloniale Perspektiven in der Erforschung von Krieg? Eine Bestandsaufnahme. Sonderband der Zeitschrift für Friedens- und Konfliktforschung (forthcoming).

Michèle Lamont is Director of the Watherhead Center for International Affairs, Robert I. Goldman Professor of European Studies and Professor of Sociology and African and African American Studies at Harvard University (USA). She is also a

Fellow of the CIFAR, where she co-directs the Program on Successful Societies. Her recent research concerns the cultural dimensions of inequality, the transformation of racial and ethnic boundaries, everyday responses to stigmatization, definitions of excellence in higher education, and evaluation processes.

Crystal M. Fleming is the Robert I. Goldman Professor of European Studies and professor of sociology and African and African American Studies at Harvard University (USA). She is also a Fellow of the CIFAR, where she co-directs the Program on Successful Societies. Her recent research concerns the cultural dimensions of inequality, the transformation of racial and ethnic boundaries, everyday responses to stigmatization, definitions of excellence in higher education, and evaluation processes.

Daniel F. Lorenz works as scientific Research Coordinator at the Disaster Research Unit (DRU) Freie Universität Berlin (Germany)). His research topics are mainly in the field of disaster research, sociology of disaster, social vulnerability, resilience, human behavior in disasters. Recent publications conclude Martin Voss and Daniel F. Lorenz: Sociological Foundations of Crisis Communication, in: Andreas Schwarz, Matthew Seeger, and Claudia Auer (eds.): The Handbook of International Crisis Communication Research, Wiley-Blackwell (forthcoming). Resilience as an Element of a Sociology of Expression, in: Behemoth (with Leon Hempel) 2014, 7(2): 26-72; The Diversity of Resilience. Contributions from Social Science Perspective, in: Natural Hazards 2013, 67(1): 7-24.

Andrea Maurer is Professor for Sociology at the University of Trier (Germany). Her research interests center on sociological theory, new economic sociology, socio-economics, and institutional analyses. She is completing a book on social mechanisms in economic spheres as well as a new edition of Max Weber's Protestant Ethic. Recently published articles: 'Social Embeddedness' Viewed from an Institutional Perspective. Revision of a Core Principle of New Economic Sociology with Special Regard to Max Weber *Polish*, in: *Sociological Review 2012, 180*(4): 1231-1413; Social mechanisms as special cases of explanatory sociology, in: *Analyse & Kritik. Journal of Social Theory 2016*/1 (forthcoming).

Renate Mayntz is Emeritus Director at the Max Planck Institute for the Study of Societies (MPIfG) in Cologne, Germany. She held chairs at several universities, served in several advisory bodies to the German government, and published numerous books and hundreds of scholarly articles. Her research fields include social stratification, technological development, the relationship between science and politics, policy formation and implementation, and the organization of government. Her theoretical interests range from social differentiation to social dynamics and institutional change. Recently she has worked and published on the financial crisis and the reform of financial market governance.

Sebastian Nessel is Assistant Professor, Department of Sociology at the University of Graz. Research areas: Economic sociology, sociology of consumption, organizational sociology, social movement theory. Recent Publications: Verbraucherorganisationen und Märkte. Eine wirtschaftssoziologische Untersuchung. Wiesbaden. Geld und Krise. Die sozialen Grundlagen moderner Geldordnungen. Frankfurt/M. 2013 (ed. with K. Kraemer).

Hendrik Vollmer is Senior Lecturer at the University of Leicester School of Management (UK). Research interests are sociological theory, sociology of organizations, microsociology, accounting. Recent publications: The Sociology of Disruption: Disaster and Social Change, Cambridge 2013; What Kind of Game Is Everyday Interaction, in: Rationality and Society 25, 2013: 370-404; Normalization and Its Discontents: Organizational Learning from Disaster (with Sven Kette), in: Heike Egner, Marén Schorch and Martin Voss (eds), Learning and Calamities: Practices, Interpretations, Patterns, London 2015: 181-198.

Jessica S. Welburn is Assistant Professor at the University of Iowa (USA). She received her PhD from the University of Harvard. Her research interests include race and ethnicity, cultural sociology, the sociology of family, and qualitative methodology. She has worked on exploring how African Americans from middle-class households conceptualize social mobility prospects. She is currently working on a book based on interviews and ethnographic observations to explore how working class and middle class African Americans in Detroit, MI navigate the city's crumbling infrastructure.

Index

A
action theory 35

B
Brazil 4, 143, 145–146, 148–149, 151, 155, 157, 166–169, 173, 175

C
consumer organisation 112, 119, 121, 128, 131, 133, 136
consumer policy 118–120, 123, 128, 131
crisis, economic 3, 12, 14, 18–19, 21, 25, 45, 49, 63–69, 71–74, 77–78, 80, 97, 99, 101–102, 104–105, 116, 130, 177, 201

D
disruption 3–4, 178–185, 187–194
disruptive event 2, 4, 85–86, 90, 93, 95–99, 103–104, 180
dissociation 184–185, 187–191, 193

E
economic sociology 3, 87–93, 96–97, 103–104, 111–114, 116–118, 130, 132, 135, 200
economy 3, 31, 64, 66–67, 73, 75–76, 78, 83, 85, 94, 98, 192
equality 147, 157

exit 90, 94–97, 104, 147, 181
explanation 96, 107–108, 160

F
field 3, 9, 26, 29, 36, 38, 40, 116, 118, 128, 178, 190–192, 194, 200
financial system 3, 63, 66–68, 70, 72–79
firm 71, 73, 76, 86, 88–90, 104, 111–118, 120–123, 125–137, 168, 177

G
Germany 16, 21, 38, 46, 101, 112, 118–123, 128, 130–132, 138–139, 172, 199–200
group, social 2, 4, 31, 38, 64, 74, 120, 126, 134, 144–145, 147–149, 151, 153–156, 160, 162–165, 167, 170, 188–189

I
identity, cultural 4, 27, 48, 64, 75, 101, 103, 144–146, 148–151, 155–156, 161–165, 167, 169, 186
identity, individual 4, 27, 48, 64, 75, 101, 103, 144–146, 148–151, 155–156, 161–165, 167, 169, 186
identity, social 4, 27, 48, 64, 75, 101, 103, 144–146, 148–151, 155–156, 161–165, 167, 169, 186
individualism 161, 166
inequality 14, 30–31, 134, 147, 150, 154–156, 160, 169, 190, 200
institution 2, 5, 14, 26, 28, 43, 45–46, 64, 66–70, 72, 74–78, 84, 86–88, 90–94, 103–104, 115–116, 150, 160

L
loyalty 3, 83, 85, 88, 90–91, 93–94, 96–99, 101–104

M
market 3–4, 32, 47, 65–67, 74–76, 84, 86–91, 94–95, 97, 99, 111–119, 121–123, 125–126, 130–137, 180

N
neoliberalism 143, 145, 147–150, 157–158, 161, 164–166
new economic sociology 3, 87–93, 96–97, 103–104, 111, 116–117, 132, 200

O
organization 1–2, 4–5, 63, ,64 65, 70, 72, 75–78, 84–88, 94, 98, 178–179, 186–189, 191, 201

Index

R
reliability 178–179, 187, 189, 191
resilience 1–5, 9–10, 12–32, 34–50, 56, 63–65, 67, 69–72, 74–80, 83–86, 88–89, 91–92, 94–95, 97–99, 101–103, 105, 111–112, 114, 117–119, 123, 132–134, 136–137, 143–145, 148–151, 162–166, 177–180, 184–185, 187–194, 199–200
resilience, concept of 1–5, 9–10, 12–32, 34–50, 56, 63–65, 67, 69–72, 74–80, 83–86, 88–89, 91–92, 94–95, 97–99, 101–103, 105, 111–112, 114, 117–119, 123, 132–134, 136–137, 143–145, 148–151, 162–166, 177–180, 184–185, 187–194, 199–200
resilience, economic 1–5, 9–10, 12–32, 34–50, 56, 63–65, 67, 69–72, 74–80, 83–86, 88–89, 91–92, 94–95, 97–99, 101–103, 105, 111–112, 114, 117–119, 123, 132–134, 136–137, 143–145, 148–151, 162–166, 177–180, 184–185, 187–194, 199–200
resilience, factor of 1–5, 9–10, 12–32, 34–50, 56, 63–65, 67, 69–72, 74–80, 83–86, 88–89, 91–92, 94–95, 97–99, 101–103, 105, 111–112, 114, 117–119, 123, 132–134, 136–137, 143–145, 148–151, 162–166, 177–180, 184–185, 187–194, 199–200
resilience, social 1–5, 9–10, 12–32, 34–50, 56, 63–65, 67, 69–72, 74–80, 83–86, 88–89, 91–92, 94–95, 97–99, 101–103, 105, 111–112, 114, 117–119, 123, 132–134, 136–137, 143–145, 148–151, 162–166, 177–180, 184–185, 187–194, 199–200
risk 10, 20–21, 24, 26–27, 31, 38–39, 47, 58, 68, 71–74, 77–78, 86, 125, 132, 157–158, 160, 177, 199

S
shock 3, 14, 19, 32, 71–73, 83, 90–91, 99, 129–130
social capital 41, 48, 98
social change 33, 63, 86, 112
social factor 3–4, 90–91, 94, 103
soundness 3, 73–77, 80
stability 1–3, 14, 23, 29, 36, 44, 63, 66–67, 69–70, 72–73, 76–77, 83–86, 88, 90–91, 112–114, 136, 183
stigmatization 4, 143–149, 152–153, 155–156, 160–161, 164–166, 169, 200
stress 3, 19, 27, 32–33, 41–42, 70–74, 76, 150, 153, 188–189
stress test 3, 70–73, 76

U
uncertainty 10, 13–15, 20–22, 24, 45, 49, 71, 86, 88–91, 104, 111, 113–115, 117, 121–123, 125–127, 133–136
USA 13, 16, 21, 199–201

V

violence 38, 47, 163, 170, 179, 182–183, 185–189, 191–192
voice 90, 94–95, 97, 104, 125, 127, 134, 137
vulnerability 24, 26–28, 30–35, 39, 45–46, 48, 56, 72–73, 77, 112–113, 115, 117, 131, 133–137, 177, 193, 200
vulnerable 3, 14, 19, 34, 73, 77–78, 123, 147, 163

W

Weber, Max 56, 85–88, 93, 96, 98, 103, 107–109, 200
Werner, Emmy 18, 24, 29, 38, 59, 83, 109